What people are saying abou

MW00988967

ALL THINGS NEW

'As a pastor leading a similar church in a similar city, I pay very close attention to Pete Hughes and KXC. Not only do I count Pete a dear friend, but I view him as one of the best emerging thinkers and leaders in the western church. The community that has grown up around them at KXC is simply incredible. Few churches manage to capture the holistic nature of the kingdom with such tenacity and clarity—from spiritual formation of the soul to the transformation of society. Pete's opening claim that "the story you live in is the story you live out" shows just how key the biblical narrative has been in the architecture of Pete and KXC's vision of church. I simply can't recommend this book enough. I want every person in my church to read this.'

John Mark Comer, Author of *The Ruthless Elimination of Hurry* and Pastor for Teaching and Vision at Bridgetown Church, Portland

'Pete Hughes has written a beautiful book. He makes the story of Scripture urgent, compelling and desirable for those seeking to do mission in our post-Christian context. Theologically deep, and resonant with the Spirit, this will re-enchant many longing hearts.'

Jon Tyson, Church of the City New York and Author of *The Burden Is Light*

'Pete Hughes is an extraordinarily gifted church leader. The central London church he started, KXC, has grown to be a significant Christian presence in a very challenging area. I am delighted he has written a book, sharing his experiences and wisdom.'

Nicky Gumbel, Vicar of HTB Church
and Pioneer of the Alpha Course

'For those fully persuaded by the narrative of Scripture, passionate about the reality of the kingdom of God and anxious to see his rule and reign breaking in to our cities and our communities, this is a book worth selling a shirt for! For years now, Pete and Bee have been practising what they preach and looking for cultural renewal in the heart of the city. They are the real deal, and this book is an outworking of their authentic experiences and is a rich resource indeed.'

Eleanor Mumford, Cofounder
of Vineyard Churches

'*All Things New* is magnificent. Deeply theological, rooted in real life and yet a prophetic call to go both deeper and further. Magnificent.'

Mike Pilavachi, Cofounder of Soul Survivor

'Pete Hughes not only leads one of London's most innovative churches, he also thinks deeply about the gospel and the culture in which it plays out today. This book skilfully relates the big story of the Bible with the particular story of planting a church in cosmopolitan, secular London. It will inspire you to reimagine not just the church but also the neighbourhood around you, in the light of the magnificent story of divine grace at work in the world.'

Rt Revd Dr Graham Tomlin, Bishop of
Kensington and President of St Mellitus College

'Wow! This book is profound. Pete helps me recapture the beauty and majesty of the Divine story and then invites and inspires me to live it out in real time—in these times! Relevant, poignant, practical and honest, this book will inspire you, challenge you and change you!'

Danielle Strickland, Speaker,
Author, Justice Advocate

'What you hold in your hand is not a manual. It's something bolder. It's a story. We have excelled in creating strategies for growing churches and reaching cities. What we desperately need is a story. We have multiplied programs for increasing our influence ... but the need of the hour is for people. People immersed in the presence of God, empowered by his Spirit who creatively and courageously live in and live out the ancient story. My friend Pete Hughes is one of those people. I have watched his journey, and that of the KXC community, as they passionately and relentlessly step into the story of God in the pages of Scripture and the streets of their city. *All Things New* tells their story and reminds us that the story of God is big. Big enough to claim the whole of our lives and beautiful enough to bring renewal to all of creation. Theologically robust, biblically immersed and culturally engaged, *All Things New* offers a way for every believer to partner with Jesus in bringing hope to hurting humanity. From the first page to the last it reminds us that everything everywhere is being swept up in a story of unforgettable, indestructible hope.'

Alan Scott, Pastor and Author
of *Scattered Servants*

'Look around at the stories our culture tells to explain the world; they either seem to be teetering on the brink of collapse or are duelling for supremacy, leaving us dizzy, dismayed and confused. In *All Things New*, Pete Hughes offers us a different story, a rich biblical drama which is not only breathtaking but true. A redemptive story which Pete and his vibrant church are living out in London's King's Cross, and which with verve and vision he invites the reader to inhabit and to see all things made new.'

Mark Sayers, Senior Pastor of Red
Church, Melbourne, and Author of
Strange Days and *Reappearing Church*

PETE HUGHES

ALL THINGS NEW

JOINING GOD'S STORY OF RE-CREATION

DAVID C COOK

transforming lives together

ALL THINGS NEW
Published by David C Cook
4050 Lee Vance Drive
Colorado Springs, CO 80918 U.S.A.

Integrity Music Limited, a Division of David C Cook
Brighton, East Sussex BN1 2RE, England

The graphic circle C logo is a registered trademark of David C Cook.

Library of Congress Control Number 2019948026
ISBN 978-0-8307-7570-5
eISBN 978-0-8307-7652-8

The Team: Ian Matthews, Keith Wall, Megan Stengel, Mark Prentice, Susan Murdock
Cover design by beatroot.media
Cover image courtesy of Forge Creative—www.forgecreative.co

Printed in the United States of America
First Edition 2020

1 2 3 4 5 6 7 8 9 10

112119

To Bee, Benj, Josh and Olive.
Thanks for filling my life with joy. I love
you more than any words could ever say and
count the adventure of living out this story
together as the greatest privilege of my life.

CONTENTS

FOREWORD

'There are five Gospels—Matthew, Mark, Luke, John and the Christian—but most people never read the first four.'

Rodney 'Gipsy' Smith

Rodney Smith was born on 31st March 1860 in a tent woven from branches of hazel and willow, deep in Epping Forest on the northeastern perimeter of Greater London. His family was Romani. They lived in a traditional horse-drawn wagon and eked a living as they traversed England selling basketry and tin.

Rodney never read the Bible as a boy—he was totally uneducated—but at the age of sixteen, his father became a Christian during one of his frequent spells in prison. The total transformation in his father's life was undoubtedly the first gospel Rodney Smith ever read, and it convinced him to surrender his own life to Jesus.

The following year, at the age of seventeen, Rodney met William Booth, founder of the Salvation Army, who immediately recruited him as an evangelist. From that moment, and for the next seventy years, he preached the gospel relentlessly, learning to read the Bible for himself so that he could teach it to others. Rodney Smith led tens of thousands to Christ and was honoured by King George VI with an MBE. His powerful witness was the fifth gospel for countless people, long before they ever got around to reading the other four.

This book, *All Things New*, is about the story of God; the one written down in the Bible and the one lived out in our lives. It's about understanding the vast metanarrative of God's purposes from Genesis to Revelation, so that we can take our place within its micronarrative today.

It is appropriate, therefore, that Pete Hughes is both a brilliant thinker and a ballsy practitioner who understands God's story in the Bible, and applies himself daily to its unfolding narrative in the world. On one hand, Pete studies God's Word diligently, intelligently and with personal integrity, seeking to 'present [himself] to God as one approved, a worker who ... correctly handles the word of truth' (2 Tim. 2:15). If you've ever heard Pete's passionate and incisive biblical exposition, or just talked with him for more than a few minutes, you know that his thinking is permeated and animated by sound doctrine.

But on the other hand, Pete is a practitioner—and here we have the power of this book. Again and again Pete insists that we outwork the magnificent, unfolding story of God in the earthly details of daily discipleship. Reading these pages was like flying at 34,000 feet with Pete pointing out the breathtaking contours of earth below, but then just as I got comfortable, he would strap a parachute to my back and push me out of the plane for a much closer look!

Pete and his wife, Bee, are fully engaged in the down-to-earth realities of building family and community in one of the most challenging and exciting parts of one of the greatest cities on earth. They have pioneered King's Cross Church, a vibrant, innovative church that has become the fifth gospel for crowds of unchurched and de-churched millennials in and around King's Cross, London. They are doing this through relational presence and cultural resistance rather than relevance and gimmickry. They know that the only way to defy the spirit of the age is to be filled, again and again, with the Spirit of the age to come.

This may sound appealing, but it is also complicated and difficult. Behind the scenes it has often been unspeakably tough for Pete and Bee. I have wept with them, and yet my presiding image of Pete is always his ready laugh and relentless enthusiasm.

Together with Pete and Bee and some other dear friends, we have embarked upon a great adventure: launching the Wildfires Festival as a gathering place for like-minded tribes to 'contend for the next Great Awakening.' We have a growing sense of expectancy because we believe that God really is, as Pete says in this book, making 'all things new.' He is in the business not just of helping a few Christians to survive and the odd church to be planted, but of rescuing, redeeming and renewing every corner of God's creation. We are all equally called—painters, programmers and paramedics alike—to participate in this urgent work of reconciliation.

I say that it is urgent because the world appears to be dying. Political and economic models are creaking. Ecosystems are breaking down. Millions of protestors are filling the streets as I write. All around us creation is 'groaning as in the pains of childbirth' (Rom. 8:22).

And this is precisely the point: these travails which feel like death throes are, in fact, labour pains. The agony of hope, not despair. And so we are actively preparing for new birth. Praying for it passionately and planning for it as intelligently as we can, believing that *'the reception of a new world from God is under way in our time. It is apparent in the staggering, frightening emergence of new communities ... Thus we are at the risky point of receiving from God what we thought God would not give; namely a new way to be human in the world'* (Walter Brueggemann, *Hopeful Imagination*).

Every now and then I read something so compelling, exciting and fresh that it creates in me a momentary crisis of faith. 'This seems so new and yet so familiar,' I think, 'such an accurate articulation of my innermost hopes and convictions, that if it's not actually orthodox Christianity I'm very much afraid I'm about to become a heretic.'

All Things New is this kind of book; it brought me to the brink of apostasy several times before reassuring me that, in fact, its message is orthodox to the very core. In other words, it takes very old, eternal truths and arms them with fresh relevance. I suspect that you're going to find yourself powerfully drawn to the vast panoramic scope of the invitation Pete presents. You may occasionally feel like someone who's been struggling to piece together a jigsaw at the moment that they are finally handed the lid.

In other words, this is the kind of book that will make sense of things and expand your vision, reminding you why you first believed and what you most deeply desire.

The canon of Scripture is of course closed, but God's story is still being written, and we feature in his plot! Our lives and communities are the fifth gospel today, just like Rodney Smith and the Salvation Army 150 years ago. How terrifying and exciting it is to be walking the earth as sons and daughters of God at such a time as this, conspiring together in Christ, by the power of his Spirit for the glory of God the Father to subvert the old order and make *all things new.*

> You should be spreading the good word. You should be etching the good word onto the glass scanning beds of library photocopiers. You should be scraping the truth onto old auto parts and throwing them off bridges so that people digging in the mud in a million years will question the world, too. You should be carving eyeballs into tire treads and onto shoe soles so that your every trail speaks of thinking and faith and belief. You should be designing molecules that crystallize into poems of devotion. You should be making bar codes that print out truth, not lies … Your new life will be tinged with urgency, as though you're digging out the victims of an avalanche. If you're not spending every waking moment of your life living the truth, if you're not plotting every moment to boil the carcass of the old order, then you're wasting your day. (Douglas Coupland, *Player One: What Is to Become of Us?*)

Pete Greig
Guildford, England
Advent, 2019

PREFACE

I started writing this book more than ten years ago. On the 28th of June 2008, I stood in St Paul's Cathedral, adrenaline coursing through my veins, making vows before God, bishops, mates and strangers. I tried to get my lines right and tried not to trip up on the priestly robes that felt, and still feel, unfamiliar. I also tried to remember how I got into this—and more than that, why I got into this. This was the point of no return. I was about to be ordained as a priest in the Church of England.

I don't remember much about that service, but one moment I remember vividly. As part of the service, those getting ordained had to publicly profess 'the faith uniquely revealed in the Holy Scriptures and set forth in the catholic creeds, which faith the Church is called upon to proclaim afresh in each generation.' With those last five words, everything slowed down. That's how I got here. That's *why* I got here. It was the call of God to 'proclaim afresh in each generation' the greatest story ever told—the story of God becoming man, living for us, dying for us, rising for us, in order to rescue, restore and redeem us. That was the beginning of a new chapter in my life, and in many ways it was the beginning of this book.

Since that moment, a primary passion of mine has been to follow through on the promise I made. This is therefore the simple aim of this book: to offer a fresh retelling of the ancient story of God's engagement with his creation, taking seriously the questions being raised within our culture today. My hope is that people will see that the key questions and longings of today are similar to those raised by God's people in their long journey through the narrative of Scripture. Furthermore, it is within this story that these questions find an answer and the longings find fulfilment. For as we follow the journey through Scripture, the longings lead us to Jesus, who leads us to the fulness of life we were made for.

So this is our task: to follow Jesus and the cause of his kingdom in the midst of a broken world. On the journey there will be breakthroughs as well as breakdowns. We will encounter victory as well as defeat. We will take hits and experience loss. But we will not lose hope. Why? Because we know the story from beginning to end—from Genesis 1 to Revelation 22. The story starts in a garden and ends in a garden city. The story begins with no sin, sickness or suffering and ends with no death, grief, crying or pain. The story gives hope to the hopeless and strength to the weak. It's the story the world is crying out to hear, and it's been placed in your hands and mine. It's time to tell the story, to shout it from the rooftops and to sing it on the streets. But to tell the story effectively we need to know the story intimately.

If we want to partner with God in rewriting the stories of our communities, workplaces and cities, we as the church have to do better at indwelling our story and communicating it to the surrounding culture. We owe it to the world around us to tell the story of God on a mission to make all things new.

Pete Hughes, 2019

THE STORY WE LIVE IN

This is my conviction: the more you intentionally indwell the narrative of Scripture, the more you care passionately about the renewal of culture.

Ten years ago, my wife, Bee, and I planted King's Cross Church (KXC) in London. One of our top priorities was to help a generation that was becoming increasingly biblically illiterate to fall in love with Scripture. We in the church have spent so much time trying to motivate and inspire a younger generation to be 'history makers,' and to make their lives count for the kingdom of God, that we have failed to equip them with a daily discipline of reading and engaging with the Scriptures. The result has been a culture of unsustainable activism that is leading towards spiritual exhaustion and apathy.

Rather than being nourished by daily bread, we've become reliant on a weekly message that will gee up troops for battle. Our preaching and podcasts have become less focussed on the inspiration of Scripture, teaching people to think and act biblically and more focussed on the inspiration of stories that build faith. Inspiring people is admirable, but do we know what we are inspiring them towards? People are increasingly unclear about what the kingdom of God actually is, evident in the way we are currently importing alternative language from the culture such as 'human flourishing,' 'the common good,' and 'the transformation of society.' I love such language, but without ever qualifying these terms on biblical grounds, the surrounding culture is beginning to redefine how the church understands the kingdom. The effect is that our understanding of the kingdom becomes less centred on Jesus the king and less connected to God's chosen instrument of kingdom change, the local church.

The challenge ten years ago was to address the crisis and put the cart back behind the horse. Our priority was to help a congregation comprised of mainly millennials immerse themselves in the story of God, feeding on Scripture as the source of their daily inspiration. The result of this pursuit, both personally and collectively as a church community, has been a deeper understanding of, and longing for, the kingdom. The biblical vision for the renewal of all things has become the cry of our hearts. More than that, time in Scriptures has created a biblical imagination for what this renewal of culture might become. What would this redemption look like in the context of politics? What about the music industry? How would the redemption of education change how we run our schools and raise our children? The questions have created both curiosity and greater longing.

Still, the more you use Scripture to fuel this imagining of the kingdom, the more you begin to see and feel the brokenness that surrounds. So much needs redeeming. The gap between what has been imagined and what currently is sometimes seems like an unbridgeable chasm. But when Jesus rose from the dead, *impossibility* was redefined. Despair becomes hope and unbelief is transformed into faith.

For the church to be an agent of cultural transformation, we need to provide people with a kingdom vision for their work, communities and families. These are the places we spend most of our time. We need to recapture a vision of the church scattered, infecting each workplace and each sector of society with kingdom values.

This book is about that journey: from the Scriptures to the culture. It's about the biblical narrative and how that narrative, when we immerse ourselves within it, affects our desires, imaginations and actions. Many books focus on the renewal of culture, but here's my challenge for those passionate about this subject: immerse yourself in the Scriptures first. Nothing will prepare and equip you for the task of transforming culture like feeding on the daily bread of God's story. As my friend Alan Scott says, 'The story you live *in* is the story you live *out*.' Now is the time to reacquaint a generation that hasn't been immersed in the Scriptures with the story of God on a mission to make all things new. The fruit of such a pursuit will result in transformed lives, families, schools, communities, businesses, offices and institutions.

For me, it was a trip to Uganda that opened my eyes to this reality, providing a new paradigm for ministry and totally resetting the trajectory of both my story and the story of KXC.

Swampland That Saved a Community

In February 2013, I travelled with some good friends to Northern Uganda. The purpose of the trip was to learn from people who were empowering others to think entrepreneurially about how to lift their communities out of poverty. The projects, all run by local churches in partnership with the development organisation Tearfund, begin the process by asking people a simple question: What resources do you currently possess that could be used to help alleviate suffering in your community? The standard answer at the start of the process is 'Nothing!' These people live in extreme poverty and experience its dehumanising effects. Dignity gradually erodes, despair sets in and hope for the future fades.

I met an individual in this condition who had come to faith in Jesus and was beginning his journey from despair to hope, from doubt to faith. Though he had few possessions to his name, this man did own a small piece of swampland. He didn't initially mention the land because it had become the breeding ground for mosquitos, which meant malaria rates in the area were sky high. It's no exaggeration to say his land was literally killing people. It had become a primary cause of poverty in the community, so understandably he didn't see it as a resource for overcoming economic troubles and bringing life to the area.

Gradually this man, along with others in his community, started thinking differently about his swampland. He began thinking entrepreneurially. Eventually a plan emerged: these people would try to dig a pond in which they could breed fish. It was a long shot, but they thought they would give it a go. So twenty men from the community started digging. For days and days, they gave their time and energy to digging in this swampland. Weeks went by with little progress. But after thirty days they had gone deep enough to hit the water level, and the beginnings of a pond emerged.

When the pond reached an adequate depth, the volunteer workers began to breed fish. Before long there was enough fish to feed his family. Over time, there were enough fish to feed not only the landowner's family, but also many others in the community. And it gets better. He began to sell excess fish at a nearby market, generating enough income to send village children to school. That's significant since education is one of the key pathways out of poverty.

Eventually, a second pond was created, and at the time of my visit there more were in the early stages of being built. The income generated from the second pond was used to employ people to manage the ponds. The vision for the next three ponds was to generate funds to construct suitable housing for community members. This swampland that once contributed to extreme poverty now provided food for the hungry, education for the unschooled, housing for the homeless and jobs for the unemployed. This is more than good news—it's incredible news. But it gets better still.

The people involved with the project began to investigate why the fish were breeding so prolifically and what made the conditions so perfect for this certain type of fish. The answer? The fish were feeding on mosquito larvae, which meant malaria rates in the area began to plummet. The land that had been killing the community was now bringing life. As I walked around the first pond, talking to the owner and other community members, I was overcome by what looked like a snapshot of Eden in the middle of lifeless terrain. The land was flourishing, but more importantly, the people were flourishing too. Why? Because one person started to think differently. He started to think like an entrepreneur.

The pond story is just one of many I could tell from my week in Uganda visiting local churches transforming their communities by becoming kingdom entrepreneurs. The old model of desperately hoping for a partnership with a wealthy western church was being replaced by a more sustainable model. Local church members realised that God has already resourced people to be agents of building his kingdom here on earth. In the process, they were eradicating the poverty that robs people of life and dignity.

So what brought about this revolution of thinking? How was the attitude of despair renewed to enable an entrepreneurial mind-set to run wild?

The answer is simple: Jesus.

Talking to church leaders and community stakeholders, the explanation was always the same. The wave of entrepreneurialism sweeping across Uganda starts with the gospel and the Scriptures. As people read the Bible and encounter the risen Christ, everything begins to change. The good news of what Jesus has done breaks the victim mind-set. People who once said 'I have nothing to give' are transformed into people who say 'If God is for me, who can be against me?' The message of the gospel restores dignity, empowering men and women to bring restoration to others.

The well-known atheist columnist Matthew Paris wrote a superb article entitled 'As An Atheist, I Truly Believe Africa Needs God,' in which he acknowledges the process of transformation. He writes:

> Travelling in Malawi refreshed another belief, too: one I've been trying to banish all my life, but an observation I've been unable to avoid since my African childhood. It confounds my ideological beliefs, stubbornly refuses to fit my worldview and has embarrassed my growing belief that there is no

God. Now a confirmed atheist, I've become convinced of the enormous contribution that Christian evangelism makes in Africa, sharply distinct from the work of secular NGOs, government projects and international aid efforts. These alone will not do. Education and training alone will not do. In Africa Christianity changes people's hearts. It brings a spiritual transformation. The rebirth is real. The change is good.

I used to avoid this truth by applauding—as you can—the practical work of mission churches in Africa. It's a pity, I would say, that salvation is part of the package, but Christians black and white, working in Africa, do heal the sick, do teach people to read and write; and only the severest kind of secularist could see a mission hospital or school and say the world would be better without it. I would allow that if faith was needed to motivate missionaries to help, then fine. But what counted was the help, not the faith. But this doesn't fit the facts. Faith does more than support the missionary; it is also transferred to his flock. This is the effect that matters so immensely, and which I cannot help observing.[1]

Although Paris' article focusses on the transformation the gospel creates in Africa, the power of change and renewal is happening all over the globe.

From Uganda to King's Cross

The people I met in Northern Uganda didn't look at me as a westerner who might give them something. Quite the opposite. They wanted to give me something—renewed confidence that the gospel changes lives and transforms communities. So I returned to London, sharing the stories with the people of KXC and inviting our community to begin asking the same question those in Northern Uganda were asking: What resources do we have that could help alleviate poverty and suffering in King's Cross and create pathways to human flourishing?

Part of the answer came in the form of office space—15,000 square feet of it! As a church we experienced the miraculous provision of three floors of rent-free office space in the heart of King's Cross, which is, in terms of real estate, one of the most expensive parts of London. Though we were given use of the space on a temporary basis whilst the landlords considered long-term plans for the building, we wanted to be great stewards of this incredible provision. So the bottom floor we immediately turned into a community area, which could be utilised by many of our compassion ministries and charity partners. But most of the second floor was empty, run-down space. So how could we use that area to serve God's purposes?

People began dreaming, and a couple in the church, Simon and Laura Willows, had a vision to turn these derelict offices into a creative space to serve the freelance community of King's Cross. Rather than working in isolation, a shared space could bring together business start-ups, social enterprises, photographers, graphic designers, web builders and filmmakers. They would work not just alongside one another, but also *with* one another to help prosper one another's businesses. Further, the vision was to build this co-working space from waste and recycled furniture.

The space, which became known as 'Tent' (acknowledging its temporary nature), soon began to take shape. Discarded scaffolding planks were sanded down and built in to tables. Three-legged chairs that had been taken to the dump were restored and put to use. Crates that had been used to transport fruit and vegetables to the market were now transformed into desks. Slowly but surely, an ugly office space became a beautiful creative environment to serve the freelance and creative community of King's Cross.

Tent first housed a few freelancers from the church, but before long it regularly had between forty to fifty workers present, with a membership of over a hundred people, most of whom had no connection with KXC. And since the church was given the space for free, we didn't need to charge any rent. All we asked was that people make donations to use the space and be part of the Tent community, which then began to generate funds to finance mission work we were doing locally to serve vulnerable people and families.

Inspired by the story of the pond, we had built a Tent. And like the story of the tent (or tabernacle) that housed God's presence as the nation of Israel journeyed from Egypt to the Promised Land, our hope was that our own Tent would be filled with God's presence and people within that community could flourish.

Rubies in the Rubble

At the same time that Tent was emerging as an entrepreneurial space, a woman at KXC experienced the emergence of her own social enterprise. Jenny Costa had been working for a London hedge fund but over time became increasingly stirred by the issues of global hunger and food waste. She could no longer ignore the troubling fact that almost a billion people on the planet go to bed hungry whilst as much as 2 billion tonnes of food (almost half the food produced around the world) is thrown away each year.[2] In 2010 Jenny quit her job at the hedge fund to start her business, Rubies in the Rubble. The simple idea was to obtain waste fruit and vegetables from the market and employ vulnerable women seeking work to make chutneys from an old family recipe. They then started selling the chutneys at Borough Market. From these small beginnings, the business began to grow.

Before long, Jenny and her team had conversations with the likes of Jamie Oliver, EAT and Waitrose, all of whom were inspired by the story of restoration. Jenny went on to receive numerous awards, including the Ben & Jerry's Sustainable Business Award in 2012, as well as The Veuve Clicquot New Generation Award, celebrating female entrepreneurs. Now you can purchase the chutneys in Ocado, eighty Sainsbury's stores, sixty Waitrose stores, Virgin Trains and more than a hundred other stores across the UK, whilst the company is exploring diversification into other food products.

Living In and Living Out the Story of God

The stories about the Ugandan swampland, Tent and Jenny Costa's enterprise are the result of people who chose to live within a 'bigger story.' When people indwell the biblical narrative, immersing themselves within that story, these redemptive outcomes are inevitable.

This 'bigger story' begins with humanity walking and talking with God in the Garden of Eden and ends with humanity walking and talking with God in a renewed heaven and earth. What starts in a garden (Gen. 1-2) ends in a garden city (Rev. 21-22). Between Eden and the renewed heaven and earth is the story of 'De-creation'—created order unravelling through sin—and the story of Re-creation, which finds its climactic moment in the life, death and resurrection of Jesus.

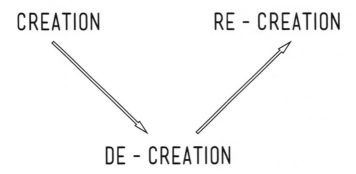

The epic ending to the biblical story puts to rest the idea that the ultimate goal of the Christian life is to leave one's body behind and ascend to the divine realm to enjoy disembodied bliss, hanging out with angels, riding clouds and drinking Red Bull. Such thinking has little to do with the New Testament and everything to do with Greek philosophy, in particular the thinking and writings of Plato. It somehow infiltrated Christian teaching and robbed people of the spectacular ending of our narrative. So much so that many people believe the Christian story can be distilled down to God making a way for those with correct beliefs, or immaculate behavior, to escape this present world in order to enjoy a blissful one in the next. I find it tragic that people outside the church genuinely believe that this is our story. I find it perhaps even more tragic that many people *inside* the church think that this is our story. It is not our story. It never has been. It never will be.

Our story is far greater than a message of escapism to another realm where God lives. Our story is of God making his home with us, healing and restoring every aspect of brokenness in this world he has given as our home. The narrative closes with a vision of heaven descending and God making his dwelling place amongst humanity on earth, just like he had done in Eden. Then, seated on his throne, indicative of his work being finally complete, the Creator declares, 'See, I am making all things new' (Rev. 21:5 ISV).

The meaning of this profound statement is lost for many people through the translation from Greek, the language of the New Testament, to English. The Greek language has two words for 'new': *neos* and *kainos*. *Neos* is something brand-new, like when you purchase a new car that has never been driven before. *Kainos* is something old that is made new, like when your car is fixed at the garage and drives 'like new.' When John has a vision of God 'making all things new,' the word he chooses is *kainos*. The world God created, the world he so loves that he would send his only son to die for, isn't banished to the garbage heap so God could create a new and improved version. Instead it is re-created or restored. Suddenly, within the twinkling of an eye, death, grief, crying and pain will belong to the past. Just like Eden—where sin, sickness and suffering had no place—God's renewed heaven and earth will be a place where all of creation can flourish. The message of Revelation 21-22 comes through loud and clear: God is in the business of renewing all things and restoring creation, including the humanity he made in his image and likeness.

This is the challenge set before us: to immerse ourselves within this unfolding drama. To find belonging there. To find fresh purpose there. To find hope for the future there. And as we do, stories of restoration will undoubtedly follow. Not just stories of ponds, offices and chutneys, but also stories of restored individuals, families, communities, businesses and schools. For God is on a mission to make all things new, and he's inviting you and I further into the story.

PART I

IN THE BEGINNING ...

Chapter 1

GENESIS, SCIENCE AND THE ART OF MYTH-BUSTING

I was one of those annoying kids who constantly asked my mum, 'Why?'

Why are we going shopping? Why do we eat three times a day? Why not four times? Why is my brother so annoying? Why do people speak different languages?

The questions never ended, exhausting for my mum. To her credit, she encouraged me to be inquisitive about everything. As a teenager, I put up a poster on my bedroom wall that said, 'All you need to be a good philosopher is the faculty of wonder.' I was full of wonder, hungry for understanding and dissatisfied with shallow answers. The first book I read as a teenager on the subject of philosophy was the fantastic and hugely popular book *Sophie's World*. The author, Jostein Gaarder, writes:

> What is the most important thing in life? If we ask
> someone living on the edge of starvation, the answer

is food. If we ask someone dying of cold, the answer is warmth. If we put the same question to someone who feels lonely and isolated, the answer will probably be the company of other people. But when these basic needs have been satisfied—will there be something that everybody needs? Philosophers think so. They believe that man cannot live by bread alone. Of course everyone needs food. And everyone needs love and care. But there is something else—apart from that—which everyone needs, and that is to figure out who we are and why we are here.[3]

These huge questions, and the pursuit of answers, energised me. I eventually went on to study maths and philosophy at university, and I wrestled to integrate my Christian faith with the weighty questions philosophers had been asking through the ages.

These fundamental questions involve our worldview, meaning that how we answer such questions shapes how we understand the world around us. We all have a worldview, a lens through which we interpret the world around us. Our worldview is shaped by our upbringing, education, painful experiences, dreams for the future and many other factors. All of these are fused together to form a framework that helps us understand and make sense of our surroundings. Sociologists tell us that our worldview is essentially an attempt to answer four core questions: Where am I? Who am I? What's wrong with the world? What's the remedy?[4]

The Bible opens up with an epic story addressing all of these questions.

The World(view) of Eden

'In the beginning God created the heavens and the earth ...' (Gen. 1:1).

The story that follows is central to our understanding of the whole narrative of Scripture. It is the story that introduces us to the key characters, establishes the key plotlines and sets the trajectory for what's to come. It's also the story that creates the worldview to help us make sense of what's happening in the unfolding drama. It would be impossible to exaggerate the importance of this text to our understanding of Scripture, which is why it is so tragic that this story is so often ignored or completely misunderstood.

Here's the problem: when we start reading Genesis 1-3, we bring our own worldviews to the text. Our interpretations of the text often reveal more about our existing worldviews than they do about the worldview of Scripture. This is inevitable and means that we need to read these ancient texts with both self-awareness and humility.

So how do we read the Genesis creation account to get to the heart of what the initial writer was saying about God, humanity and the world? How do we take off the cultural lens through which we currently see and make sense of everything around us?

To do this we need to lay some foundations and do some myth-busting.

Text or Pretext?

It has been said that a 'text without a context is just a pretext.'[5] Anyone can rip a part of Scripture out of context and use that Scripture to defend or justify a particular position. Parts of the church, in their darker moments in history, have used the Bible to defend and justify slavery, the Crusades, apartheid and other forms of oppression and discrimination. How? Leaders and communicators took a text out of context and used it to support their agendas.

To avoid this, Terence Fretheim advocates what he calls a 'Three Worlds Approach' to reading Scripture. He argues that when we read Scripture, three worlds are colliding: the world of the text, the world behind the text and the world in front of the text.[6]

The task of interpretation is to read the text, and before applying it to our culture (the world in front of the text), we need to delve into the world behind the text to better understand the context the writer was speaking into. Once we have a better grasp of that world, we are more likely to answer the question of what the author was trying to say to his intended audience. We will then be equipped to do the work of translation in figuring what the author might want to say to us, his unintended audience.

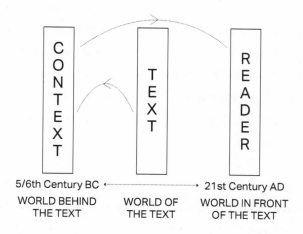

5/6th Century BC ← · · · · · · · · · · · · · · · → 21st Century AD

| WORLD BEHIND THE TEXT | WORLD OF THE TEXT | WORLD IN FRONT OF THE TEXT |

The text is what connects readers in the twenty-first century with, for example, the author of Genesis 1 writing from perhaps the fifth century BC from Babylonian captivity. None of this threatens our belief that all Scripture is God-breathed and inspired by him. But it does highlight that by speaking through certain people in certain times from certain contexts, a work of interpretation is necessary for us to hear the timeless words of God.

How does this help when it comes to reading the Genesis creation account? The answer is that this approach encourages us to read the Bible 'literately' not just 'literally.' Reading the Bible literately means recognising that Genesis 1-3 is not a scientific account. It belongs to an entirely different genre of literature.

The Elephant in the Room: Genesis as 'Lousy Science'

You've probably heard the argument of the new atheists: 'the biblical account of creation has no rational basis, it can't be explained on scientific grounds and hence must be dismissed. For progress to be made, we must liberate ourselves from the old way of thinking that keeps us in the dark.' The problem is that throwing out the bathwater (treating Genesis 1-3 as a scientific account of creation) inevitably leads to throwing out the baby (all of the truths contained within this creation account).

To dismiss Genesis 1-3 as lousy science is to miss the very heartbeat of these creation accounts. Genesis 1-3 is not science. It's relatively disinterested in the question of *how*, being far more concerned with *why* God created the earth. To impose the genre of science upon an ancient text is something any historian would describe as an elementary error. Though Richard Dawkins, for example, acknowledges that not all Christians are creationists, holding to a literal understanding of the Genesis creation account, he proceeds to state: 'Of course irritated theologians will protest that we don't take the book of Genesis literally anymore. But that is my whole point! We pick and choose which bits of scripture to believe, which bits to write off as symbols or allegories. Such picking and choosing is a matter of personal decision....'[7]

However, faithful reading of any historic document, let alone Scripture, has nothing to do with 'picking and choosing' but about reading that document contextually, according to its genre. Genesis 1-3 belongs to the genre of mythology, so to appreciate the purpose of the text, we need to understand this genre.

Mythology and Ancient Trash-Talking

The story of Genesis 1 was written either in or under the influence of Babylonian exile in the sixth or fifth centuries BC. This means it was written hundreds and hundreds of years before the Enlightenment and long before 'scientific literature' as we know it today. In fact, it was written before the genre of philosophy rose to prominence with the Greeks. So before scientific ways of knowing and before philosophical discourse, the ancients told stories about the world as they knew it, and they called these stories 'myths.'

The term *myth* is often used these days to refer to a fable or false story, but academic use of the term generally does not pass judgement on truth or falsehood. To ask if Genesis 1-3 is true, or if Adam and Eve really existed, is to impose Enlightenment categories on a premodern text. That is not to say Adam and Eve didn't exist, only that Genesis 1-3 is not addressing such a question. In the study of mythology, a myth is a sacred narrative explaining how the world and humankind came to be in their present form. Myths are 'true,' not in the way that scientific data is true, but in that these stories answer the big questions about the nature of God, humanity and the world around us. So how do we access these 'truths' contained in the Genesis story?

One way to dig for these truths is to compare the Hebrew creation myth with other ancient Near Eastern creation stories—for example, the Babylonian myth of Enuma Elish, the Canaanite myth of Baal or the numerous Egyptian creation accounts. The fact that so many of these stories significantly overlap terrifies many Christians. Questions and doubts begin to emerge: Is our story borrowed? If so, does that undermine its authenticity? How do we now interpret the story?

These are all important questions, but they don't threaten the integrity or authenticity of Genesis 1. The strong similarities between these creation accounts make sense when you consider that each of the myths was attempting to explain the cosmos as they commonly experienced it. The structure and order of creation is pretty much consistent in each account: the separation between light and darkness, day and night, the heavens above and the earth below, the land and the sea, humanity and the animal kingdom.

The strong similarities also make sense when you consider the long time the people of Israel spent in Egypt and the fact that Genesis 1 was written either in or under the influence of Babylonian exile. The people of Israel had spent centuries immersed in these other creation stories elevating Marduk, Baal and other such deities. No doubt these myths had been imposed upon the Jewish people: they knew them thoroughly.

Genesis 1 therefore borrows key elements of these creation stories from the surrounding cultures, and then twists them in order to differentiate the Hebrew God from the competition. It is subversive literature at its best, a form of ancient trash-talking if you like. The writer confronts and challenges Mesopotamian theology (whether Babylonian or Egyptian) and provides an account of creation that points to the God of Israel, rather than any of the Mesopotamian gods, as the supreme, unique and sovereign deity. Genesis trumps all the other stories. It puts those stories, and the deities they point to, firmly in their place as subservient to the Hebrew account and the one true God it showcases.

Digging for Gold: The Explosive 'Truths' of Genesis 1

What are the truths contained in the Hebrew creation account? If the similarities are to be expected, the explosive truths about the character of God and the nature of humanity are most likely to be found in how it stands apart from the alternatives on offer. Let me outline three major differences:

Firstly, Israel's God has no myth of origin, and he transcends all cosmic matter. He was and is and will always be. This strongly contrasts the polytheistic creation accounts throughout the ancient Near East, where most gods have a story of origin and fail to transcend nature. Reading or hearing the creation accounts side by side, one would swiftly conclude that Israel's God is uncreated, unrivalled and supreme. He has no match.

Secondly, the means of creation are quite different. Most ancient Near Eastern creation stories involve warfare and violence. Two of the gods engage in battle, with the conquering god using the defeated victim as the raw materials for creation. Compare that with the Hebrew account where there is a complete absence of bloodshed. Instead, Israel's God creates through divine speech. He's that powerful. His breath has the power to form planets. He says 'Let there be light' (Gen. 1:3), and there is light. Our worldviews today mean we miss the shock and awe that Genesis 1 would have created: a creation story without violence, a deity creating through speech.

Last is the great difference in the descriptions of how and why humanity came to be. In the Enuma Elish and numerous other ancient myths, humanity is made from the blood of the defeated gods and created to be the servants of the gods, but in the Genesis account God created man in his own 'image and likeness' (Gen. 1:26). And rather than making him a slave to the gods, God gave him dominion over creation.

Reading these ancient myths begins to make sense of why the Greeks and Romans spent so much time appeasing the deities, living in genuine fear and terror as to what they might do and how they might act. However, this unparalleled Hebrew story features a god who created the world out of the overflow of love, and then created humanity to be his friend, to share in his rule and to walk and talk together in a garden of delight. It's a story so beautiful, so profound, that rather than trying to make it fit our worldview, we need to allow it to create a whole new worldview.

Let's explore then this new world and, in particular, the climactic moment of the creation story: God creating humanity in his image and likeness.

Chapter 2

CREATION AND THE IMAGE-BEARERS OF GOD

I remember vividly the day our eldest son, Benj, was born. Bee and I had opted to give birth at the nearby birthing centre, a setting somewhere between a home birth and the hospital labour ward. When we had visited in the weeks building up to Benj's birth, we had been impressed with the sense of calm and order. It felt more like a spa than a medical facility. The whale music was unbelievably relaxing, people calmly strolled the corridors and no screaming could be heard. I concluded that the women here, behind closed doors, were painlessly giving birth in jacuzzis (otherwise referred to as 'birthing pools'). The midwife mentioned that if we chose the birthing pool option, then it was fine for me to be in the pool too. Enjoying a soak in the jacuzzi whilst having our first child seemed like a great idea.

So the big day arrived. We rushed to the birthing centre feeling stressed and on edge. The warm welcome and whale music immediately put us at ease. We were shown to our room and offered an herbal tea. I was getting ready for the jacuzzi when plans began to head in a different direction. The midwife examined Bee and identified some complications, suggesting we should go downstairs to the labour ward. We were whisked away, leaving the whale music and herbal teas behind to embrace the chaos of the labour ward. We heard women screaming, and we saw doctors and nurses rushing from room to room.

We arrived at the bed reserved for Bee, who by now was in tremendous pain. Nurses placed a heart monitor around Bee's waist to track the baby's heart rate, which each contraction caused to slow. This went on for a while, and then during one contraction, the intensity levels rose. The heartbeat had almost disappeared, so the midwife pulled a red chord. From nowhere, doctors and nurses emerged and surrounded Bee. There must have been seven or eight of them in the room.

One of the doctors explained that there was no time for an epidural and that the baby desperately needed to come out during the next contraction. They all began to urge Bee to push as hard as she could. She did, but the baby didn't come. They gave Bee another pep talk that the baby really needed to come out. The stress levels were high, way too high for my liking. So out of nowhere, I stepped forward, placed my hands on Bee's waist and loudly declared, 'In the name of Jesus, I command this baby to come out!'

Every eye turned from Bee to me. I could read their minds. *Who is this idiot! Someone tell him to calm down. He's hysterical. Give him some gas and air.*

I actually was really keen for some gas and air. One of the nurses, no doubt a Christian, nodded her head approvingly as if to add her 'Yes and amen.'

Benj emerged with the next contraction. Doctors checked that he was fine, and then immediately said they needed to take Bee off for surgery. I was overcome with emotion at meeting my newborn son and equally overwhelmed with pride at the courage of my wife, who had done the whole thing without any pain relief. As they wheeled her away, I proudly proclaimed, 'Bee, you are incredible! I'm going to buy you a DVD player!' To this day, I have no idea why I said that. We already had a perfectly good DVD player. It made no sense, but I guess nothing communicates love like the promise of a new DVD player.

They rushed Bee off and for the next two hours I sat alone in a room with my son Benj. The feelings of joy, relief and love were overpowering. I said over Benj again and again, 'You are my son, whom I love, with you I am well pleased.' I couldn't take my eyes off him. This little boy was made in my image and likeness. He carried my DNA. This was day one of his life, and though I knew nothing about him, I knew that I loved him with every bit of my human heart. From that moment until now, this is the truest thing about my son: he is loved with every bit of his father's heart.

Throughout human history every generation has sought to answer the question regarding what it means to be human. I have read multiple books on the subject, but something moved from the head to heart in those two hours with my son. To be human means to be made in the image and likeness of God the Father, to be loved by every bit of his heavenly heart.

What Does It Mean to Be Human?

'When I look at your heavens, the work of your fingers, the moon and the stars, which you have set in place, what is man that you are mindful of him, and the son of man that you care for him?' (Ps. 8:3-4). The psalmist is not alone in confronting the question of human identity. The philosopher Carl Becker sarcastically poses a similar question to the psalmist, whilst providing his own answer:

> What is man that the electron should be mindful of him? Man is but a foundling in the cosmos, abandoned by the forces that created him. Unparented, unassisted and undirected by omniscient or benevolent authority, he must fend for himself, and with the aid of his own limited intelligence find his way about in an indifferent universe.[8]

Becker's modern-day answer to the timeless question of what it means to be human suggests man is insignificant, forgotten, abandoned, unparented and undirected in the cosmos. The psalmist, however, paints a different picture of human identity. The psalmist is clearly overwhelmed by God's greatness and majesty, which culminates in the question 'what is man that you are mindful of him?' Surely the answer will involve man being nothing but dust?[9] Yet the answer that the psalmist provides is more than surprising.

Psalm 8 carries on by saying: 'You have made them a little lower than the angels [elohim] and crowned them with glory and honour. You made them rulers over the works of your hands; you put everything under their feet' (vv. 5-6). An alternative translation of Psalm 8 would be that humanity has been made 'a little lower than God,'[10] who has bestowed on them a royal identity and with it the invitation to share in his rule. In complete contrast to the idea of being abandoned by benevolent authority, and having to fend for oneself, the psalmist echoes Genesis 1 in affirming that we are made in the image and likeness of God.

The Language of Image and Likeness

Genesis 1 records God's creation of humankind on the sixth day as both the climax of the creation story and the final act before a period of divine rest (day seven). God says: 'Let us make mankind in our image, after our likeness. And let them have dominion over the fish of the sea and over the birds of the heavens and over the livestock and over all the earth and over every creeping thing that creeps on the earth' (v. 26 KJV). God then blessed humanity and commanded his creations to be fruitful and to multiply, filling the earth. Human beings are therefore not only created in the image of God (this is who they are); they are also created to be the image (this is their role in the world).[11]

These verses have attracted an enormous amount of attention from biblical scholars seeking to understand what the writer meant by the terms "image" (the Hebrew word is *tselem*) and 'likeness' (*demût*). At the heart of such research lies the biblical answer to the timeless question regarding our human identity.[12]

Like Father, Like Son

The only other place in Scripture where the two terms *image* and *likeness* appear side by side is in Genesis 5: 'This is the written account of Adam's family line. When God created mankind, he made them in the likeness of God. He created them male and female and blessed them. And he named them "Mankind" when they were created. When Adam had lived 130 years, he had a son in his own likeness, in his own image; and he named him Seth' (vv. 1-3).

The author provides a summary of Genesis 1, calling to mind the creation story, before adding the details of the birth of Seth, using the same two Hebrew terms *tselem* (image) and *demut* (likeness). The clear suggestion is that what Seth is to Adam, humanity is to God—a beloved son.

This 'sonship' identity of humanity, central to the creation story, is then reaffirmed in the story from Genesis 12 onwards. Abraham is called to be a father to many nations, but specifically to the nation of Israel, formed through his offspring. This nation is then adopted through the epic Exodus narrative and invited afresh to be God's son. The command given to Moses is simply to go to Pharaoh with the message: 'This is what the LORD says: Israel is my firstborn son, and I told you, "Let my son go, so that he may worship me"' (Ex. 4:22-23).

The writer of Deuteronomy echoes this theme when describing the disobedience, idolatry and subsequent fall of Israel. Mirroring the fall of Adam and Eve, the writer states: 'You deserted the Rock, who fathered you; you forgot the God who gave you birth' (Deut. 32:18).

If the fall (or De-creation) amounts to disconnecting from the father and walking away from the benefits of sonship, then salvation (or Re-creation) amounts to the restoration of that relationship. It shouldn't surprise us therefore that our rescuer, Jesus, the true 'image of God,' is affirmed in his sonship from the start.

At his baptism, the heavens open, and with the Spirit present in the form of a dove, the Father speaks over Jesus, 'This is my Son, whom I love; with him I am well pleased' (Matt. 3:17).

This affirmation comes at the beginning of Jesus' ministry and serves as both an affirmation of his identity and an affirmation of his mission, to 'seek and to save that which was lost' (Luke 19:10 NKJV). The key question here is what has been lost? The answer, at least in part, is that Israel and humanity at large have lost their connection to the father, and in disconnecting from the source of life, they have inevitably embraced death and are settling for far less than the fulness of life they were created for.

The driving force in this mission is God's mercy. The Hebrew term for mercy is *rahamim,* based on the Hebrew word *raham*, meaning 'womb.' The word *rahamim* is translated as 'the visceral feeling a mother has for the child of her womb.'

What would a mother do to rescue one of her children if in danger? Jump in front of bus to save a son? Take a bullet to rescue a daughter? The more apt question would be, what *wouldn't* a mother do to rescue one of her kids? The love of a mother is fierce. The umbilical cord may get cut at the moment of birth, but a bond remains that is pretty much unbreakable.

That same fierce connection is what drives the mission of God. It's his compassion for his children who need rescuing from inevitable death. We see this at its clearest in the ministry of Jesus. What drives his pursuit to restore lepers, to liberate the oppressed, to place the lonely into families and to bring sight to the blind? The answer is that God in Christ is rescuing his children, driven by the powerful force of mercy. This is God's mission and he invites you and I to share in it.

Consider Matthew 25 as a great example. Jesus says, 'For I was hungry and you gave me something to eat, I was thirsty and you gave me something to drink, I was a stranger and you invited me in, I needed clothes and you clothed me, I was ill and you looked after me, I was in prison and you came to visit me' (vv. 35-36). The obvious response from the disciples would have been shock. When was Jesus in prison? When was he naked? And then comes the punchline: 'Truly I tell you, whatever you did for one of the least of these brothers and sisters of mine, you did for me' (v. 40).

We read that list as an example of what a Mother Teresa–type character might give their time to. This is how the heroes of the faith live, but not you and me. Still, any parent will tell you that most of that list is a regular day looking after the kids. Every day, mothers and fathers feed the hungry, give a drink to the thirsty, clothe the naked and look after the sick. Why? Because they love their kids.

The logic of Matthew 25 seems to be this: what you naturally do for your own children is what God wants to do for his children. If your son were homeless, you would give your best energy to finding him suitable accommodation. If your daughter were starving, you would do anything to provide food. If your son were addicted to drugs, you would try to find a pathway to rehabilitation. And what you would do for your own children is what God wants to do for his children: rescue them in order to lead them to life.

Humanity as God's Royal Representatives

The language of 'image and likeness' is borrowed from the realm of royal ideology from Mesopotamia and Egypt. At that time, kings (and sometimes priests) were designated the image or likeness of a particular god, tasked with representing that deity and mediating divine blessing to the earthly realm. Remember the subversive nature of the Genesis creation account, which we see again here: what is true of the king in the surrounding cultures is true of all humanity in the Hebrew Bible. Therefore all human life is sacred and of exquisite value.

The task of royalty is to rule, which is exactly the task humanity is invited into as God blesses his image-bearers and commissions them to 'be fruitful and increase in number; fill the earth and subdue it' (Gen. 1:28). So with a royal identity, humanity is given a royal task, to rule and extend God's kingdom throughout the world. Having been placed in Eden, Adam and Eve were to extend the garden by transforming the outer chaotic region of the wilderness into habitable territory.[13] The biblical vision of God's glory filling the earth is to be accomplished through the rule of humanity as God's royal representatives. Their multiplying and filling the earth is the means by which God's own glory fills the earth.

It's worth noting here that this royal identity is also priestly in nature. The description in Genesis 2 that 'the LORD God took the man and put him in the Garden of Eden to cultivate it and keep it' (v. 15 NASB) contains the two Hebrew verbs *abad* (cultivate) and *samar* (keep). This word pair appears elsewhere in the Old Testament to describe priests who *cultivate* and *keep* the Temple in Jerusalem.[14] The point is that before the fall, humanity was given both a royal identity and a priestly identity. The people were called not only to rule, but also to bless, to extend Eden as well as to cultivate and keep it. The two go hand in hand, for it is only after the fall that priesthood and kingship are separated.

This royal (and priestly) understanding of what it means to be human has huge ramifications regarding the mission of the church. We demonstrate the love of God by treating people according to the royal identity they have in the eyes of God. A key aspect of our mission is to restore a royal identity to those who tossed the heavenly crown aside in trying to become the king of their own kingdom. This sin, of life centred around the self, leads to dehumanisation. Human life loses value, which affects how we treat one another. Far from treating one another like royalty, we treat one another as if we are but dust.

Mother Teresa demonstrated this understanding of humanity crowned with glory and honour in the most profound way. She was once visited by a journalist from the UK wanting to write a piece about her work in the slums of Calcutta. One day, they found a beggar on the street with open wounds and maggots eating away at the rotting flesh. The beggar was undoubtedly dying, but the nuns wanted to provide this man with a comfortable and dignified death. They took him back to their base and nursed his wounds. The journalist then took Mother Teresa aside to explain how deeply unstrategic it was for them to be nursing a dying man who had no chance of surviving, particularly when they could be searching the streets to find people who they might genuinely be able to rescue. Mother Teresa gently responded that their role and mission was to provide dignity to people, whether in life or at the point of death.

The journalist and Mother Teresa returned to the beggar's bedside for the final few moments of his life. His last words revealed the impact of the sisters' ministry. He simply said, 'All my life I have lived like a dog. Today I die like a king.'

The radical hospitality and love of these humble sisters in Calcutta have provided a reminder to the church: the mission we have been entrusted with is not about adding value to something worthless but restoring value to something priceless. Likewise, the mission of God is to restore people, not just to their royal identity, but also to their royal vocation.

Humanity as God's Statues

Throughout the Old Testament the Hebrew word *tselem* (image) primarily designates a cult statue. People reading the creation account in its original language would have concluded that humanity represents God's statues on the earth. Imposing our modern worldview on the text, this makes little sense, but in the context of ancient Near Eastern literature, it is utterly profound. In such a context, it was common for powerful kings to erect an image of themselves in the parts of the empire where they would rarely appear. The statues of the reigning kings were a constant reminder of the one who was sovereign over the people. The clear implication of Genesis 1 is that humanity has been placed upon earth as God's sovereign emblem. These statues are therefore to be regarded as sacred.

In the context of the ancient Near East, to desecrate or deface a statue of the king was considered the same as attempting to attack the king in person. It was impossible to differentiate between the statue and that which it represented. This mind-set is present in numerous biblical texts, including Proverbs 14:31: 'Whoever oppresses the poor shows contempt for their Maker, but whoever is kind to the needy honours God.' To oppress someone made in the image of

God is to oppress God himself. The same logic also drives the Great Commandment that Jesus describes as the key to understanding and summarising all the Law and the Prophets: First, love the Lord your God with all your heart, soul, mind and strength. The second commandment, which Jesus says is like the first, is to love your neighbour as you love yourself (Matt. 22:37-40). Loving someone made in the image of God is to love God himself.

There is, however, another layer of meaning to this idea of humanity as God's statues. In the ancient world, every god had a temple, and placed inside each temple was a statue of that god. It was inconceivable for a temple not to have a statue present of the god who dwelt there. This is one of the ways in which the people of Israel, and in particular the Temple in Jerusalem, were so unique. As part of God giving Israel the Law as a pathway to human flourishing, he explicitly said within the Ten Commandments, 'You shall not make for yourself an idol [statue], or any likeness of what is in heaven above or on the earth beneath or in the water under the earth' (Ex. 20:4 NASB).

The Jerusalem Temple was therefore devoid of any statues. Why? The reason is God doesn't need statues of stone or bronze because he has living statues that contain his breath. Unlike the manufactured statues that have eyes but can't see, ears but can't hear, and mouths but can't speak, God's living statues can very much see, hear and speak. This is why the Israelites were not allowed to make any images of their God. To do so would be to ignore the call and identity God had placed upon them. To build an idol or a golden calf would be to deny God's call on their lives and the identity he bestowed on them.

God has made each of us to be his living statues in the world. The man-made replicas are an offence; they have no life in them. They can't love their Maker and enter into relationship with him. But we can. As God's living statues, we are created to be God's real presence in the world, filling the earth with the glory and presence of God.

I was reminded of this recently when the square outside King's Cross Station was opened to the public as part of the redevelopment of the area. To mark the occasion, the square was filled with fairground rides, candy floss machines, jugglers and magicians. Other street performers stood motionless until money was placed in a hat to initiate robotic movements. I was intrigued to read the headline the next morning in a local newspaper: 'Living Statues Bring New King's Cross Station Square to Life.'

What is God's plan to restore and re-create King's Cross? How is he going to restore your street, town or workplace? The answer: he has living statues, filled and energized by God's own breath, and their presence ushers in the presence of God himself. And these statues, restored as sons and daughters of God, with both a royal and priestly identity and vocation, become God's agents of restoration in the world. A restored humanity restores humanity.

Chapter 3

DE-CREATION AND THE DISTORTION OF THE IMAGE

At the Arctic Circle, there is a tribe of Eskimos who have developed an effective trap for wolves. They screw a razor blade into a block of wood and then bury the contraption in the snow. They then drip some blood onto the snow, with the trap hidden below.

Wolves have an amazing sense of smell, so they eventually find the blood and start licking the snow. The snow is so cold that it begins to numb the tongue. Having tasted the blood, the wolf wants more and keeps licking. It eventually licks through the snow and begins licking the blade. By this point, the tongue has been entirely numbed, so it can't feel the cuts inflicted by the blade. More blood appears, but the wolf keeps licking. The cycle goes on, until the wolf eventually collapses.

I've shared the story on numerous occasions as an illustration of the disastrous effects of sin. It's never gone down well. But the illustration dramatically makes the point. Sin is essentially seeking to satisfy our deepest needs outside of God. We take our soul's longings and desires to people, places and pursuits in hope of finding acceptance, healing and salvation. Our appetites drive us to what we think will satisfy, and when we find such a thing, we start licking. However, we fail to realise that rather than satisfying the soul, we are killing it.

Our pursuit of life outside of God leads us to death. To disconnect from God, the source of life, must surely mean embracing death. Idolatry leads to De-creation—which happens to be the story presented in Genesis 3.

Leaving Eden

The narrative flow of Genesis 1-3 moves from humanity living under God's blessing towards humanity living under the curse of exile, having been thrown out of the Garden of Eden. Already in Eden you have a precursor to the Law, with God providing boundaries in which humanity can flourish. God said to Adam, 'You are free to eat from any tree in the garden; but you must not eat from the tree of the knowledge of good and evil, for when you eat from it you will certainly die' (Gen. 2:16-17). Obedience to this simple law will be the key to remaining under God's blessing. Disobedience will amount to stepping outside of such blessing and embracing the curse of exile.

This is the story of De-creation: created order breaking down. Adam and Eve, created in the image and likeness of God, decided they would like to go it alone. Rather than living in God's kingdom and God's garden, they preferred to create their own kingdom in which they could be in charge. The serpent offered them the opportunity to 'be like God.' The tragedy is that they were already 'like' God, made in his image and likeness. But in choosing to be God's rival rather than his friend, they are thrown out of Eden and find themselves lost in the wasteland.[15]

Martin Luther famously defined sin as a life turned in on itself. Rather than orbiting around God, we want everything to revolve around us. This was the choice of Adam and Eve, and the effect of their decision—choosing independence over dependence and their will over God's will—had ramifications for all created order. Everything began to unravel. In the wasteland outside of Eden, Cain killed his brother Abel and the created order that God declared good started to spiral into chaos.

The absolute low point in the De-creation story comes in Genesis 6, where it states that the earth was 'filled with violence' (v. 13) and that God was 'grieved in His heart' (v. 6 NASB). This story in which Adam and Eve had been commissioned to multiply and fill the earth, expanding the presence and glory of God, got thrown off course. God's heart, filled with delight in chapter 1, was filled with pain, and humanity became overcome with violence.

Adam and Eve's role as God's royal representatives was to extend the boundaries of the garden until Eden covered the whole earth. This task became impossible when they were expelled from the garden. They no longer had access to the abundance of life and vegetation in Eden that is necessary to bring life to the wasteland beyond. How could they extend blessing when they were now under a curse?

A Lost and Stolen Identity

By wanting to have 'a likeness to God' independent from him, humanity loses its identity. The image of God is distorted. If our purpose is to mirror or image God to the world, the mirrors crack and the image that we are meant to reflect gets distorted in the process. No wonder so many people today have such a distorted image of God as some angry, distant deity wanting to rob people of life. They have a distorted image of God because they've seen so many distorted 'images of God' in the world.

It's not that people cease to be God's image-bearers from Genesis 3 onwards; it's that they stop living out their true identity in the world. They are sons and daughters separated from their father. They have a royal identity but have taken off the crown. Their identity has, at least in part, been lost and can only be recovered by God (in Christ) leaving the garden to 'seek and to save that which was lost' (Luke 19:10 NKJV).

However, there is a sense in which the identity of humanity has been more than just lost. It has been stolen. When people choose their own will rather than the will of God, they surrender to the will of the serpent. This act of idolatry is the defining moment leading to De-creation, as true identity is relinquished and given to another. That is the true and tragic effect of all idolatry. As CS Lewis noted, idols always break the hearts of their worshippers.[16] For in worshipping another, we give away an identity that was meant to be ours and receive an identity that we should never own. In worshipping money, we allow our wealth, or lack thereof, to define our identity and levels of happiness. In worshipping success, we define ourselves by our achievements. In worshipping sex, we begin to define ourselves by how much we are or aren't getting. All of these are tried and tested ways of guaranteeing a broken heart.

Adam and Eve's primary sin was idolatry. They had been called to be stewards of the garden, protecting and ruling over God's created order.

Submitting to the voice of the serpent therefore represents an abdication of their responsibility. So how did we end up in the mess of De-creation? Humanity (represented by Adam and Eve) neglected the call to rule under God and listened to the voice leading us away from God.

One of the tragedies of the De-creation narrative is evident in the New Testament title given to Satan, who is called the 'prince of this world.' If Genesis 1 stresses that to be human amounts to being the King's child, with a royal identity, then that can only mean humanity was created to be God's prince, with authorised power to share in God's rule. To describe Satan as the prince of this world is a tragic reminder that an identity was stolen in Eden.

Idolatry as the Pathway to De-creation

The apostle Paul lays out the effects of idolatry in Romans 1. Referring to the nation of Israel, and perhaps also to Adam and Eve, he states:

> For although they knew God, they neither glori-
> fied him as God nor gave thanks to him, but their
> thinking became futile and their foolish hearts
> were darkened. Although they claimed to be wise,
> they became fools and exchanged the glory of the
> immortal God for images made to look like a mor-
> tal human being and birds and animals and reptiles.
> Therefore God gave them over in the sinful desires
> of their hearts to sexual impurity for the degrading
> of their bodies with one another. They exchanged
> the truth about God for a lie, and worshipped and

> served created things rather than the Creator—who
> is for ever praised. Amen. (vv. 21-25)

Paul emphasizes that idolatry is the sin that opens the door to every other sin. We were created to be worshippers of the one Creator God. We were created to live in perfect harmony with the one from whom all life flows, with this connection leading to a full and joyful life. That's why the first of the Ten Commandments is a mandate against idolatry. Central to the vision of human flourishing is right worship, remaining connected to the Creator. Conversely, wrong worship (idolatry) leads to human suffering. Disconnection from the source of life will inevitably lead towards death, and this journey begins when we walk through the door of idolatry.

We've discussed that God's mission is to renew all things through humanity, his living statues, animated and empowered by his breath. It follows, then, that the worst thing that can happen is for these living statues to lose the breath of God, becoming dead and inanimate. It is through the act of worship, remaining connected to the Creator, that we breathe in the breath of God. Without breathing in, we would have nothing to breathe out. Our mission would become powerless. The restoration of all things would be impossible without God's breath. So a fundamental question, critical to God's mission in the world, is how to ensure that we don't lose God's breath. And the answer is simple: steer clear of idolatry.

The Bible reiterates again and again that the main effect of idolatry is becoming like the objects of our worship. When we worship Jesus, we become like Jesus; when we worship idols, we become like them. Psalm 135 puts it like this:

> The idols of the nations are silver and gold, made by human hands. They have mouths, but cannot speak, eyes, but cannot see. They have ears, but cannot hear, nor is there breath in their mouths. Those who make them will be like them, and so will all who trust in them. (vv. 15-18)

This idea is a major theme for the Prophets and is also found in the teachings of Jesus.[17] The clear implication is that Israel became like their idols and consequently became spiritually blind, deaf and unable to breathe properly.

My guess is that most people reading this book haven't actually built a statue from wood and then proceeded to bow down and worship it. If idolatry in the ancient world did look like that, what does idolatry in the twenty-first century look like? What does it look like in my life? Louie Giglio, in his book *The Air I Breathe,* writes:

> So how do you know where and what you worship? It's easy. You simply follow the trail of your time, your affection, your energy, your money and your loyalty. At the end of that trail you'll find a throne; and whatever, or whomever, is on that throne is what's of highest value to you. On that throne is what you worship.[18]

Idolatry was the door out of Eden into the lifeless wasteland outside. It is the door through which we begin our journey towards dehumanization.

Trying to Get Back to Eden without God

Having described the process of hitting rock bottom through idolatry, Genesis goes on to tell the story of the Tower of Babel. It's the story of humanity trying to retrieve in their own strength their heavenly home, and with it their heavenly identity. They said to one another, 'Come, let us build ourselves a city, with a tower that reaches to the heavens, so that we may make a name for ourselves' (Gen. 11:4). Humanity has been attempting that same goal ever since.

The Tower of Babel is not alone in failing to deliver the heavenly identity and home that we long for. There are numerous 'towers' trying to achieve the same goal. Different worldviews—whether religious, political or otherwise—aim to provide different remedies to the fall of humanity. The message of Babel is that all such efforts are doomed to failure. We can't build a tower high enough. We are not strong enough, wise enough or good enough.

The Tower of Babel story is placed where it is as a firm warning and reminder as to what the wider narrative of Scripture is *not* about. The Christian message is not about how we can make our way back to God. It is not about trusting in human strength, wisdom or morality to retrieve a heavenly identity and a heavenly home that we lost in Eden. That's the endeavour of religion and this is a story of grace: not of our works, but of his work. Such radical grace can be hard to comprehend. It's much easier to settle for a set of rules whereby we can measure how close to God we might be getting.

Thankfully, there is one other story in the opening eleven chapters of Genesis that points us in the right direction, towards a remedy, and this story serves as a taster as to what Genesis 12 through to Revelation 22 will be about.

Ark Theology: The Story of Noah

The story of Noah begins with humankind increasing in number, fulfilling the command in Genesis 1 to be fruitful and multiply. Evil, however, begins to take over, causing God to declare his intent to wipe out humankind and with it the evil that humankind had allowed to exist. God invites Noah, the one righteous and blameless man, to build an ark to survive the flood that will devastate the land and eradicate the rest of humanity. Noah takes two of every kind of living creature with him in the ark, and when the waters eventually subside after the flood, Noah and his family start afresh. They enter into a covenant relationship with God and go about filling the earth as humanity was created to do at the very beginning. The covenant with Noah is really just a renewal of God's covenant with Adam, highlighting that this flood story is fundamentally a story of restoration.

The flood that covers the earth symbolizes the primordial chaos before creation takes place. The dove, sent out from the ark by Noah, hovering over the floodwaters, calls to mind the Spirit of God hovering over the waters in Genesis 1:2. The waters then subsiding after the flood are reminiscent of God separating the waters from the land on day three of creation. The message contained within this story is that God will never give up on creation. Though created order has fallen through humanity's sin, God's plan is to restore and re-create his broken world.

In Genesis 1-2, created order is to be sustained through right worship and obedience. For Re-creation to take place there needs to be a reversal of the disorder, which involves eradicating evil and restoring right order. Both are in view in the flood story. The violence that has filled the earth is judged, before order is restored.[19]

The flood story contains the new creation theology that dominates the whole biblical narrative. DL Moody, the remarkable nineteenth-century evangelist, used to talk about the church being like a lifeboat rescuing people from this world drowning in the waters of sin to live in a better world (heaven). Such theology, however, misses what the Noah story, as well as the wider narrative that it points towards, constantly emphasises: that salvation isn't simply *from* this world, but *for* this world. Ark theology, as opposed to 'lifeboat theology,' doesn't allow for the dualistic thinking that separates the material and the immaterial, the earthly and the heavenly. Noah is rescued both from the world and for the world, so that his family might be agents of Re-creation, spreading God's blessing throughout the world as Adam and Eve were meant to.

The Noah story functions as a foretaste of what the rest of the biblical narrative will be about: God's plan to renew and restore all things. For those who have read the Noah account, the end of the biblical story in Revelation 21-22 is no surprise. God, the judge and restorer of life, sits on his throne and simply declares, 'Behold, I am making all things new' (Rev. 21:5 NASB). Or, to borrow the language from the Epistle of Barnabas 6:13, one of the earliest extra-canonical sources we have from the first century, God will proclaim, 'Behold, I will make the last things like the first things.'

Chapter 4

PERSONAL REFLECTIONS: LOST AND FOUND

In my mid-twenties, I went through a number of experiences that left me totally disorientated. God felt far off, and I felt disconnected both from him and myself. A friend suggested I see a counsellor, which I did. Like a visit to the doctor, I went with my presenting symptoms, hopeful for a quick diagnosis and some pain-free treatment to find myself again.

For those who have had counselling, you know the drill. The presenting issues are the starting point, but they are just the presenting issues. The real pain is often found in the stuff that is not presenting, hidden deep down. So with the counsellor, I talked about the immediate pain, disappointment and loss. It was hard, but I felt like I was making progress.

I had been hiding in ministry for the previous year, trying to nurse my wounds in private, and now I finally found a place where I didn't have to hold myself together as a 'church leader.' For the first time I could own parts of my heart I'd been busy disowning. I got in touch with anger, grief and other foreign emotions. But just when healing felt close, the real blow came. We'd been treating the symptoms, but now was the time to explore the source of the symptoms. It was time to go back to when the wound first began. We would return to the moment when, like Adam and Eve, I realised I was naked and needed to cover up.

The counsellor asked if I had any memories of feeling shame from my childhood. I spent a few moments thinking, and a couple of random memories emerged, but neither felt significant. I said that nothing substantial came to mind. I should have realised that the 'nothing substantial' comment was careless, providing an open door for the counsellor.

'Well, tell me about the insubstantial memories then.'

It's a strange moment when an insubstantial memory gets vocalised in the presence of someone. You realise that what was potentially insubstantial a few seconds ago is anything but insubstantial as the full force of emotion hits you in the retelling. I nonchalantly said that when I was ten years old I still regularly wet my bed. I was half expecting to laugh as I said it, but instead I began sobbing. Suddenly I was transported to those moments waking up at a friend's house in a wet bed, feeling such embarrassment and shame. At eleven, I went on a football tour with the county team. Even at eleven the lad culture was beginning to kick in, and whilst on tour I woke one morning with another wet bed. Desperately trying to cover up, I had to find the fairly unempathic coach to explain what had happened. Each experience deepened the shame.

Much has changed since then, and I've been controlling that magic muscle now for almost thirty years, but hidden shame was still lurking, manifest perhaps most in my drivenness at work.

One of the non-presenting issues for me in counselling had been the desperate desire to achieve something remarkable. I was a driven athlete, not just wanting to win, but wanting to win well. I was driven when it came to academia, not just wanting to perform well academically, but to do something spectacular. Why? Because when you experience shame, you swallow the lie that you are unworthy of love. Salvation for me therefore looked like achieving something remarkable to prove to the world and to myself that I was indeed worthy of love. Every exam was an opportunity for healing, every game an opportunity for redemption. The problem was that great results weren't providing the healing and redemption they promised.

This pattern continued in ministry. Every sermon and every pastoral encounter felt like an opportunity for healing or disgrace. I arrived at the counsellor exhausted and defeated. I'd idolised success, hoping it would be to me like the fig leaves Adam and Eve used to cover their nakedness. I've no doubt Adam's fig leaf was bigger than it really needed to be! That's what shame does. I lived with the constant fear of failure, and the experiences of success just weren't enough. Worshipping success was breaking the heart of this fragile worshipper, and I was done with it. I could envision God coming to find me, like he did for Adam and Eve in the garden, saying 'Pete, where are you?'

In the months that followed, I found myself again, but far more importantly, I found the love of God. I had to let go of pursuing the crown of success to realise I'd already been given a more beautiful crown, the crown of sonship. Like Adam and Eve in the garden, I'd lost sight of what it meant to be made in the image and likeness of God. So I went in search for an identity outside of God.

A key moment in the counselling for me was when I heard my counsellor say to me that the driving motto of my life had become, 'I perform in order to be loved.' He was right. My best energy was spent trying to win the love of the crowds, my family and my friends. The tragedy was that I already had all of the above (or at least the love of my family and friends). But shame always blinds us to the beauty of what we already have. I was performing by preaching, leading, playing sports or taking classes to win a love I already possessed.

The counsellor suggested a new motto, 'I perform because I'm loved.' In other words, the activities may remain the same, but the motivation is entirely different. So simple, but this paradigm shift felt like discovering fire. Love is the beginning of the journey, not the destination. It's the fuel, not the reward. Jesus heard his father say 'this is my Son whom I love, with him I am well pleased' at the very beginning of his ministry before he'd achieved anything. That's what enabled him to stay true to his identity and mission, not distracted by the adulation or opposition of the crowds. I was beginning to hear those same words over my own life. And so I began to increasingly open myself to the love of the Father, finding identity less in my failures and successes and more in his unchanging affection towards me, his son.

This is my story of healing, from De-creation towards Re-creation, of journeying back to the life of Eden, where shame doesn't rob me of intimacy with God and others. Fifteen years on, I still feel in the early stages of it. The journey from the garden to the wilderness is the story of every human heart. The journey where freedom overcomes shame and intimacy overcomes isolation can also be the story of every human heart. But tragically it isn't. God has come searching for us in the person of Jesus, simply asking, 'Where are you?' The journey back to the life of Eden begins when we respond to the invitation to be found. Not all respond, though, unaware that the response transforms everything.

The wilderness becomes a garden of delight the moment we allow God to walk into the room. This is the beauty of the gospel and the beauty of the story of Scripture. The moment we say yes, his story from life to death to resurrection, and the wider story from creation to De-creation to Re-creation, becomes our story.

PART II

THE STORY OF ISRAEL

Chapter 5

FROM SLAVERY TO THE PROMISED LAND

Our kids love to hear the story of how Mum and Dad got together. For them it's an origins story: an account that explains how they came to be. It helps that it involves a drunk burglar, the police and Bee and I being stuck together in the dark for an hour.

I was studying for my finals at university at the time. My housemates had finished their exams so were out celebrating. The phone rang, and though tempted to ignore it, I answered. It was a good friend from the church I attended in Nottingham. He had just received a call from a girl in the church who was in distress.

Bee was home alone that night, having opted for a quiet evening in. Whilst on the phone to a mate, she heard a banging at the door. She went to open it, but no one was there. She continued the conversation on the phone, before hearing a rattling at the window. She opened the curtains to find a man trying to break in. He started screaming at Bee, trying to open the window. Beginning to panic, Bee quickly and breathlessly described the situation over the phone. The friend told her to run across the road to the shop and wait there. He would immediately call the police. So Bee put the phone down, grabbed her coat and ran out of the front door.

A minute later, the friend called my house. I could hear fright in his voice. He said a girl from the church was in distress as a burglar was breaking into her house. He explained the events and then asked if I could run over and meet the girl at the shop. I said I'd leave right away, but then realised I should know who I was looking for. I asked if she was anyone I knew? Was she single? How old was she? I thought key bits of information might be helpful. He responded, 'It's Bee Jones. You know, from our small group.' My heart started racing. He didn't know this, but I had been keen on Bee for ages and was desperate to get to know her more. This was an enormous answer to prayer. This was my big moment.

Time was of the essence, so I ran upstairs to do my hair, put on aftershave and change my shirt. If this was my opportunity to be a knight in shining armour, I wanted to look good, feel good and smell good. So I ran out of the house and sprinted round to the shops. 'Eye of the Tiger' played in my mind and adrenaline coursed through my veins.

Soon I arrived at the shop and met Bee. She was looking beautiful, but also quite anxious, and asked what we should do next. I had no idea, but blurted out that we should go back to the house to check if all was okay. We made our way back to the house and nervously opened the front door. We went inside and then Bee asked again, 'What now?' I replied that we should search the whole house to check that no one had broken in. We climbed to the third floor, and then made our way down, checking every room on route, until we ended in the lounge.

I confidently declared that the house was safe, with no sign of the burglar or a break-in. Bee seemed less confident and walked over to the window in the lounge where she had previously seen the burglar. There on the patio, beneath the window, was the burglar. He had passed out and was lying unconscious on the ground.

My adrenaline started pumping again. We called the police once more and were told not to wake the would-be thief. Police would arrive within the hour. So we sat down on the sofa in the lounge, lights turned off so as to not wake the burglar, and waited. For an hour we sat and talked, getting to know each other through whispered conversation, with the sound of the burglar snoring in the background. The police eventually showed up and took the burglar off. Bee's housemates then returned home. We told them the story and shared the excitement and drama of the evening. I then said my goodbye, knowing deep down this was the start of something beautiful.

I walked home that night with swagger. Life felt great. Over the next few days, rumours spread through our group of friends and acquaintances that I had rescued Bee from a dangerous burglar, before handing him over to the police and securing the house. Details became exaggerated and people celebrated my bravery, but I felt little need to correct the embellishments. Within a week, Bee and I went on our first date, and the rest, as they say, is history.

A number of our friends have suggested that perhaps the burglar was an angel in disguise. Though there is no biblical precedence for angels excessively drinking and being arrested by the police, I think it's a lovely idea.

Here's the point: this story is so special to our family because it belongs to a much greater story. Fast-forward eighteen years, Bee and I now have three amazing kids, Benj, Josh and Olive. We have been married for sixteen of those years and are unbelievably grateful to God for the journey we have been on. The burglar story is meaningful to us, and our kids love to hear it because hidden in the drama is the origins of our family, the place where their identity and belonging are secure.

So let's explore the origins story of the family of Israel. It is the account of God rescuing Israel from the threat of Pharaoh, marrying her at Mount Sinai and establishing a whole new family as a result. To fully understand who we are and what we are about, it's pivotal to understand this origins story.

Father Abraham Had Many Sons

If Genesis 1-2 is the story of creation, and Genesis 3-11 is the story of De-creation, then the rest of the biblical narrative is the story of God's movement towards Re-creation. This chronicle begins in Genesis 12 with the call of Abraham to be a father to the nation Israel, which was chosen to be God's vehicle of blessing to the rest of the world. Israel, a second Adam of sorts, is now to be the true humanity, showing the rest of the world what it means to be human.

In Genesis 12:1-3, the Lord declares to Abram (who was later renamed Abraham):

I will make you into a great nation, and I will bless
you; I will make your name great, and you will be a
blessing. I will bless those who bless you, and whoever curses you I will curse; and all peoples on earth
will be blessed through you.

Abram was seventy-five years old at the time and no doubt
confused as to how God would accomplish this through a man
without an heir. Such a promise would have seemed ridiculous to
Abram, who together with his wife, Sarai, were trying to process
the pain of potentially never having a child of their own. But this
promise is then reiterated in Genesis 15, as God says to Abram,
'Look up at the sky and count the stars—if indeed you can count
them … So shall your offspring be' (v. 5). Into this context of
pain and heartbreak came the promise, highlighting that God
much prefers to choose the weak things to shame the strong and
the foolish things to shame the wise.

So what does Abram bring to the table in this emerging partnership, through which God is going to make all things new? The
answer is faith. Rather than rejecting God and his ability to open
Sarai's womb that had been barren, Abram simply believed, and
it was credited to him as righteousness. But such radical obedience and faith still leave room for questions. Abram rightly asked
how God would bring such things about, and God answered by
making a covenant with Abram. He asked Abram to slaughter
a number of animals and lay out the carcasses in the form of a
tunnel:

> As the sun was setting, Abram fell into a deep sleep,
> and a thick and dreadful darkness came over him....
> A smoking firepot with a blazing torch appeared and
> passed between the pieces. On that day the LORD
> made a covenant with Abram and said, 'To your
> descendants I give this land.' (vv. 12, 17-18)

In the ancient world this would have been a common method for two parties to enter into a binding agreement. Once the animal carcasses had been laid out in the form of a tunnel, the two parties would then walk between the slaughtered animals as if to say, 'May what has happened to these animals be done to me if I do not keep my oath with you.'[20]

What differentiates this covenant with Abram from more typical covenants from the time is that Abram was asleep, and God alone, in the form of a fire, passed between the carcasses. This amounts to God saying that he alone will bring about this plan to create a nation through Abram, and that he alone will bear responsibility for covenantal disobedience. God makes a divine pledge that he would rather die than give up on his plans to restore created order and make all things new. And that's exactly what God does through Christ at the cross. God in Christ bears the punishment of covenantal disobedience, leaving Abraham's descendants to enjoy covenantal blessing and the fulness of life they were made for.

Abraham went on to have a son, and the many descendants that followed eventually settled in the land of Egypt. The promises given to Abraham therefore provide the backdrop for the book of Exodus as the sons of Abraham become the children of God.

The Exodus Narrative: The Defining Story of the People of Israel

The story of Moses, and the narrative of liberation that follows, is enormously important for understanding Israel's identity and faith. The Exodus narrative is the birth story for Israel as a people. It all begins as God hears the cries of his people during their four-hundred-year period of slavery in Egypt and then intervenes to rescue them from oppression. The rescue mission gets underway when God revealed himself to Moses. Many other Hebrew boys were drowned in the Nile by Pharaoh's decree, but Moses was 'drawn out' of the Nile by Pharaoh's daughter, who took pity on him. Thus, Moses experienced God's rescue very early in his life.

Moses was then adopted by Pharaoh's daughter, who named the child, saying, 'I drew him out of the water' (Ex. 2:10). It's almost impossible to miss the fact that Moses' rescue is a foretaste of Israel's rescue. Moses, the one drawn from the water and adopted into a new family, led Israel to be drawn from the waters of the Red Sea into a covenant relationship with God, who adopted Israel as his own. As we see with Moses, rescued people rescue people. Liberated people in the kingdom are always called to become agents of liberation, and so the calling of Moses to liberate his fellow Israelites became a key moment in the story.

The Burning Bush and the Great I Am

God grabbed Moses' attention through a burning bush. Drawn by the strange sight of a bush on fire without being consumed, Moses approached the bush before God began to call his name and reveal to him the mission to liberate his people. In this encounter at the burning bush, Moses was confronted with three questions: Where do you stand? Where is your land? What is in your hand?

Moses was standing on holy ground. It's holy for the simple reason that the Holy One is there. The one who walked and talked with Adam and Eve in the garden was present in the desert, talking with Moses. And what does he say?

> I have indeed seen the misery of my people in Egypt. I have heard them crying out because of their slave drivers, and I am concerned about their suffering. *So I have come down to rescue them from the hand of the Egyptians and to bring them up out of that land into a good and spacious land*, a land flowing with milk and honey—the home of the Canaanites, Hittites, Amorites, Perizzites, Hivites and Jebusites. And now the cry of the Israelites has reached me, and I have seen the way the Egyptians are oppressing them. So now, go. I am sending you to Pharaoh to bring my people the Israelites out of Egypt. (Ex. 3:7-10, emphasis mine)

Notice the language used to describe God's rescue: *he will come down to bring them up*. This provides a foretaste of God's ultimate rescue plan in Christ, who came down by taking on human flesh, dying for the sins that led to the unravelling of created order, and rising again to establish God's new creation and bring resurrection life to God's redeemed people. God always redeems by coming down to lead us up, and here Moses was drawn into God's redeeming plans.

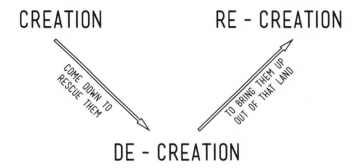

Moses was reminded of the promise given to Abraham that God had a land set aside for Israel—and not just any old land, but the very best, a land flowing with milk and honey. Moses responded with the obvious question: 'Who am I that I should go to Pharaoh and bring the Israelites out of Egypt?' (v. 11). In other words, 'I'm out of my depth! I don't have what it takes to confront the most powerful man, and empire, on the planet.' Interestingly, God didn't directly answer Moses' question. He simply says, 'I will be with you' (v. 12). Moses' ability, or lack thereof, is a secondary matter. What counts here is who God is, and his ability for the task at hand. This is why he goes on to reveal not only that he will be with Moses, but also his name, and therefore his identity.

In such a context, the revelation of one's name is an invitation into relationship, which is perhaps why it says in Exodus 33:11 that 'The

LORD would speak to Moses face to face, as one speaks to a friend.'
God is not a distant deity. He sees, he hears, he speaks, he draws close
and he reveals his name. In his interaction with Moses, God was binding himself to the nation of Israel in his mission of restoration.

Human Agency and the Purposes of God

In such an intimate encounter with God, Moses is changed into the
image of the one he worships. From this new sense of being, Moses
begins to act, and through his actions, Pharaoh experiences God
himself. This is highlighted in the remarkable statement made by
God to Moses: 'See, I have made you like God to Pharaoh' (Ex. 7:1).
Pharaoh experiences the one in whose image Moses has been made.
Consider the following process:

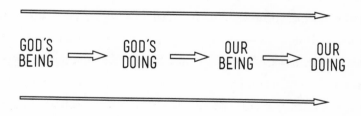

THE ART OF BECOMING

GOD'S BEING ⟹ GOD'S DOING ⟹ OUR BEING ⟹ OUR DOING

CULTURAL RENEWAL

How do we go about renewing culture and partnering with God
to transform our cities and communities? The answer is that we need
to become 'like God,' which starts with the issue of God's identity.

The mission of God always centres on his nature and character. From God's identity, all of his actions flow, and it is in the activity of God that we are redeemed and transformed. God's *doing* redeems and transforms our *being*, and our *being* then overflows in our *doing*. This is what happens when we partner with God. This is why the Great Commission to extend God's purposes throughout creation is essentially about making disciples and forming people into the likeness of Jesus. For as we are transformed into God's likeness, our actions become the vehicles through which people come face to face with God.

Plagues and Partings of Waters

Once God has revealed his name and the assignment set before Moses, God then asked him, 'What is that in your hand?' (Ex. 4:2). The answer is a staff, the tool of the trade for a shepherd. With the staff, Moses could move sheep from point A to B, but he was unlikely to move a nation from Egypt to the Promised Land with the same staff. It works with sheep, but doesn't work quite as well with whole nations or vast armies. So God invited Moses to throw the staff on the floor, and immediately it became a snake. When Moses picked up the snake, it turned back into a staff. God was telling Moses that this isn't about *his* ability or suitability for the task at hand. This was God's mission, and it would be God's power made perfect in Moses' weakness that will bring liberation into being. God then proceeded to demonstrate this power and sovereignty to his people through a series of plagues.

The climax of Israel's liberation story takes place in Exodus 14 and 15. Through the crossing of the Red Sea and the destruction of the

Egyptian army, God rescues Israel after four hundred years of oppressive slavery. The theme of Re-creation is strong here as Israel passes through the sea from certain death to new life. The creation language, including the separation of light from darkness (Ex. 14:20) and the separation of waters to reveal dry land (Ex. 14:21),[21] is lifted straight from Genesis 1 to underline the point that liberation is for the sake of Re-creation. Evil and injustice, embodied by the Egyptian army, are destroyed and judged so that right order might be established.

Mount Sinai and the Pathway to Human Flourishing

The covenant made at Mount Sinai was a royal covenant in which Israel came under the rule of Yahweh. The words of God in Exodus 19:4-6 provide a foundation for what follows in the establishment of the Sinai covenant:

> You yourselves have seen what I did to Egypt, and how I carried you on eagles' wings and brought you to myself. Now if you obey me fully and keep my covenant, then out of all nations you will be my treasured possession. Although the whole earth is mine, you will be for me a kingdom of priests and a holy nation.

The call to be a 'kingdom of priests' points to God restoring to Israel the royal identity that was given to Adam and Eve in the very beginning. Redemption always amounts to Re-creation.

As well as being a 'kingdom of priests,' God calls Israel to be 'a holy nation.' This refers to a people set apart, not simply from other nations, but for a specific purpose. Israel's liberation was for the sake of bringing blessing once again to all of creation. Throughout the Exodus narrative, the text constantly reminds us that God doesn't work alone. He works in and through his image-bearers. Augustine described the partnership between God and humanity by saying, 'Without God we cannot; without us he will not.'

Central to Israel's vocation is the gift of the Law, given to Israel at Mount Sinai. The purpose of the Law is to create the boundaries in which Israel can flourish and know God's blessing. This is of critical importance, for to extend God's blessing to all of created order, Israel must know, enjoy and carry the blessing themselves.

Temples, Tabernacles and Homes

The book of Exodus ends with the glory of the Lord filling the tabernacle. Israel's journey through the narrative of the book of Exodus is from slavery under Pharaoh to sonship under Yahweh, from enforced construction of buildings for Pharaoh to willingly building a dwelling place for God. This represents a significant change in the way God relates to his people. Having drawn near and revealed his name and nature, God was now present amongst them, journeying with them as they proceeded towards the Promised Land.

The construction of the tabernacle is central to the Re-creation theme.[22] In Jewish thinking, the act of creation was understood as the building of God's temple. If Eden had been God's original temple, then the construction of the tabernacle marks a movement towards Re-creation, restoring what was lost in Genesis 3.[23]

The first five books of the Bible (known as the Pentateuch) end with God's rescued people getting ready to enter the Promised Land. Like Adam and Eve being given a land to call home (Eden) and a base from which to extend God's blessing to all created order, the nation of Israel were about to be given their land and with it the same commission. The Pentateuch ends as it begins, highlighting the nature of the wider narrative to which it belongs: a story of Re-creation.[24]

Belonging, Purpose and Hope

As Israel looked back upon their journey from slavery in Egypt to worship at the tabernacle, three powerful bonds held the people together as a community. They stood as the people of God with a shared *history*, a shared identity and purpose in the *present* and a shared hope for the *future*. For any subsequent generation in Israel, the people first had a story to belong to of how God miraculously delivered them from Egypt and provided for them in the desert. Second, the Sinai covenant would always remind the people that God had called them to be his chosen people, with a purpose as a 'kingdom of priests and a holy nation' to bring blessing and further God's purposes on earth. Thirdly, until Joshua led the people into the Promised Land, they also had the future hope and expectation that a land flowing with milk and honey awaited them.

This strong sense of belonging, purpose and hope that unites the people of Israel on their adventure points to the very heart of what it means to be human. In and through the Exodus narrative, and more specifically through relationship with Yahweh God, these deep longings finally find fulfilment.

We live at a time when people are desperately searching for a sense of belonging, purpose and hope. People are searching for fulfilment, for a story, a remedy or a map to lead them home to life as it was meant to be. The yearning for Eden, for a promised land, is hidden in the depths of every human heart. But people are losing hope that such a home even exists.

Proverbs 13:12 tells us that 'hope deferred makes the heart sick.' A huge amount of the sickness in our culture is caused by the huge amount of hope deferred. So what do people do with the pain? The common response is to either bury it or numb it. Many people self-medicate with drink, drugs, workaholism, illicit sex, co-dependent relationships, obsession with food, gambling and the list goes on. These addictions are the epidemics of our time. The UK has recently been named the 'addictions capital of Europe,' with the abuse of drugs and alcohol alone costing the nation a total of £36 billion each year.[25] Why? Because people are losing hope, living without a story that brings belonging and purpose.

This search for home drives so much of human behaviour. If deep longings are unfulfilled and unsatisfied, we will forever be in search of their fulfilment. But there is such a home, a place where our deepest needs are met. This is what the Jewish people experienced as God rescued them from Egypt, dwelled amongst them as his presence filled the tabernacle, and journeyed with them to the Promised Land. They discover that human flourishing is only possible when one is connected to the source of life.

Chapter 6

FROM THE PROMISED LAND TO SLAVERY

When I was young, I read the story of the 'Old South Indian Monkey Trap.' The trap consists of a hollowed-out coconut tied to a tree. The Indian natives placed an orange or lemon within the hollowed-out coconut, creating a small hole just big enough for the monkey's fist to enter the coconut and grab the orange. The monkey's clenched fist, however, can't fit back out, and the monkey is suddenly trapped. The monkey's freedom to roam and enjoy the expanse of the jungle has been robbed by refusing to let go of the fruit.

This journey from freedom to slavery, from wide-open space to imprisonment, became Israel's story. Like Adam and Eve grabbing the prohibited fruit and being exiled from Eden as a result, Israel grabbed the forbidden fruit of idolatry and likewise traded their freedom for slavery. Idolatry always opens the door to De-creation. So let's follow the story from the Promised Land back into slavery.

The Kingdom Established and the Kingdom Demolished

As the people of Israel stood on the edge of their inheritance, Joshua took on the leadership from Moses and eventually led the people into the Promised Land. They took the land, drove out their enemies and settled. After Joshua's death, a series of 'judges' brought leadership to the nation, and throughout this reign of judges, a cyclical pattern emerged: the Israelites turned away from God and towards the idols of the surrounding nations. This results in God's judgement, manifest in the surrounding nations rising up against God's people. The people then cried out to the Lord for rescue, and God responded by raising up leaders through whom he threw off the foreign oppressors and restored the land to peace.

Israel eventually asked God for a king. This request signalled, at least in part, Israel's rejection of God as King, as well as a lack of understanding of Israel's true identity. The people knew that to be human meant being a child of the King with a royal identity. They shouldn't have needed an earthly king because they have all been invited to share in God's rule.

Nevertheless, God granted their request and chose to rule from heaven through a representative king on earth, starting with King Saul. This privileged position then enabled David, Saul's successor, to reconquer all the nations that had previously dominated Israel. David and his son Solomon proceeded to lead Israel to a high point in their history: a time of peace and prosperity. Under Solomon, in fulfilment of God's promise to Abraham, 'the people of Judah and Israel were as numerous as the sand on the seashore' (1 Kings 4:20).

The kingdom of God was present, and this was a time of kingdom fruit and abundance. The building of the Temple, a key motif in the Re-creation story, fittingly takes place during this season of prosperity.

The Oppressed Become the Oppressors

Something tragic began to happen during this period of kingdom prosperity. As we read in 1 Kings 9:15, 'Here is the account of the forced labour King Solomon conscripted to build the LORD's temple, his own palace, the terraces, the wall of Jerusalem, and Hazor, Megiddo and Gezer.' The same people rescued from forced labour in Egypt enslaved others to build a temple for their God. The irony is tragic. The people of God became so blind that they couldn't spot the problem of using slaves to build a temple for the God who liberates slaves. The commandments given to Israel at Sinai slowly slipped from their memory, and the clear instruction to 'not mistreat or oppress a foreigner, for you were once foreigners in Egypt' (Ex. 22:21) is long forgotten. What began as establishing God's kingdom soon became about building their own empire and holding on to the blessing themselves.

Hazor, Megiddo and Gezer were military bases established to protect the wealth of Solomon's empire. As described in 1 Kings 10:

> Solomon accumulated chariots and horses; he had fourteen hundred chariots and twelve thousand horses, which he kept in the chariot cities and also with him in Jerusalem. The king made silver as

common in Jerusalem as stones, and cedar as plentiful as sycamore-fig trees in the foothills. Solomon's horses were imported from Egypt.... They also exported them to all the kings of the Hittites and of the Arameans. (vv. 26-29)

This highlights how far Solomon fell. Like the fall in Genesis 3 where Adam and Eve seek to build their own kingdom centred around their own desires and will, Solomon followed in their path. He knew the Torah inside out, including the words of Deuteronomy 17:

The king, moreover, must not acquire great numbers of horses for himself or make the people return to Egypt to get more of them, for the LORD has told you, 'You are not to go back that way again.' He must not take many wives, or his heart will be led astray. He must not accumulate large amounts of silver and gold. (vv. 16-17)

Solomon's response is essentially, 'Not your will be done, but mine.' Having acquired thousands of horses and chariots from Egypt, he effectively became an arms dealer, making money from war. In a tragic turn of events, the people forgot their past and became the new Egypt with Solomon as the new Pharaoh. The identity and purpose God gave Israel at Sinai gets forgotten, and rather than becoming a vehicle of God's blessing, Israel became a vehicle of oppression. At the root of this downward spiral is idolatry.

The Tragedy of Idolatry

In 1 Kings 11, we read that Solomon had 'seven hundred wives of royal birth and three hundred concubines, and his wives led him astray. As Solomon grew old, his wives turned his heart after other gods, and his heart was not fully devoted to the LORD his God, as the heart of David his father had been' (vv. 3-4). As Solomon turned his heart to the gods of the surrounding nations, things began to go horribly wrong. God had made it clear at Sinai that covenantal obedience would lead to blessing, and the people had enjoyed such blessing under David and then Solomon. But Sinai also made it clear that covenantal disobedience would lead to a curse. To disconnect from God, the source of life, can only amount to disconnecting from life itself.

As the story unfolds, the kingdom of Israel became divided into the northern kingdom of Israel (ten tribes) and the southern kingdom of Judah (two tribes). The northern kingdom was led by a series of kings who constantly did 'evil in the eyes of the Lord,' turning the people again towards the idols of the surrounding nations.[26] The southern kingdom followed a similar path, with the occasional righteous king that turned the people back to the living God.

The people knew that covenantal disobedience would eventually result in the curse of exile, which is exactly where the story headed. The northern kingdom of Israel was overpowered by the Assyrians in 722 BCE and the southern kingdom of Judah taken by the Babylonians, who destroyed Jerusalem and the Temple in 587 BCE. The people were deported, and like Adam and Eve departing Eden, Israel and Judah departed the Promised Land to live in foreign territory.

The Curse of Exile and the Psalms of Lament

The people of Israel found themselves back in exile. But it was a self-inflicted exile: they walked away from God, turned their back on the covenant, and exile was the result. This is what makes the lament of Psalm 137 so deep:

> By the rivers of Babylon we sat and wept when we remembered Zion. There on the poplars we hung our harps, for there our captors asked us for songs, our tormentors demanded songs of joy; they said, 'Sing us one of the songs of Zion!' (vv. 1-3)

Such psalms provide a behind-the-scenes account of how exile felt for the people of God. Anger, disappointment, confusion, regret and pain flow from the pages of such psalms as the writers emotionally process all that they are going through. And yet in the midst of these laments, we find psalms of hope. These remind the people that the God who restored Israel in the past, most notably in their deliverance from Egypt, will restore them once more.

The worshipping life of the nation of Israel reveals the story that has shaped them as a people, and it is a story of redemption and renewal. It is the nature of God to not only create, but also to re-create. He is the God who makes all things new. Therefore, though the people may be weeping by the rivers of Babylon, they are not beyond redemption. With God, there is always hope. It is these themes of judgement and restoration that dominate the writings of the Prophets, which we will look at next.

Chapter 7

EXILE, HOMESICKNESS AND THE HOPE FOR NEW LIFE

Malcolm Muggeridge was one of the great English journalists of the last century. On one occasion whilst working in India, he took a stroll down to a nearby river for a swim. Across the river he could see an Indian woman bathing in the water. Driven by lust, Muggeridge pushed thoughts of marital fidelity to one side and began swimming furiously towards the woman. This is how he recounted the story in a letter written to his father:

> She came to the river and took off her clothes and stood naked, her brown body just caught by the sun. I suddenly went mad. There came to me that dryness in the back of my throat; that feeling of cruelty and strength and wild unreasonableness which is called passion. I darted with all the force of swimming I

had to where she was, and nearly fainted, for she was old and hideous and her feet were deformed and turned inwards and her skin wrinkled.... She was a leper ... showing a toothless mask.[27]

Muggeridge fell back in the water, shaken by the encounter. He muttered under his breath, "What a dirty lecherous woman!"[28] It was only later that he came to realise that it was not the woman who was lecherous. It was his own heart.

In later life Muggeridge came to faith in Christ. He likened this encounter in his youth to that of a running boy chasing the 'lusts of the flesh.'[29] It was only when he was far from home that he recognised that he was the one in need of salvation, more than the leprous woman. For Muggeridge and every heart far from home, the gospel of the Father who runs to embrace us is unbelievably good news. The boy running after the lusts of the flesh, like Israel chasing the idols of the surrounding nations, will always end up in a far-off land. Thankfully for Israel, God did not abandon his treasured possession in the far-off land of Babylon. The major focus in the prophetic writings of the Old Testament is the promise of judgement (in the form of exile) and future restoration, of death followed by new life. In the darkest place of De-creation, promises of a future light stir hope in the Jewish people.

It would be tempting here to rush to the stories of Jesus and the formation of a whole new world. But to bypass the prophecies and promises that gave hope to a nation lost in darkness might rob us of the opportunity to taste how sweet this restoration and Re-creation was. So let's delve into these promises, spoken to Israel in the midst of the curse of exile.

The Promise of a Faithful Husband

The Hebrew creation story includes a wedding, as God and humanity become one. A sense of celebration enlivens the opening chapters of Genesis, with feasting, abundance, intimacy and blessing accompanying the great wedding. Humanity's first sin of idolatry equated to marital unfaithfulness. Despite this betrayal, God remained faithful, constantly pursuing those who turned their backs on him. It is this pursuit that drives the narrative of the Exodus, where Israel isn't simply rescued from Egypt, but also rescued for the purpose of entering into a covenantal relationship with God.

The image is of God and Israel getting married at Mount Sinai, with the gift of the Law (and the Ten Commandments) functioning as the wedding ring that marks out the Jewish people as God's bride, his treasured possession.[30] It is worth highlighting here that the Law wasn't given to an enslaved people as a pathway to freedom but to a free people as a pathway to living under God's blessing. Obedience to the Law was first and foremost about honouring the marriage vows in order to enjoy a healthy and life-giving marriage. But for God to be truly loving, he has to give his 'treasured possession' free will to choose obedience or unfaithfulness.

Ezekiel 16 provides a brutal account of Israel's descent into marital unfaithfulness. God is portrayed as a wounded lover, recounting the story of rescuing, marrying and elevating Israel above the surrounding nations only to watch her take her love elsewhere. We learn how God felt with the statements, 'You trusted in your beauty and used your fame to become a prostitute,' followed by 'You adulterous wife! You prefer strangers to your own husband' (vv. 15, 32). We see

God's anger and his pain as Israel breaks the covenant and wanders off into a distant land. Jeremiah picks up on this theme:

> The LORD said to me, 'Have you seen what faithless Israel has done? She has gone up on every high hill and under every spreading tree and has committed adultery there. I thought that after she had done all this she would return to me but she did not, and her unfaithful sister Judah saw it. I gave faithless Israel her certificate of divorce and sent her away because of all her adulteries.' (3:6-8)

The wedding celebrations in Eden were a distant memory, the marriage at Sinai had long been forgotten, and here in Jeremiah 3 the prophet addressed the pain of betrayal and divorce. Israel had to face the trauma of exile, separated from God and his blessing. But the deeper pain resided in the heart of God, who declared, 'Return, faithless people ... for I am your husband' (v. 14).

Incredibly, right in the middle of pain and mess was found the invitation and promise of restoration. Similarly, Ezekiel 16 ends not with judgement but with a promise of God remembering the covenant he made with Israel in the days of her youth and establishing an everlasting covenant with her.

This promise of covenant renewal is the source of huge hope when Israel are lost in exile, separated from their lover. A time is coming, say the Prophets, when God will return to remarry his bride and lead her back to fulness of life.[31] What God had done at the

Exodus in liberating his people and wedding himself to them, he would do again.

The message is clear: their future will contain a wedding—a wedding to the Creator of life himself—and such a wedding can only mean fulness of life awaits. Their past contained such a wedding, and though they now experience the pain of separation, God is coming to marry them once more.

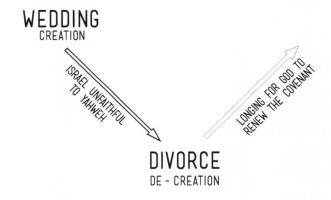

The Promise of a Returning King

In his book *Kingdom Conspiracy*, Scot McKnight summarises the narrative of Scripture with three key stages:

> 1. God rules the world through his elected people, but God is the one and only King.
> 2. Israel rejects God as their King, yet God accommodates Israel's desire to elect their own King.

3. God returns as King (in the person of Jesus, the Messiah) to rule over his people and establish his reign throughout the earth.[32]

McKnight refers to these stages as Plan A, Plan B and Plan A Revised. Within this framework, the primary sin of Adam and Eve, and later Israel as a whole, is the desire to rule 'like God' as his rival instead of 'under God.' The fall amounts to living in a world where our will is done rather than God's. The request of Israel recorded in 1 Samuel 8 to have their own earthly king like other nations that surround them mirrors the sin of Adam and Eve. Samuel's displeasure at such a request is met with God's own displeasure.

Plan B then kicks into gear with some high points and some real low points. The highest point in Plan B, which still falls short of how God intended things to be, is the reign of David. But the lows outweigh the highs as the story unfolds, culminating in the invasion of the Assyrians in the north and the Babylonians in the south, before the southern kingdom of Judah is deported to Babylon.

However, promises fuel hope, and God had promised to set David 'over my house and my kingdom for ever; his throne will be established forever' (1 Chron. 17:14).[33] When things got tough, these promises stirred within the Jewish people a longing for a new Davidic King to come and establish again God's reign over the earth. These messianic longings fill the prophetic literature of the Old Testament. Isaiah 9 is one of the best-known examples:

> For to us a child is born, to us a son is given, and
> the government will be on his shoulders. And he

will be called Wonderful Counselor, Mighty God, Everlasting Father, Prince of Peace. Of the greatness of his government and peace there will be no end. He will reign on David's throne and over his kingdom, establishing and upholding it with justice and righteousness from that time on and for ever. The zeal of the LORD Almighty will accomplish this. (vv. 6-7)

The Old Testament concludes with the longing for God to return as King, summarised in the following diagram:

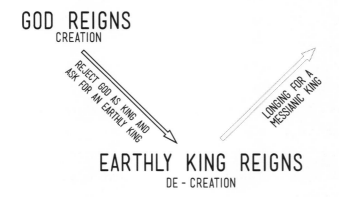

GOD REIGNS
CREATION

REJECT GOD AS KING AND ASK FOR AN EARTHLY KING

LONGING FOR A MESSIANIC KING

EARTHLY KING REIGNS
DE - CREATION

The Promise of a Good Shepherd

Related to the theme of kingship is the idea of God as Israel's shepherd. Borrowing Scot McKnight's framework, we could also say that Plan A meant God would shepherd his people, with Plan B being earthly shepherds ruling instead of God. David famously declared that, 'The LORD is my Shepherd' (Ps. 23:1), but his people looked to David to shepherd them.

Plan B is littered with stories of Israel being mistreated by their shepherds. One of the defining Old Testament phrases describes Israel as 'sheep without a shepherd.'[34] The people became scattered, with 'scattered sheep' another popular metaphor for the Prophets when describing Israel in exile.

Hopes for a return from exile inevitably centre on these lost sheep being found. But found by whom? The people cry in Psalm 80: 'Hear us, Shepherd of Israel … Awaken your might; come and save us. Restore us, O God; make your face shine on us, that we may be saved' (vv. 1-3). In other words, salvation will be dependent on the 'Shepherd of Israel.'

The Prophets repeatedly highlight that Re-creation will be dependent on both judgement and restoration. The shepherds who misled the nation will be judged so right order can be restored. In Ezekiel 34, the Lord announces judgement for the shepherds who have misled his flock, before stating:

> For this is what the Sovereign LORD says: I myself will search for my sheep and look after them. As a shepherd looks after his scattered flock when he is with them, so will I look after my sheep. I will rescue them from all the places where they were scattered on a day of clouds and darkness. I will bring them out from the nations and gather them from the countries, and I will bring them into their

own land ... I myself will tend my sheep and make them lie down, declares the Sovereign LORD. I will search for the lost and bring back the strays. I will bind up the injured and strengthen the weak. (vv. 11-16)

The promise is that God will come as a Good Shepherd to lead his people out of exile and into the green pastures reminiscent of Eden. In fact, Ezekiel goes on to prophesy that people will see this restoration and say: 'This land that was laid waste has become like the garden of Eden' (Ezek. 36:35). As we know, the great hope, deep in the heart of the Jewish people, was to walk and talk with God again in his garden of delight. And the good news is that God is coming, in the words of Psalm 23, to guide Israel 'along the right paths for his name's sake' (v. 3). And where do those paths lead? The short answer is to the place where heaven and earth are one, and where there is no death, grief, crying or pain.

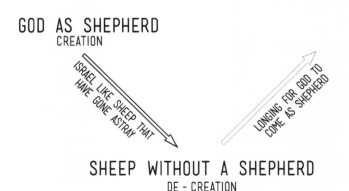

GOD AS SHEPHERD
CREATION

ISRAEL LIKE SHEEP THAT HAVE GONE ASTRAY

LONGING FOR GOD TO COME AS SHEPHERD

SHEEP WITHOUT A SHEPHERD
DE - CREATION

The Promise of a Loving Father

Marriage isn't the only metaphor to describe the relationship between God and Israel. In fact, in the Jewish worldview, the highest form of love is not the love of a husband for their wife, but the love of a father for a son. Thus, the final promise involves God appearing as a Father to adopt Israel afresh as his chosen Son.

Hosea 11 beautifully captures this father heart of God, rescuing his beloved son, only to experience the pain of his son rejecting him and wandering back into the wilderness:

> When Israel was a child, I loved him, and out of Egypt I called my son. But the more they were called, the more they went away from me.... It was I who taught Ephraim [*one of the tribes of Israel*] to walk, taking them by the arms; but they did not realise it was I who healed them. I led them with cords of human kindness, with ties of love. To them I was like one who lifts a little child to the cheek, and I bent down to feed them. (vv. 1-4)

The betrayal is strong, but the love of a father is stronger. God, the loving father, can't turn his back on those who have rejected him, promising to lead his people out of exile and resettle them in their homes. In exile, Israel's longings resurfaced for reconciliation with their Father. Their salvation would be dependent upon their Father gathering them back in their land and adopting them afresh as his son. Only then could they experience all the benefits of sonship, walking and talking with their Father in the garden they were made for.

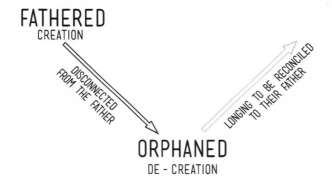

Standing on the Edge of the New Creation

The Old Testament ends here: with longings and hopes. Longings for God to come as a husband to marry his people once more; hopes of God returning as King to rule and reign over his people, as well as all the earth; longings for God to appear as the Good Shepherd to lead his people back to green pastures; and hopes of God returning to father them once more, pouring his blessing out upon his children.

The narrative of the Old Testament is the story of Israel seeking to recover what was lost at the fall and to experience the life of Eden once more. But the doorway to Eden remains shut, and every human effort to open it has failed. Only one will be found worthy. Only one knows what it will take. And Israel's future, as well as the future of all creation, and the hope of heaven and earth being married once more, lies entirely now with that 'only one.'

Chapter 8

PERSONAL REFLECTIONS: THE POWER OF STORY

Every Passover, the people of God would gather together to retell their story. As they looked back at their journey, gratitude swelled as they reminded themselves of God's faithfulness. What's more, remembering stirred fresh hope and deep longing for God to show up again as a Father, King, Husband and Good Shepherd.

When we look back at our stories, we can trace the contours of God's faithfulness and experience growing hope. For this reason, we regularly remind ourselves of our story at KXC, not to make much of us, but to make much of God. Bee and I planted KXC full of hopes and dreams. The story that followed has been far more about discovering God's hopes and dreams for this church and this city.

Let me back up. Bee and I got married in 2003, and immediately began working in Watford with Soul Survivor, a Christian organisation running worship festivals and conferences for young people. Soul Survivor was a spiritual home for us. We fell in love with the place, the people and ministry flowing out from there. Mike

Pilavachi, the founder and leader of Soul Survivor, had mentored me from my early teenage years, so working for and doing life with Mike over those years was an incredible gift.

But the time came when Bee and I felt a new calling and, with much heartache, decided to leave Soul Survivor. After shedding lots of tears, we set out on an adventure to plant a church, with training as the first step. We moved into central London to join the leadership team of St Mary's Bryanston Square, where we would spend the next five years studying theology, getting ordained in the Church of England and learning as much as we could from John Peters, the vicar.

Looking back, it was during this transition from Watford to London that the King's Cross piece of the jigsaw puzzle emerged. We sold our one-bed flat in Watford and naïvely thought we could buy a one-bed flat in central London, failing to realise that our budget would barely buy us a garage. So we spent the next six months sofa surfing, trying to figure out how we could afford to live in central London. Then we received a phone call that changed everything.

An amazing couple called David and Fiona Saunderson rang us out of the blue. They owned a family house in walking distance of King's Cross and were making plans to move to Cambridge. They loved the area, had lived in King's Cross, and prayed for it for many years. They decided to remain invested in the area by keeping hold of their house and were looking for people to housesit for six months. The phone call was to see if we would be interested. I asked if I could take a moment to think and pray about it, and after less than a millisecond, said, 'Yes! Absolutely!' We moved in, and what was meant to be six months housesitting became five years. Their extraordinary generosity over that time led to the birth of KXC.

When it comes to the subject of calling, it's hard to discern things whilst looking and moving ahead. When, however, you stop and look over your shoulder, joining the dots of what God has done and where he has moved in your life, it creates a trajectory. Follow that trajectory, and the future becomes clearer. After a few years of living in King's Cross, we were beginning to seriously wrestle with where God was calling us to plant a church. We would have gone anywhere. Well, almost anywhere. We were moving at quite a pace and finding it hard to hear God. So we stopped. We looked over our shoulder and realised that God's extraordinary provision for us in London was more than coincidence. It was God's way of moving us into the place where we would eventually plant. Over the years living there, we fell in love with the area. We also began to get in touch with the desires stirring within and, in particular, a passion for this amazing part of London.

The psalmist says, 'Delight in the LORD, and he will give you the desires of your heart' (37:4). God knows us intimately. He knows that some of my desires, perhaps like some of yours, are slightly (and sometimes entirely) wayward. Nevertheless, in his grace, he still chooses to both speak and use the desires at work within us. Perhaps it is in the process of delighting yourself in the Lord that God's desires become our desires, which then drive our activity.

For Bee and I, what followed was a wave of the prophetic. We started prayer walking around the area. At the time, the area behind the station had been marked out for redevelopment. Argent, the redevelopers, had fenced off the area, ready for action. They had placed a huge billboard on the entrance to the site, which read: 'King's Cross is being delivered.' This was at the time of the credit crunch, back in

2009, during the global financial crisis. Conventional wisdom would have said this was not the best time to take on a multi-billion-pound regeneration scheme. No doubt people were questioning Argent, wondering if it had bitten off more than they could chew.

We stood outside the entrance to the site, looking up at the bill-board, with a strong sense of God's nearness and an inner-knowing that those words represented a prophetic statement. It had far more to do with the heart of God than it did the plans of Argent. This part of London, known for poverty and prostitution, had always been close to God's heart, but we were now being drawn close to his heart and his plans for King's Cross.

By this point it honestly felt like all our church-planting plans and ideas—developed over years of dreaming, training and preparing—were placed to one side as we got swept up into God's plans. So we went to see the Bishop of London to share our heart and vision. He sent us with his blessing and commissioned us to plant a new church in King's Cross, serving alongside the many other churches in the area.

So the journey began. We launched on Sunday 14th February 2010. Being Valentine's Day, those who didn't have a date joined us as we cast vision for the adventure ahead. We had a simple mission statement: to recklessly give ourselves away to God, each other, the people of King's Cross and beyond. In the ten years since we planted, we've seen God do remarkable things, even as we made plenty of mistakes. Through all the ups and downs, I held on to the promise, 'He who began a good work in you will carry it on to completion' (Phil. 1:6).

The apostle Paul spoke those words to the church in Philippi when they were experiencing significant persecution by the Roman

Empire. If ever there had been the temptation to throw in the towel, to settle for a more comfortable life, to bow the knee to Caesar and proclaim him as Lord rather than Jesus, that was the time. But Paul encouraged them to remember their story of the church's beginning (as told in Acts 16). It's an incredible story of miracle after miracle: the miraculous conversion of Lydia, the demonically oppressed slave girl and the jailer who was about to kill himself. Throw in an angelic visitation, Paul and Silas' imprisonment and a supernatural earthquake leading to their escape, and it makes for great reading. Paul reminds his readers therefore that their church was built on the miraculous acts of God.

I look back and take courage from similar stories at KXC's beginning. Planting the church during the financial crisis in one of the most expensive parts of London, we knew we needed a financial miracle to get going. We were renting space for Sundays and covering three part-time salaries with not much coming in. But in the first week, we received an anonymous gift of £50,000. I would have kissed the donor had the person not remained nameless. I have since learnt that if something is God's plan, he'll resource it. If it's simply *your* plan, there's a good chance you'll have to resource it.

That same week, I received a message from the borough commander of the police. He was a Christian and heard we were planting a church in King's Cross. We had met at Soul Survivor years before, but I had no idea that he was now based here. He gathered other Christian police officers fortnightly to pray for the area and invited me to join. Through his friendship and encouragement, we connected with organisations doing amazing work to alleviate suffering and tackle poverty. We had been clear to the congregation that we as a church weren't the answer for the challenges facing King's Cross, nor did we know the answers. Our task was to take the posture of learners, serving and supporting what others were doing in the area. The connection with these local charities provided that opportunity to learn, grow and develop relationships in the community. These incredible relationships, which came from the initiative of the borough commander, were another reminder that this was God's idea and not ours.

We also experienced miraculous provision of space. In the first year, the KXC office was the spare room of our house—three small desks with a bed in the corner. A year into the adventure, we needed to grow the team, while Bee and I were expecting our second child. The office needed to move, so we started praying. Around that time I got a phone call from my friend Jon Burns. A friend of his had invested into property in King's Cross just before the financial crash. He was left with empty office space and asked Jon to help him find charities to move in so that he could get rate relief on all the space. Jon asked if we would like 2,000 square feet of office space rent-free. The only condition was that there would only be a one-day notice period on the tenancy. As soon as the market picked up, whether that was in six years or six weeks, we would have to be out. We took the risk and moved in, and what a gift it was.

After eighteen months at Tileyard Studios, we got another call. It wasn't the 'please be out tomorrow' call, but it was a warning that the market was picking up and that the move-out call was coming. So we began praying again, and again we received a miraculous answer. This sounds like an exaggeration, but this is the absolute truth: My colleague Andy Kitchen took a phone call from Singapore from a lady who was the part owner of a seven-story office block on Pentonville

Road in King's Cross. The owners wanted to redevelop the building but needed a few years to get their plans together. She had done a Google search for suitable charities to offer space to and found KXC. The phone call was the offer of 5,000 square feet of office space right down near the station. We honestly thought it was a joke to begin with—the kind of joke one of my brothers might play. But it was true, and in 2012 we moved into York House. We actually ended up being given 15,000 square feet of space and spent the next three years establishing a mission base for kingdom-minded charities.

This is a small part of the story of the early years of KXC. Like the people of Israel being formed through breakthrough moments (such as the Red Sea deliverance) as well as breakdown moments (such as worshipping the golden calf), we as a church have had both the breakthroughs and the breakdowns. Both have been an opportunity to discover something of God's character, heart and essence. We have been formed through these experiences.

These stories matter. Communities are formed through shared stories and experiences. The more intense the experience, the deeper the bonds. The people of Israel experienced a journey intense beyond words—from Egypt to the Promised Land, from the Promised Land to Babylon, and from Babylon towards awaiting redemption in Jerusalem. But through the journey, God's people found a shared identity and a shared sense of belonging, purpose and hope. And this is what we all crave. Their story has become part of our story, now fulfilled in the life, death and resurrection of Jesus. The story of every follower of Jesus, the story of every local church, belongs to this bigger story.

PART III

JESUS AND THE NEW CREATION

Chapter 9

THE SECOND BEGINNING

I came to faith at the age of four. I had been wrestling with substitutionary atonement theology and came to the conclusion that through the cross, Christ had offered both a propitiation for my sins and an expiation of those sins. I'm joking, of course! I was too busy watching *Thomas the Tank Engine*, too young to understand most of the words in that previous statement, and too young to remember what actually happened at that early salvation experience.

However, this is how my parents tell the story: Before bed one night, I told my mum and dad that I wanted to become friends with Jesus. They led me in a prayer, and I added my 'amen' to follow Jesus and live for him. My immediate response was to run through to my brother's room. I asked Tim if he had been 'born again,' using the language I had picked up from Sunday school. He looked fairly confused, so I called Mum and Dad through to his room. I told them that Tim wanted to become a Christian and that they should lead him in a prayer. They did, and Tim gave his life to Jesus.

The next day Tim and I fought over who had led whom to faith. Here it is in print: I led Tim. Perhaps one day people will tell stories of the four-year-old evangelist, with flawless atonement theology, who led the great worship leader Tim Hughes to faith. I'll leave you to judge whether I should take a small cut of his song-writing royalties.

However profound your story of coming to faith is or isn't, Christians believe that turning to Jesus, whether as a four-year-old or a ninety-four-year-old, amounts to a rebirth. The language of being born again, borrowed from John's gospel, points to this. We have our 'birth' day, the day of our physical birth, but we also have a story to tell of our 'spiritual' birth. When we come to Christ, we become, in the words of Paul, a new creation, or more specifically a 'renewed' creation—what we might also call a new or second beginning.

In the Beginning ... Again!

John's gospel begins with three familiar words: 'In the beginning ...' (1:1). For the reader who opened up the Bible and started reading in Genesis, John chapter 1 is potentially confusing: Why are we back at the start of the story? Can a book even have two beginnings? But this is John at his best as a writer, taking the reader back momentarily to provide a platform for everything he wants to say in his account. His message is simple: in Jesus, a new creation is being established. Genesis was the story of creation; John's gospel is the story of the Re-creation.

Each of the gospels in its own way starts with this same theme of Re-creation. Matthew's opening words—'a record of the genealogy of Jesus Christ'—are perhaps better translated 'a book of the genesis of Jesus Christ' (1:1). Any reader of these words in the first century would hear the parallel words of Genesis 2:4: 'this is the book of the genesis of heaven and earth.' Interpreted this way, these opening words of Matthew's gospel are more than just an introduction to the genealogy that follows. If Genesis 1 and 2 provide the story of creation, then Matthew is suggesting that his book provides the story about the new creation that takes place in and through Jesus Christ.

The Creator Steps into Creation

Names matter. In the ancient world, a person's name was intimately connected to his or her identity. Names were chosen with care, which is why the angel specifically told Mary that the baby born to her should be called Jesus. Why Jesus? The Aramaic name for Jesus is Yeshua, which is derived from the longer Hebrew name Yehoshua, which simply means 'Yahweh saves.' But if you keep digging, you discover that the root word of Yehoshua is the Hebrew word for salvation, *yasha*, meaning to be led into a wide-open space.

Jesus' name carries within it his mission. This is God in human flesh, leading people from slavery to the wide-open space of salvation. It was Joshua (Yehoshua) who eventually led the people into the Promised Land, and now Jesus (a second Joshua) has come to lead people to the true Promised Land—a renewed heaven and earth. He will restore things to how they were meant to be. The flourishing associated with Eden will no longer be a story from the past but also a vision of their future.

Jesus' Baptism and the New Creation

The baptism of Jesus in Luke 3 is another key moment in the story for understanding the theme of Re-creation. When all the people were being baptised, Jesus was too. And as he was praying, heaven was opened and the Holy Spirit descended on him in bodily form like a dove. And a voice came from heaven: 'You are my Son, whom I love; with you I am well pleased' (v. 22).

When we read this text, we're aware that something hugely significant is happening because heaven was opened, but most of the meaning gets lost in translation. God doesn't just open heaven to speak, as he regularly speaks throughout the Scriptures without opening heaven. The language of heaven being open therefore must point to something significant.

The mention of God's Spirit being present in the form of a dove is more than just a nice addition to make this a Trinitarian moment. This is loaded language of deep significance to the Jewish people.

When the Jewish people were exiled in Babylon, they left their homes as speakers of the Hebrew language. When they returned to Jerusalem seventy years later, they came back speaking Aramaic, the language of the Babylonians. This change in language meant that the Hebrew Scriptures needed to be translated into Aramaic so a post-exile generation, less familiar with the Hebrew language, could immerse themselves in the story they belonged to. This Aramaic translation of the Scriptures came in the form of a collection of spoken paraphrases, provided by the Jewish rabbis, to help explain and sometimes expand the Hebrew Scriptures. The collection of spoken phrases became known as the Targum.

So what's this got to do with the Spirit appearing as a dove? Why not some other bird? The significance of the dove is clear when reading the Targum's translation of Genesis 1. The translation best known by first-century Jews, and the translation perhaps most familiar to

Jesus himself, paints a picture of the Spirit of God hovering over the waters 'like a dove.'

In other words, the same Spirit hovering over the waters at the beginning of creation is now hovering over Jesus at the beginning of the new creation. The dove is symbolic of the new creation. Heaven is torn open. Jesus, anointed by the Spirit, is here to usher in God's will on earth as it is in heaven. And to make all things new.

The Temptations: 'If you're the Son of God ...'

The key to fulfilling God's purpose to make all things new is living in the knowledge that you are God's beloved. That's why the words of affirmation spoken over Jesus at his baptism come before he has done anything: before any miracle, any creative parable, any act of compassion. It was as if God were saying, 'I'm already proud. I couldn't love you more. There is nothing to prove, no love to win. Now, knowing that you already have it all, go and live a radical life.'

In Luke 4 we read about the temptations Jesus faced, which was really a battle over this identity rooted in the love of God. The statement 'If you are the Son of God' (v. 3) is the enemy's attempt to sow doubt regarding Jesus' sonship. The enemy knows that if Jesus, and humanity, live from this secure identity, then it's game over. The new creation will dawn, which is why the temptations are so fierce.

In reading the temptation narratives, there seems to be two layers to the text. The first and most obvious layer is that these temptations are centred around Jesus (and us) finding our deepest needs and longings satisfied outside of God. In other words, they are about enticing us into idolatry.

The first temptation—to turn stone into bread—is about stepping out of the relationship of dependency with the Father and providing for one's own needs. It's essentially about self-sufficiency and building a secure life for oneself. The second temptation—being offered the kingdom by submitting to the enemy—is about finding significance not in serving others but in having power over others. The last temptation—to jump from the temple and allow the angels to catch Jesus—is about doing something spectacular to win the love of the crowds.

These aren't arbitrary temptations. Sociologists say that the three deepest longings of humanity are for love, security and significance. These longings drive us, and whatever or whoever satisfies them (even if only partially) becomes our god, the one we centre our lives around. The temptations Jesus faced are the same temptations we face day in and day out. We all deeply long to feel loved, secure and significant, but such longings cannot be fully satisfied outside of relationship with the Father.

The second layer of meaning to these temptations is one rooted in the wider narrative. As noted in previous chapters, if created order is to be sustained through right worship, then it is always idolatry that destroys that order. For humanity to be restored, there needs to be both an embracing of judgement as well as a reversal of this tendency towards idolatry.

Humanity's identity, stolen in Genesis 3, is the target again in Luke 4 as Satan repeatedly says to Jesus, 'If you truly are the Son of God....'[35] This blatant attempt to undermine Jesus' identity (and thus humanity's) is dealt a heavy blow as Jesus stands firm in his identity as God's beloved son. Secure in his sonship, and having overcome Satan's attack, Jesus returns from the desert 'in the power of the Spirit' (v. 14) and then begins his ministry of pushing back darkness, driving out evil spirits and taking back territory from Satan. This is the story of Genesis 3 being reversed, and having won back humanity's identity as sons and daughters, Jesus immediately trains up his disciples to share in his ministry of proclaiming the gospel, healing the sick and casting out demons.

Lost and Found: Jesus Reclaiming Lost Identities

Describing his mission, Jesus said he came 'to seek and to save the lost' (Luke 19:10). This involves reclaiming humanity's true identity as sons and daughters of God with a royal identity. Many of Jesus' interactions are best understood as Jesus reclaiming such an identity for people.

Consider the lady caught in the act of adultery in John 8. We are told that she was caught in the act and therefore most likely naked (or at least indecently clothed). She was then dragged into the temple courts. Ready armed, the crowds gathered to stone her—not because they were particularly aggressive, or even caught up in the mob mentality, but because they were a Jewish crowd. In other words, they knew the Torah clearly stated that the punishment for adultery was stoning to death. So out of respect and obedience to the Torah, the crowds were ready to execute her.

It's hard to imagine what the woman must have been thinking and feeling. Obviously she was terrified and humiliated, but the intensity of the situation is hard to comprehend. She was facing death, publicly exposed, with the full weight of the Torah against her, and with nowhere to turn to. Until Jesus stepped in. He said, 'Let him who is without sin throw the first stone.' The crowd hushed. The woman, cowering still, waited to receive the first hit. And then she heard the thuds as rocks fell, not on her body, but onto the dusty floor of the temple courts. The same crowd poised to stone her dropped their stones and dispersed. Only Jesus and the woman were left.

'Where's the crowd?' he asked. 'Do they condemn you?' She gradually lifted her head to look around. All the people were gone. She nervously shook her head before hearing words she would never expect from the Torah-giver himself: 'Then neither do I ... Go now and leave your life of sin' (v. 11).

If you had the opportunity to look into the face of God and glimpse his expression as he gazes upon you, would you take it? Most people would answer that question with an adamant, 'No!' Their view of God, perhaps shaped by their experience of the church, is that God's face would appear angry or, worse still, menacing—the kind of face that the adulterous woman might have expected from Jesus. But the woman saw something much different—a face full of compassion and grace. In the face of Jesus the woman realises that God's mercy triumphs over judgement. And having seen such a face, how can she not be changed.

This adulterous woman was ready to die, encircled by a crowd ready to punish her, naked and ashamed. It's the complete opposite of the picture of human flourishing painted in Genesis 1 and 2, where Adam and Eve are naked and unashamed, living fully as they ran around the wide-open space. In this beautiful encounter, Jesus opened the door to freedom. Sin was washed away. Dignity was restored, and this daughter walked away from the encounter with a new identity. Why? Because Yeshua seeks and saves that which is lost.

Jesus' encounter with Zacchaeus is another such story. Zacchaeus was a tax collector, which meant he was in league with the Romans, the very people oppressing the Jewish community. One strategy the Roman Empire employed to crush nations underneath them was to impose a heavy tax system. This would cripple the defeated nation, reducing the threat of uprising and ensuring compliance. To make the plan work, the Roman authorities needed a group of Jews willing to betray their own people by collecting taxes. The incentive for such betrayal was the ability to keep a portion of the tax revenue.

Over time, the Jewish community became poorer and the tax collectors became richer. So unsurprisingly such tax collectors were despised. Zacchaeus may have been wealthy, but he would have been lonely. He was trapped, being used by the Romans and hated by his fellow Jews.

Luke 19 tells us that Zacchaeus heard through the grapevine that a rabbi, Yeshua, would be passing through the area. Driven by intrigue and perhaps desperation, Zacchaeus travelled to see the rabbi in person. As the crowds gathered, Zacchaeus had to climb a tree to observe the action because he was short. As Jesus passed by, he stopped, looked up and called Zacchaeus by name. I imagine that the crowd fell silent. Jesus, a rabbi who taught the Torah with great authority and insight, wanted a conversation with the notorious tax collector. All the people watching the scene unfold probably expected Jesus to publicly rebuke Zacchaeus for betraying God and his people.

Like the lady caught in the act of adultery looking up to see Jesus' face radiating love and mercy, Zacchaeus looked down from the tree to the see the very same face. Jesus simply said, in essence, 'Zacchaeus, let's go hang out at your place.' In other words, let's be friends.

The crowd would have been confused and outraged. Whilst we don't know the details of the conversations that followed between

Jesus and Zacchaeus, it resulted in Zacchaeus giving away half of his possessions to the poor and paying back those he had cheated four times the amount. Jesus then declared to the crowd, 'Today salvation has come to this house, because this man, too, is a son of Abraham. For the Son of Man came to seek and to save the lost' (vv. 9-10).

What happens in this short encounter? Simple: Yeshua led Zacchaeus to the wide-open space. Because that's what Yeshua does.

Jesus Manifesto

When Jesus had returned from the desert, he began his ministry by quoting Isaiah 61 and Isaiah 58. He announced:

> The Spirit of the Lord is on me, because he has anointed me to proclaim good news to the poor. He has sent me to proclaim freedom for the prisoners and recovery of sight for the blind, to set the oppressed free, to proclaim the year of the Lord's favour. (Luke 4:18-19)

The year of the Lord's favour points to legislation described in Leviticus 25, which stipulated that every fifty years the people must celebrate the Year of Jubilee by freeing all slaves, releasing all those in prison, cancelling all debts, and dividing up the land equally amongst the twelve tribes of Israel (as Moses had done at the beginning). This Jubilee year represented good news, particularly for those who had spiralled into poverty. It was like a reset button for Jewish society, because their society, like ours, was broken, greedy and selfish. Certain people rose to the top and others plummeted to the bottom. Then, over time, the gap between rich and poor continued to grow. And because God hates such inequality, every fifty years the Torah stated that they had to wipe the slate clean.

The Jubilee year pointed back to Eden, to life as it was meant to be lived, without greed, slavery and debt. But it also pointed forward. The Prophets had spoken of a time when God would hit the reset button once and for all by sending a messiah to deliver them. Then they would celebrate not just a year of Jubilee, but also a reign of Jubilee. God's good creation would be restored to how it was meant to be.

Luke 4 is powerful because Jesus quotes this promise to a people living under Roman oppression. If there was ever a moment when people were crying out for freedom, this was it. Isaiah 61 was a prophecy that gave them strength and hope that light might be at the end of this tunnel. And so Jesus, having just read this prophecy, quietly took his seat again. We are told that every eye in the synagogue is fastened on him. Why? Because you can't just quote such a passage without commenting on it. You can't tap into the deepest longings of a nation living under oppression, without adding a few words of hope. Maybe they were hoping Jesus would say, 'Stay strong, that moment will come,' or 'Don't forget that light exists at the end of this dark tunnel.' But he says nothing. He just sits down. And when every eye is fixed on him, he speaks the words that bring light into the darkness. He simply says, 'Today, this Scripture is fulfilled in your hearing' (v. 21). For all those wondering when this reign of Jubilee would begin, Jesus provided a clear answer. Today. When Jesus said, 'The Spirit of the Lord is on me,' he meant it. He was the anointed one, the promised messiah, the agent of creation and the agent of

Re-creation, now on a mission to usher in a reign of Jubilees and lead people from exile to their true heavenly home in the new creation.

Jesus, the Second Moses

This reign of Jubilee was associated with the Jewish people returning from exile. The people had come home from Babylon to Jerusalem under the leadership of Ezra and Nehemiah, but they were still in a state of semi-exile, being ruled over by the Romans. The prophecies of returning from exile remained unfulfilled (or at best, only partially fulfilled), and the Jews were still hoping for another Moses to come and liberate them, and another David to come and reign over them.

Israel's return from exile is critical to understanding Jesus' kingdom message. For Israel, this return was thought to involve liberation from Roman rule, but for Jesus a larger return was in mind. This was more than just a return from exile; it was also a return to the life of Eden. This was something the Jewish prophets pointed towards, including these words from Ezekiel:

> For I will take you out of the nations; I will gather you from all the countries and bring you back into your own land.... I will resettle your towns, and the ruins will be rebuilt. The desolate land will be cultivated instead of lying desolate in the sight of all who pass through it. They will say, 'This land that was laid waste has become like the garden of Eden.' (Ezek. 36:24, 33-35)

These prophetic texts, full of imagery from the Exodus story, highlight that the new creation will come about through a new exodus. This then becomes the backdrop in Matthew's gospel where Jesus retraces the steps of Israel's history in order to fulfil her calling and usher in a new age.

The diagram below summarises the journey from Egypt to the Promised Land. The people left Egypt, passed through the waters of the Red Sea, began their journey through the wilderness and stopped at Mount Sinai to receive the Law and enter into covenant relationship with God. He provided bread from heaven to sustain them on their journey towards the land God had marked out for them.

THE EXODUS

EGYPT	WATERS	WILDERNESS	MOUNT + LAW	HEAVEN'S BREAD	PROMISED LAND

Notice how Matthew structured his whole gospel account to mirror this journey. After the birth of Jesus, Mary and Joseph escaped to Egypt with Herod on a mission to kill this baby who was born as king of the Jews. Once safe, they came 'out of Egypt' and returned to Nazareth (Matt. 2). In the very next chapter, Matthew described Jesus passing through the waters of baptism, before beginning his journey of forty days in the wilderness (Matt. 4), surely representing the forty years his ancestors spent there. In Matthew 5, Jesus ascended the mountain to deliver his famous 'Sermon on the Mount,' providing a new pathway towards blessing, not through Torah obedience but through the relationship he invited them into. Any Jew reading this biography of Jesus would know exactly what Matthew was trying to say: Jesus was fulfilling their story.

Jesus then provided bread from heaven by feeding five thousand hungry people, paralleling God's provision of manna (bread from heaven) during the wilderness wanderings. Matthew could not have been clearer: Jesus was the second Moses, leading a second exodus, not simply out of slavery to Egypt or Rome, but from slavery to all sin, darkness and death. Jesus led his people to the promised land of the new creation.

THE EXODUS 2ND EXODUS

→

The Exodus	2nd Exodus	Reference
LEAVING EGYPT	LEAVING EGYPT	MATTHEW 2
WATERS	BAPTISM	MATTHEW 3
WILDERNESS	TEMPTATIONS	MATTHEW 4
MOUNT + LAW	SERMON ON MOUNT	MATTHEW 5
HEAVENS BREAD	FEEDING 5000	MATTHEW 14
PROMISED LAND	NEW CREATION	

The kingdom language constantly used by Jesus is best understood with this Exodus backdrop in mind. Jesus' announcement of the arrival of the kingdom meant that a new creation was being inaugurated through a new exodus.[36]

The healings and exorcisms of Jesus described as manifestations of the kingdom are equally to be understood as signs of Re-creation: Jesus restored people to how they were always created to be. For example, in Luke 11:20, Jesus states: 'If I drive out demons by the finger of God, then the kingdom of God has come to you.' The term 'the finger of God' is lifted from the Exodus narrative, where in response to the plagues against Egypt, Pharaoh's magicians exclaim, 'This is the finger of God' (Ex. 8:19). In fact, Jesus also associated his healings with the new exodus, quoting Isaiah 35 to explain his mission:

> Be strong, do not fear; your God will come, he will come with vengeance; with divine retribution he will come to save you. Then will the eyes of the blind be opened and the ears of the deaf unstopped. Then will the lame leap like a deer, and the mute tongue shout for joy ... and those the LORD has rescued will return. They will enter Zion with singing; everlasting joy will crown their heads. Gladness and joy will overtake them, and sorrow and sighing will flee away. (vv. 4-6, 9-10)

The language of blind eyes opening and deaf ears hearing again suggests the curse of exile that was a result of idolatry was being reversed. Israel had been warned that those who worship idols would become like them, having eyes but not seeing and ears but not hearing.[37] But the idolatry that had led to De-creation was being transformed into Re-creation through the perfect obedience of a second Moses, who was bringing about a second exodus.

Chapter 10

RECOGNIZING JESUS

An old story about Abraham Lincoln (probably apocryphal) depicts him visiting a slave auction years before he rose to prominence and became the US president. According to the legend, he stood at the back of the auction and noticed the atmosphere change as a number of slave girls were paraded through the room. It was abundantly clear what these slave girls were going to be used for.

The first slave girl was auctioned and the bids flooded in, each bid met with cheers. Lincoln was repulsed by what he saw. From the back of the room, he loudly offered his bid, silencing the crowd in the process. His bid went well beyond what the slave girl was worth and well beyond what anyone else could afford. The crowd was stunned. What kind of man would pay that amount of money for a slave girl? It made no sense. The slave girl looked terrified, frightened at the prospect of what such a master would do.

The auctioneer closed the bids and pointed the slave girl in the direction of her new master. She made her way to the back of the room with every eye fastened on her. As she approached Lincoln, he looked her in the eye and simply said, 'Young lady, you are free.' The crowd leaned in, totally perplexed. She asked what his words meant.

'It means you are free,' he responded.

'Does that mean,' she said, 'that I can say whatever I want to say?'

Lincoln said, 'Yes, my dear, you can say whatever you want to say.'

'Does that mean,' she asked, 'that I can be whatever I want to be?'

'Yes,' Lincoln replied, 'you can be whatever you want to be.'

'Does that mean I can go wherever I want to go?'

'Yes,' he replied, 'you can go wherever you want to go.'

The girl paused for a moment to take this all in, and then, with tears streaming down her face, responded, 'Then I want to go with you.'

If you were to ask any Christian about their decision to follow Jesus, each person would have a unique story to tell. But behind each story would be the same response as the slave girl. 'When I realised who this man was and what he was like—his generosity, grace, mercy and kindness—then following him was the easiest decision in the world.' In other words, when we recognise Jesus for who he is, the rest takes care of itself.

The Promise of Re-creation

The fulfilment of Old Testament prophecies is key to understanding the gospel narratives. Israel's hope of a new creation centred around God coming as a husband, father, shepherd and king to rescue his children. The gospels are littered with stories of Jesus revealing his identity as the one spoken of by the Prophets, but again and again people fail to recognise him. As John 1 states:

He was in the world, and though the world was made through him, the world did not recognise him. He came to that which was his own, but his own did not receive him. Yet to all who did receive him, to those who believed in his name, he gave the right to become children of God. (vv. 10-12)

For the ones who received him, life began to flow as they entered the wide-open space. For the ones who didn't, the dream of walking and talking with God remained a distant hope. The same is true today. For those who recognise Jesus and see him for who he is, what is on offer is nothing short of new life.

The Promise of a Faithful Husband

In Mark 2, we read that Jesus was heavily criticized for partying with the wrong crowd. At a time when the disciples of John the Baptist and the Pharisees were fasting, people found it offensive that Jesus was wining and dining—with tax collectors and sinners, of all people. Jesus responded to the criticism:

How can the guests of the bridegroom fast while he is with them? They cannot, so long as they have him with them. But the time will come when the bridegroom will be taken from them, and on that day they will fast. (vv. 19-20)

Who's the bridegroom? Why is he going to be taken away? What on earth is going on? A key text for understanding Jesus' answer is Zechariah 8:19, a prophecy spoken to God's people in exile in Babylon:

> This is what the LORD Almighty says: 'The fasts of the fourth, fifth, seventh and tenth months will become joyful and glad occasions and happy festivals for Judah. Therefore love truth and peace.'

The four fasts mentioned emerged from Israel's painful history in Babylon. Each fast was an opportunity to remember and mourn what had been lost, as well as to cry out to God their redeemer to come and rescue them. The Jewish people knew they had broken the covenant and walked away from their lover, resulting in separation from God. Exile was their choice before it was God's choice. So these fasts fuelled the longings of the Jewish people for God to come and fulfil the promise to marry them once more.

Zechariah therefore prophesied a time when the fasts associated with exile will be replaced by joyful festivals, with lots of eating and drinking. It will feel like a wedding, because that is exactly what it will be. God is coming to marry his bride, and there will be a party to end all parties.

With this context in mind, Jesus is essentially saying, 'I am the bridegroom you've been waiting for. I am God, come to marry you and lead you to the life I made you for.' Such a wedding banquet was being realised in the eating and drinking with the tax collectors and sinners. Having experienced the pain and agony of separation, they could now experience through Jesus the joy and ecstasy of union with God.

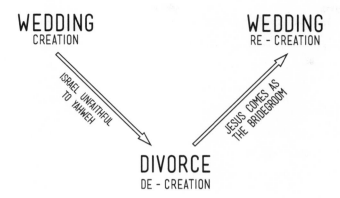

The Promise of a Loving Father

Scripture is the story of a loving father leaving his home to find his lost beloved son to bring him back home. This wider story is condensed into one of the greatest parables of all: the parable of the lost son.

Jesus told this story to a crowd of first-century Jews. So to understand this very Jewish story, it's essential to understand three things.

Firstly, Israel's title, given in the Old Testament, was 'God's Son.' Although many of the Jews had returned from Babylon, they were still ruled over by the Romans, separated from God, and therefore in a state of spiritual exile.[38] Their great hope was to be reconciled to their Father and to feast in his home once more. When the crowd heard Jesus tell the story of a son turning his back on his father, ending up in far-off land, then longing to return to feast in his father's house, they would have realised this retelling was their story.

The second thing to know is that there was a well-known Jewish ceremony called the 'kezazah ceremony.'[39] If a son ever behaved in the manner equivalent to the son in Jesus' story, wishing his father dead by asking for an early inheritance, and then tried to return home to his father and community that he had humiliated, then the people of that village would give the son a taste of his own medicine. They would line up on the threshold of the village, and once the son was standing at the same threshold, they would take a clay pot and smash it at the feet of the returning son. This was a symbolic way of saying that the relationship between the son and the community was like the clay pot, broken and irredeemable. The word *kezazah* meant to 'cut off,' and through this brutal ceremony the son was cut off from the community, with no hope for a return.

As Jesus told the story, the crowd would have been expecting a kezazah ceremony. They knew Jesus was a prophet speaking into their story as a lost son. They longed for restoration and wanted to find their way home, but now feared they would be cut off eternally from the Father's presence.

The third thing to know is that in the Middle Eastern culture of the time, dignified men didn't run. In order to run, you would have to pull up your robes and expose your bare legs, a shameful thing to do. Boys would run, male slaves might run, but a Hebrew father would never, ever run.

So why was this story such a shock to the crowd? They were expecting the smashing of clay pots, but there was no such mention. The kezazah ceremony never happened. The father didn't pour out his wrath on his son. In fact, quite the opposite, the son was not humiliated because the father humiliated himself instead. We are told in the text of Luke 15 that his father saw him from a long way off, which implies he was watching and waiting. Instinctively, the father lifted his robes and ran. Why? Because if the people of the village got to the young man first, they would perform the kezazah ceremony and cut the son off from the community. Driven by love and mercy, the father ran to meet his son.

His son could hardly begin his speech before the cloak was around his shoulder and the signet ring was on his finger, the symbols of full sonship. The son was only going to ask for the position of a hired servant, thinking that perhaps he could pay back his debts and eventually earn his way back to the table. But that's religion, and this is a story of grace.

I imagine the crowd listening to Jesus was stunned and silent, probably thinking, *What kind of father would do that?* Which is exactly the point of the story. God is a good Father, full of grace and truth. Through Jesus, he is on a mission to seek and save that which is lost.

The story is deeply prophetic, because within a short space of time, they would visibly see God pick up his robes, embrace the shame and humiliation, and start running to welcome his children home. As Jesus hung naked on the cross, mocked and ridiculed, his arms were outstretched to offer an embrace to any lost son or daughter who wanted to come home and experience the life they were made for.

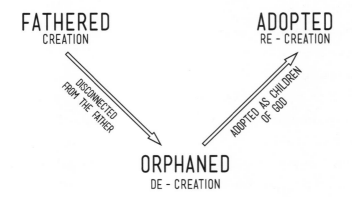

FATHERED
CREATION

ADOPTED
RE - CREATION

DISCONNECTED FROM THE FATHER

ADOPTED AS CHILDREN OF GOD

ORPHANED
DE - CREATION

Jesus, through this parable, is telling the story of the restoration of Israel, but he is simultaneously telling the story of humanity's restoration. Adam and Eve leaving the garden (and their father) in a bid for independence is humanity's story as well as Israel's story. But Jesus, the true Israel and the second Adam, has come to lead us home to our father. In other words, this is more than just the story of Israel's return from exile: it's the story of the Re-creation of all things.

The Promise of a Good Shepherd

In Matthew 9:36, we read that Jesus saw the crowds and had compassion on them, 'because they were harassed and helpless, like sheep without a shepherd.' Later in the same gospel account (chapter 15), Jesus described his mission as being 'sent only to the lost sheep of Israel' (v. 24). This statement reveals God's plan of salvation: first to rescue Israel and then through Israel to bring healing and restoration to all created order. The starting point, however, will be the lost sheep of Israel, who have no shepherd to rule over them and therefore have gone without green pastures and still waters for too long.

The backdrop to all these statements is the prophecy of Ezekiel 34—that God would come himself as a shepherd. He declares, 'I myself will search for my sheep and look after them.... I will search for the lost and bring back the strays' (vv. 11, 16).

This prophecy finds its fulfilment in Jesus, who told a parable to declare that this promise had been fulfilled in him. In Matthew 18 and Luke 15, Jesus told the story about a lost sheep being found. The context in the lost sheep parable, as with the story of the prodigal son, is Jesus talking about the banquet of the age to come (in Luke 14) and being accused of wining and dining with the wrong crowd. The Pharisees were outraged by his behavior, and he responded to their mutterings with the lost sheep parable.

This parable, like many others told by Jesus, was allegorical, so each of the characters in the story represented characters in the earthly and heavenly realm.

PARABOLIC WORLD	HEAVENLY WORLD (V7)	EARTHLY WORLD NARRATIVE SETTING
FRIENDS	ANGELS	TAX COLLECTORS
SHEPHERD ⬇ LOST SHEEP	GOD ⬇ LOST SINNER	JESUS ⬇ SINNERS / ISRAEL
NEIGHBOURS	ANGELS	SINNERS

So Jesus told of a shepherd who left ninety-nine sheep to find one that was lost, and when he eventually did, he threw a party with his friends and neighbours. The story highlights that in the heavenly world this represents God finding one lost sinner and then partying with the angels.

But heaven and earth are colliding in Jesus, and therefore the heavenly party and banquet was being actualised in the earthly realm as Jesus ate and drank with tax collectors and sinners. So far so good. But what we often miss is the outrageous claim right at the heart of this parable: Jesus claimed to be God, finding lost sinners, and then equated these redeemed tax collectors, prostitutes and adulterers with the angels. This is nothing short of a radical claim to divinity, identifying himself as God in human flesh, fulfilling the promise of Ezekiel 34. He is the Good Shepherd finding the lost sheep.

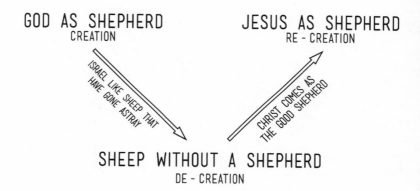

In John 10, Jesus boldly declared, 'I am the good shepherd. The good shepherd lays down his life for the sheep' (v. 11). This statement is one of the famous seven 'I am' statements of John's gospel. In each statement, Jesus applied to himself the divine name (Yahweh, meaning 'I AM') revealed first to Moses in Exodus 3. In this specific example, by declaring 'I am the good shepherd,' he was more than just making a claim to divinity—he was equally proclaiming that the promises of Ezekiel 34 are being fulfilled. In and through Jesus' ministry, God is searching for the lost, bringing back the strays, binding up the injured and strengthening the weak. This is everything the Jewish people had been longing and praying for. The Good Shepherd was on the move to find his lost sheep.

The Promise of a Returning King

The last prophecy was of God returning to be their king. This is why Luke's gospel opens in the way that it does, with the accounts of the births of both John the Baptist and Jesus, playing on the Jewish expectation of the arrival of a royal messiah to usher in the kingdom of God. The angel Gabriel's statement to Mary—that God would give her child the throne of his father David and an everlasting kingdom (1:32-33)—suggested the fulfilment of God's promise to David that his throne would be established forever.[40] The 'Song of Zechariah' in Luke 1 also proclaims that God 'has raised up a horn of salvation for us in the house of his servant David' (1:69). The use of such language surely pointed to the imminent arrival of the kingdom and the fulfilment of Israel's longings.

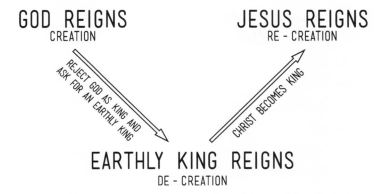

The kingship of Jesus continues to be front and centre in the story of Herod seeking to kill this baby 'born king of the Jews.' It remains front and centre as John the Baptist declared:

> Prepare the way for the Lord, make straight paths
> for him. Every valley shall be filled in, every moun-
> tain and hill made low. The crooked roads shall
> become straight, the rough ways smooth. And all
> people will see God's salvation. (Luke 3:4-6)

John the Baptist quoted Isaiah 40:3-5, calling to mind the ancient Near Eastern custom of sending representatives ahead to prepare the way for a monarch's visit. By applying this prophecy to himself, John the Baptist prepared the people for a king's visit. Jesus then arrived on the scene, building on John the Baptist's use of Isaiah's prophecies regarding a return from exile, quoting Isaiah 61 and declaring: 'The Spirit of the Lord is on me, because he has anointed me.' The Jewish people were waiting for the messiah to rule over them and lead them to freedom, and Jesus claimed to be such a king. His words were backed up with his actions as the kingdom was made manifest through signs and wonders. The blind began to see, the deaf began to hear and the lame began to walk, all of which Isaiah said would accompany the return from exile and the arrival of the kingdom.

Momentum continues to build, the disciples recognise Jesus' true identity as Peter confesses Jesus as 'God's messiah' (Luke 9:20). Then you reach the climactic moment of Jesus' triumphal entry into Jerusalem: Jesus comes riding into Jerusalem on a donkey. This ful-fils the prophecy of Zechariah 9:9, 'See, your king comes to you … lowly and riding on a donkey,' making it abundantly clear that he really is the long-awaited returning king.

The crowds began to shout 'Blessed is the coming kingdom of our father David!' This is a quote from Psalm 118, known as the

'Conquerors Psalm.' The psalm was written to commemorate the victory of Judas Maccabeus over the Syrian King Antiochus, who had made it his goal to humiliate the Jewish community and to wipe out their faith. It was at this low point in Israel's history that a military hero emerged, Judas Maccabaeus. In 163 BC he drove out the Syrian king and purified and re-consecrated the temple. Then, returning victorious, he entered Jerusalem with the crowds shouting, welcoming home their hero with branches of palm trees, with harps, cymbals and songs.

There is no doubt that as the crowds welcomed Jesus into Jerusalem, shouting out Psalm 118 and laying down branches of palm trees, they were full of hope and expectation that they are welcoming in another military hero, who like Maccabeus before him, will overthrow the enemy and usher in a time of peace and prosperity. Such is their hope and longing that they fail to notice the colt. Jesus was very much their long-awaited king, but he wasn't riding a war horse. He was on a lowly donkey, symbolising peace. Jesus, Israel's promised king, was on a mission to establish his kingdom, but it's a very different type of kingdom.

The crowd, blinded by their own nationalist dreams, were preparing to enthrone their king, but what followed was a very different enthronement. Jesus would be crowned but with a crown of thorns. He would be lifted up, but not before being stripped naked, beaten and then nailed to the cross.

A key passage for understanding Jesus' claim to be king appears in John 18. Pontius Pilate asked Jesus if he is indeed the king of the Jews. Jesus responded by saying, 'My kingdom is not of this world' (v. 36). Jesus was claiming to be king, but subverting their understanding of kingship. This king rides donkeys not war horses, and his kingdom is a heavenly one rather than just an earthly one. But make no mistake about it—this heavenly kingdom is breaking into the earthly realm. In the narrative context of the gospels, Jesus was about to be enthroned on the cross as king, and what seemed like the king's greatest defeat and the final end to his kingdom would turn out to be his ultimate victory and the beginning of a brand-new day.

Chapter 11

JESUS, THE GOSPEL AND THE KINGDOM OF GOD

I hate rats. Most people do, but I really hate them. It began when I was four years old. I had a hamster, and one night it escaped from its cage. I was fast asleep when, in the middle of the night, I felt a scratching sensation on my chest. I looked up and saw what I thought was a rat, staring me down whilst perched on my bare chest. It felt like its black eyes were staring into my soul. I squealed and slapped the rodent off my chest. I reached across to turn on the light, jumped out of bed and, with adrenaline coursing through my veins, started searching the bedroom to find the rodent.

I eventually caught a glimpse of it, limping towards shelter, and only then realised that it wasn't a rat, it was my pet hamster, Hobby. It had somehow made its way up onto the bed. The adrenaline was still pumping, so I grabbed Hobby, threw it into the cage, shut the cage door and over the next few days proceeded to starve it to death.

That last bit was a joke, by the way. I didn't do that. I just fell out of love with Hobby. We became roommates who didn't interact. But I think that episode was the activating event for my phobia. Fast-forward a decade, every night before bed I would check my room for rodents. Armed with a baseball bat, I would look under the bed and check the wardrobes. I would then get into bed and wrap the duvet around me, making sure that every part of my body, except my face, was inaccessible to a vicious rat.

Fast-forward another five or so years, I remember being at university unable to sleep during my finals, convinced that our run-down student flat had a rodent problem. My brothers, aware of my vulnerability, would send encouraging messages reminding me that in the cities of the UK, we are never more than six feet away from a rat. One friend even sent me a newspaper story of some giant rats that had been growing huge through cannibalism.

For those who have studied Cognitive Behavioural Therapy (CBT), you may have come across the work of Albert Ellis, considered the grandfather of cognitive therapies. He developed something known as the ABC of CBT. His thesis was that our behaviours are the consequences (C) of our beliefs (B), which are shaped by activating events (A). My night-time encounter with Hobby, the activating event (A), created an irrational belief that rodents would attack me (B), which led to behavioural consequences (C) affecting my sleep.

According to CBT, the pathway towards healing involves deconstructing the irrational beliefs and replacing them with rational ones. For example, how much more scared would a rodent be of me than the other way around? What are the chances of a rat being in my bedroom?

And what harm could a rat do anyway? Leaving the 'Black Death' of the 1300s to one side, which potentially took the lives of up to 200 million people across Europe, the answer is not much. As these rational beliefs replace the irrational ones, new patterns of behaviour emerge.

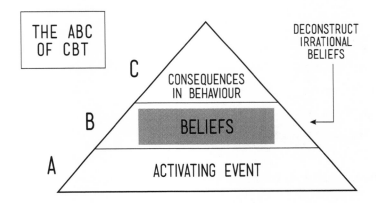

CBT is a huge gift helping thousands of people live with greater freedom. I've personally benefitted from such a therapy. But if CBT represents good news, the gospel represents unbelievable news. God is more than just a divine therapist helping renew our minds by deconstructing irrational beliefs and replacing them with rational ones. Far beyond that, God takes on human flesh in the person of Jesus, and through his life, death and resurrection provides a whole new activating event. As we build on this foundation, new beliefs emerge, that we are loved, have been chosen, forgiven, adopted into a family, called out with a purpose to live for and a hope to live with. The new beliefs begin to transform every part of our lives, bringing healing and liberation to us and through us.

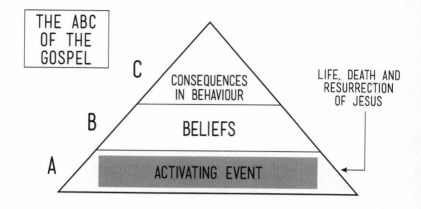

Put simply, the gospel changes everything.

What Is the Gospel?

So far we have explored how Jesus fulfilled the prophecies of the Old Testament, brought to completion Israel's story, inaugurated God's kingdom and ushered in God's new creation. These are all major themes of the four gospel accounts, but how do they relate to what we refer to as 'the gospel'? Is the gospel simply the message that God's kingdom has now broken in? Or is the gospel the story of how God is remaking his broken world? Is the gospel the good news that we are justified by faith in the one who died for our sins and clothed us in the righteousness of God? Is it all of the above?

It may surprise some to read that this question, even after the last two thousand years of church history, is a fairly hot subject in the church right now, debated by some of the great thinkers and theologians of our time. In the midst of the disagreements, everyone seems to agree that 1 Corinthians 15:1-8 is the key text to examine, where Paul defines the gospel for us:

> Now, brothers and sisters, I want to remind you of the gospel I preached to you, which you received and on which you have taken your stand. By this gospel you are saved, if you hold firmly to the word I preached to you. Otherwise, you have believed in vain. For what I received I passed on to you as of first importance: that Christ died for our sins according to the Scriptures, that he was buried, that he was raised on the third day according to the Scriptures, and that he appeared to Cephas, and then to the Twelve. (vv. 1-5)

The word *gospel* simply means 'good news.' This is important because it highlights that before the gospel is a life to live, or an ethical code, or a set of beliefs, it is a piece of news to proclaim. That is why Paul said twice that he 'preached' it. Obviously he embodied the message in his life and demonstrated it in his actions, but first and foremost he preached it. This emphasis is highlighted in Paul's statement in Romans 10:17 that faith comes through hearing the message. Put simply, the gospel is good news that needs to be proclaimed and heard.

Historically, the word *gospel* would have been used to describe the good news of a king's victory in battle. Once the enemy had been defeated, the commanding officer would send messengers from the battlefield with the good news (gospel) that the king had been victorious, the enemy had been overcome, the people were free and could live in peace. Nothing needed to be done, because everything necessary had already been done.

Dr Martyn Lloyd-Jones, one of the great British preachers of the twentieth century, builds on this understanding of the term 'gospel.' He invites us to imagine the scenario where the king hadn't yet been victorious, and the battle raged on. In that case, rather than sending messengers with good news, the commanding officer might send some military advisers with strategies of what needs to be done in the ongoing battle. Lloyd-Jones proceeds to compare the good news of Jesus with the good advice of religion:

> Every other religion sends military advisers to people. Every other religion says that if you want to achieve salvation, you will have to fight for your life. Every other religion is sending advice saying 'here are the rites and the rituals; here's the transformation of consciousness and laws and regulations.' We send heralds. We send messengers not military advisers.[41]

The gospel is the message of what Christ has done. Jesus cried out at the cross, 'It is finished.'[42] Everything necessary for salvation has been done. The battle is over. The king is victorious. The response to such news is celebration. We are free. The response, however, to religion, to good advice rather than good news, is fear: a job still needs to be done, a battle needs to be fought and defeat remains a possibility. Tragically, both inside and outside of the church, people mistake the gospel for good advice and remain terrified of both the present and future. It is critically important that we remember that the gospel is good news.

Died, Buried, Raised ... According to the Scriptures

So the gospel is good news, but about what? Paul describes the following good news as of 'first importance: that Christ died for our sins according to the Scriptures, that he was buried, that he was raised on the third day according to the Scriptures, and that he appeared to Cephas, and then to the Twelve' (vv. 3-5).

In this statement, Paul highlights the key facts: Jesus died, was buried, was raised on the third day and then appeared to his followers. But he also emphasises two other important points. Firstly, Jesus died 'for our sins' (which we will address in the next chapter). Secondly, he did all of this 'according to the Scriptures.' This phrase is repeated, so can't be ignored or brushed off. This simple phrase is Paul's way of saying that this all happened to fulfil the story of God's engagement with his people and his world. Jesus died, was buried and rose again to fulfil not just Israel's story, but also the story of God on a mission to make all things new.

Paul's use of the phrase 'according to the Scriptures' means that the death and resurrection of Jesus are the means through which this story is fulfilled.

The Story of God Fulfilled in the Story of Jesus

Scholars suggest that Philippians 2:6-11 is one of the worship songs of the early church. It is a worship song about the good news of what Jesus has done for us, and therefore a song about the gospel itself. The song is structured around three movements: the incarnation, the cross and the resurrection/ascension.

The first stanza, focussing on the incarnation, references Jesus, who being 'in very nature God,' makes himself nothing by taking on human flesh. The word *incarnation* comes from the Greek 'in carne,' meaning 'in flesh.' In the first movement of the song, the Creator God takes on human form and enters our condition. The language used here of Jesus not considering 'equality with God something to be grasped' is intended to draw us back into the wider narrative by reminding us of Adam and Eve grasping for the forbidden fruit. By comparing Jesus to Adam, Paul is highlighting again Jesus' life, death and resurrection as the fulfilment of the story that began in Genesis 1. The incarnation is the first move Jesus makes in his mission to rescue us. Athanasius, in his *On the Incarnation*, famously stated that 'God became man so that man might become God.' The emphasis here is surely that we can only participate in the divine nature (2 Pet. 1:4) because God first participated in our nature.

The second stanza of the hymn goes on to state that being found in the appearance of a man, he humbled himself by becoming obedient to death—even death on a cross. The use of 'even' highlights that crucifixion wasn't just any old way to die. It was chosen specifically by the Romans as a form of execution for revolutionaries because of how humiliating it was for its victims. Victims were stripped naked publicly and then left to slowly suffocate in agony.

So why did Jesus die? There are two questions involved here: the historical question (why did the Romans kill him?) and the theological question (what did his death accomplish?). Normally the answers to these questions are held apart, as if the historical and theological are entirely separate. But 1 Corinthians 15 emphasises that Jesus died both for our sins and according to the Scriptures. In other words, perhaps the theological answer and the historical answer relate.

The historical answer is that Jesus died based on the charges brought by the Jewish leaders that he was a revolutionary, claiming to be Israel's true messiah. Jesus told Pilate that his kingdom was 'not of this world' (John 18:36). But this kingdom was being birthed in the earthly realm. A revolution was spreading, and the Romans had a proven strategy for wiping out revolutions: take out the revolutionary leaders, make a public spectacle of them through crucifixion, and the revolution will gradually die out. So Jesus died as a revolutionary leader, accused of posing a threat to both the Jewish authorities and the Roman Empire.

In the next chapter we will examine the theological answer to Jesus' death. But it's worth underlining here that whatever theological answer we provide, it has to be consistent with the historical answer that Jesus died as a revolutionary inaugurating a new kingdom. Theories of the atonement, when extracted from the wider narrative of Scripture, can distort not only our understanding of the cross, but also our understanding of salvation.

The third stanza of the hymn in Philippians 2 focusses on the ascension and resurrection of Jesus, who is exalted to the highest place. By conquering death and rising from the grave, Jesus became the firstborn of the new creation.

After defining the gospel for us in 1 Corinthians 15, Paul proceeds by preaching to the church in Corinth about the resurrection. People there had been debating Christ's resurrection and whether a future resurrection would be part of their story. Paul brings clarity to the debate:

> If Christ has not been raised, our preaching is useless and so is your faith.... If Christ has not been raised, your faith is futile; you are still in your sins.... If only for this life we have hope in Christ, we are of all people most to be pitied. (vv. 14-19)

The resurrection is the hinge point in the story and a critical ingredient to the gospel. Without it, the whole thing falls apart.

But let's note again that when Paul defines the gospel in 1 Corinthians 15 he emphasises that Jesus rose from the grave *according to the Scriptures*. Like the cross, we can't extract the resurrection from the story without distorting its meaning. When this happens, the resurrection becomes an event that simply validates Jesus' claims to be God, proving the cross to be effectual in dealing with our sins and saving us from God's wrath. The resurrection does do that, but it does far more. This is the moment where the new world breaks in. In the former order, dead men don't rise, but in this new order they very much do. Paul goes on to state in this epic sermon on the resurrection:

> But Christ has indeed been raised from the dead, the firstfruits of those who have fallen asleep. For since death came through a man, the resurrection of the dead comes also through a man. For as in Adam all die, so in Christ all will be made alive. (vv. 20-22)

The resurrection, like the cross, belongs to the story of Jesus, which in turn belongs to the story of Israel, which in turn belongs to the story of God's engagement with the world he so loves. What 1 Corinthians 15 and Philippians 2 make abundantly clear is that the gospel is the good news that through the life, death and resurrection of Jesus, this wider narrative has been fulfilled. God is making all things new.

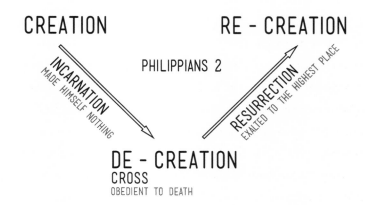

Did Jesus Preach the Gospel?

The four biographies of Jesus carry the name 'gospel' for the simple reason that they tell the story of Jesus' life, death and resurrection as the fulfilment of the wider story of God. However, a question often asked is whether Jesus himself actually preached this gospel.

If one simply equates the gospel with justification by faith, as some seem to do, then Luke 18:9-14 is the only clear example of Jesus preaching about justification. If one equates the gospel with substitutionary atonement, then the pivotal texts become Mark 10:45 (about the Son of Man giving his life as a ransom for many) and Luke 22:37 (where Jesus quotes Isaiah 53, a prophecy about the suffering servant who embraced our punishment to bring us peace). These passages highlight that justification by faith and substitutionary atonement are at the heart of the gospel message, but if the gospel is only defined in these terms, then one would have to argue that Jesus didn't spend much time preaching the gospel.

However, if we define the gospel as the story of Jesus told as the fulfilment of God's engagement with the world, then Jesus is constantly telling his story as the saving story that completes what began in Genesis 1. For example, we have already explored how Jesus referred to himself as the awaited bridegroom, the good shepherd and the returning king. Each of these titles points to the fulfilment of the wider story that has been derailed through sin, and Jesus is claiming to be the central figure that completes this saving story. These narrative threads both highlight the effects of sin as well as how God is going to deal with sin through judgement. Time and time again Jesus points to himself as the agent of salvation, the central figure of the wider story, inviting people to repent and warning them of the coming judgement that awaits those who reject him. Add to this certain parables in which Jesus tells the story of the coming kingdom with himself (and more specifically his life, death and resurrection) as the saving agent.[43] Then add the three occasions where Jesus predicts his own death and resurrection, knowing that these central acts will both accomplish his mission and be the lens though which people will understand his teaching. We have to conclude that Jesus was constantly preaching the gospel.

The Gospel of the Early Church

Paul proclaimed the message that in Christ's death and resurrection, the story of God redeeming the world had been fulfilled. Jesus preached the same gospel. So what about the early church in the book of Acts?

There are seven recorded sermons in the book of Acts: 2:14-39; 3:12-26; 4:8-12; 7:2-53; 10:34-43; 13:16-41; 17:22-31. Each of these gospel sermons focusses on the story of Jesus' death and resurrection, rooting these events in the Old Testament and the wider story of Israel, before issuing a call to repentance and to receive forgiveness of sins. None of these seven sermons mentions hell, only one mentions justification and there is no full articulation of substitutionary atonement. These central doctrines, more fully unpacked in Paul's letters, explain how this story and these events save.

The gospel sermons in Acts, however, focus less on the how and more on the why (the fulfilment of Israel's story and the forgiveness of sins) and the what (the specific events of Jesus' death and resurrection). This doesn't undermine these doctrines but rather places these doctrines within a story that underlines their significance. It is through faith alone in Christ (his life, death and resurrection) that we are justified, declared not guilty, clothed in his righteousness, forgiven of our sin and reconciled to the Father. This is the cause and the effect of the gospel. The cause is the news that in King Jesus the story of God's engagement with the world has been fulfilled. The effect is that whoever responds to the news and repents is justified, forgiven and declared righteous. One cannot separate the cause from the effect. Without the gospel there cannot be justification and without justification there cannot be salvation.

Put simply, the gospel is the news that through the life, death and resurrection of King Jesus, the kingdom of God and God's new creation has broken in, and all things are being made new.

Chapter 12

PERSONAL REFLECTIONS: DESTINY HIDDEN IN HISTORY

Every person has an 'in the beginning' part to their story. To be born again as a follower of Jesus means we also have a second 'in the beginning.' This is how things work in God's kingdom, as Jesus restores and redeems people to be who they were designed to be. God is in the business of making all things new. This means people are made new, but it also means places and communities are made new.

So back in 2009, as we stood outside the fenced-off redevelopment site of King's Cross, reading the placard declaring 'King's Cross is being delivered,' we had no idea of the adventure that would lie ahead. We didn't know what joy and fun would be around the corner. Thankfully, we also didn't know the challenges and costs that would be part of the story. These included moments of working incredibly hard for no reward, seasons of pushing against doors that just won't open, and times when it felt like we were grasshoppers in a land of giants.

A moment of revelation in the middle of a tough season came when Alan Scott spoke at our weekend away in January 2016. During one of his talks, he began prophesying over KXC, and King's Cross more generally. He said, 'Your destiny is hidden in your history.' That one phrase has echoed in my mind and heart ever since. In one sense, it mirrors what this whole book has been about. The story of Eden isn't just a story of our past, but equally contains clues to our future. Jesus has come to seek and save that which was lost in Eden. Our destiny really is hidden in our history. But more than that, I felt God was inviting me further into the story of King's Cross. As someone who is passionate about cultural renewal, I was excited to explore and imagine what would happen if the unfolding story of Scripture began to interact with the unfolding story of King's Cross. When an individual jumps into the story of Jesus we use the language of 'born again' or 'new creation.' What if King's Cross as a place became immersed in the story of God? You would expect new creation. 'King's Cross is being delivered' is fitting language. A new baby is being delivered: a restored and redeemed King's Cross.

Inspiration kicked in. I began dreaming again. What would a restored and redeemed King's Cross be like? How would the business community operate? How would the residential estates be different? What would the atmosphere be like? If destiny is hidden in the history of King's Cross, it felt like a good starting point would be to dig out some history books and start reading. I lie. Wikipedia was my starting point.

King's Cross was given this name in the mid-1800s. Before that, it was known as Battlebridge, providing a crossing over the River Fleet. It took its name because it was the site of a major battle in AD 61 between the Romans and the Celtic Iceni tribe, led by Queen Boudica. Two empires collided, with the victorious Romans establishing a settlement on the site. As I read that part of the history, I was reminded of the words of Augustine, who stated that whilst most earthly cities had been established by blood taken, the city of God (his metaphor for God's kingdom) had been established by blood given. In other words, heaven invading King's Cross is possible because of the blood given by the King himself. How beautiful therefore that the area is named King's Cross.

The history also made sense in another way: why it felt like a spiritual battle trying to minister in this part of London. The place was birthed in kingdoms battling for dominance, and perhaps something of that spirit remained. Part of our job would therefore be praying for the blood of Jesus to break the power of this territorial spirit in order that God's kingdom would reign over this land once more. If De-creation in King's Cross looks like rivalry and competition, Re-creation will look like peace and reconciliation. This continues to be our prayer, that King's Cross would be delivered.

There's a second part of the area's history that interested me. In AD 597 a mission of Roman monks arrived in Essex with the relics of the martyr St Pancras. Their aim was to convert Britain to Christianity. The monks eventually built a church at Battlebridge, where St Pancras Old Church is today, making it one of the oldest sites of Christian worship in Europe. This means before King's Cross was known as a transport hub sending people and goods all over Britain and Europe, it was known as a mission centre sending out good news. If its destiny is hidden in its history, then God's plan to deliver King's Cross must in part be about rediscovering these apostolic and missionary roots. And that too has become our prayer: that the blood of Jesus would redeem the past and usher in a new future; that this place where empires have collided would become a beating heart of the gospel and of God's kingdom in this nation.

Fast-forward to the 1800s, the area had developed a rather tarnished image. A statue of King George IV was erected at the Battlebridge crossroads in 1830 to try and redeem its reputation. The statue attracted ridicule and was demolished in 1842, but in the process the area was renamed King's Cross and the name stuck. I believe that names matter, so choose to believe the name is prophetic, pointing both back to the cross and forward to the future God has prepared for this part of London. My prayer is that King's Cross would be known as a place of redemption, restoration and renewal. With the redevelopment that has taken place, this reputation is already emerging, and our prayer is that what has emerged physically with the redevelopment would increasingly emerge spiritually and socially as the story of King's Cross interacts with the story of God's kingdom.

Why does this matter? Because God has placed you as an instrument of restoration exactly where you are. To follow the way of Jesus is to do what he did. He entered time and space, he died and rose again, to bring renewal and redemption to people and places. He invites us to follow his way. Where you live and work therefore matter. The story of your city matters. The story of your community matters. Do you know it? Because the hope for your city and community is found in being introduced and immersed in the story of God, and God has perfectly positioned you to bring those two stories together.

PART IV

THE DARKNESS OF NIGHT AND THE DAWN OF NEW DAY

Chapter 13

THE DEATH OF THE KING AND THE LIFE OF THE KINGDOM

I was nineteen at the time and had one simple job: to chauffeur Mike Pilavachi to the showground on time for a morning meeting. We were staying off site at Cole Manor, about fifteen minutes from the Royal Bath and West Showground, where the Soul Survivor festival was taking place. We set off early that morning, and I began to drive Mike down the winding country lanes to the site. The car, which belonged to Mike, had definitely seen better days, which is what I kept telling myself, and Mike, in the weeks that followed.

We climbed a steep single country lane, heading towards a sharp left turn. We were travelling at approximately twenty-nine miles per hour, just below the limit, which I also kept telling Mike in the weeks that followed. We began to turn sharp left, over the brow of the hill. There, right in front of us, was a huge black Land Rover, travelling approximately thirty-one miles per hour and therefore over the limit. I slammed on the brakes, as did the driver in the Land Rover. All I remember next was the sound: BANG!!! Silence descended and remained for what felt like an hour. I eventually broke the silence: 'Sorry, Mike, I think I've broken your car.' And by broken, I meant written off. We sat in silence for a bit longer. He then broke the silence: 'I forgive you.'

We eventually both got out of the car. We were both uninjured. The car less so. The bonnet had completely crumpled in. I looked to see what kind of damage had been done to the Land Rover. The answer was nothing. The bumper and grill hadn't even been scratched. We then had to push Mike's car into a field and leave it there to begin the walk of shame back to Cole Manor. I knew Mike well enough to know that when he said he forgave me, he meant it. But I was concerned about the car and how much it might cost to fix or replace. I knew Mike would never let me pay for it, but I also knew he wouldn't be able to afford to pay for it either. It was an awkward walk back.

We eventually arrived at Cole Manor and the owners were very understanding, offering to drive us to the site. I suggested that I drive, but for some reason they declined the offer. We arrived on site just in time for the morning session, and Mike thoroughly enjoyed telling ten thousand teenagers that I had written off his car. In fact, someone kindly gave Mike their Audi estate at that conference. I had been instrumental in upgrading his rusty Astra to an Audi estate. Mike didn't quite see it that way.

Looking back many years on, the bit I vividly remember is knowing that my relationship with Mike would be okay, because he had forgiven me, but I wasn't sure what would happen to the car. My sin, although mainly the sin of the driver of the Land Rover, had been forgiven, but the car was in a field in the middle of Somerset unable to start.

Some of us have a theology of the cross that is big enough to forgive sin but too small to restore creation; big enough to cover the offence but too small to repair the damage; big enough to pardon the crime but too small to transform the criminal. But the good news of the cross is that Jesus has more than just forgiven sins, he's overcome all that would stand in opposition to his kingdom purposes to restore all things. I learnt it the hard way, that God more than just cares about my relationship with Mike; he also cares about Mike's car!

The Cross and Re-creation

For Re-creation to take place, there has to be both a reversal of the disorder as well as the restoration of right order. In the story of Noah's ark, it was the flood (judgement) that enabled a fresh start. In the story of the Exodus, the evil of the Egyptian empire is judged at the Red Sea, enabling a liberated Israel to journey to the new life of the Promised Land. Judgement and new life go hand in hand. Sin and its consequences have to be dealt with for everlasting life to begin to flow. Both are in view at Calvary.

The cross reverses disorder and restores right order. The cross is therefore to be seen as both the place of judgement and the perfect act of worship that reverses the disobedience and idolatry of sinful humanity. Both are taking place simultaneously.[44]

Placing the Cross within the Biblical Narrative

In the last chapter we stated that there is both a theological as well as historical answer to the question of why Jesus died. The historical answer is that he died as a revolutionary seeking to establish a kingdom that posed a threat to both the Jewish and the Roman authorities. The theological answer, at least how it is most often presented, is that he died for our sins that we might be reconciled with the Father. But rather than separating the historical and theological, what happens if we unite them? The answer is that a fuller understanding of the cross emerges. Our theology of the cross becomes big enough to not just pardon individuals, but to transform all of created order. Through the forgiveness of sins, God's kingdom project to redeem and re-create all things becomes possible. He died for our sins in order to fulfil the wider narrative of Scripture.

The way to hold together the historical and theological is to make sure our theology of the cross is rooted in the biblical narrative. This sounds obvious, but Tom Wright suggests that the standard theories of atonement have often located the cross within narratives other than the biblical one:

> Anselm cut the cross loose from its scriptural moorings and placed it within a feudal system of honour and shame; Abelard, within a story of a divine teaching programme; the Greek Fathers, within the world of mythical satanic powers. None of these is without biblical resonance, but equally none

grapples with the actual story the biblical writers tell, and the way in which the gospel writers in particular present the meaning of Jesus' death primarily through a narrative, a narrative which offers itself not just as an echo of bits and pieces of the ancient scriptures of Israel but as the continuation of that story and the bringing of it to its climax.[45]

The challenge set before us is to place the cross back in the wider story, as both the climactic moment of the story as well as the moment of fulfilment and completion. The cross, as we will discover, is the scene of ultimate judgement, final victory, perfect worship and new birth.

The Scene of Ultimate Judgement

To examine the idea of Christ embracing judgement on our behalf, often referred to as penal substitution, the key ingredients of the doctrine (sin, law, God's wrath and justice) have to be defined in the context of the biblical narrative. The inability to do this has caused some to place their understanding of the cross within the world of Roman criminal law. But the judge who acts at Calvary is not the judge acting according to Roman law, balancing crime with punishment and injury with recompense. Instead, this is the judge of the Old Testament law, acting according to the Torah in order to maintain and restore his covenant relationship with his people.

Within this covenant context, sin is to be defined as more than just transgressing a law, but as rebelling against a person. Sin is as much a relational term as it is a legal one. Our infidelity towards God from Eden onwards has ramifications: God's wrath is his divine response to human unfaithfulness and can be only understood within the context of his love. Tom Wright states:

> The biblical doctrine of God's wrath is rooted in the doctrine of God as the good, wise and loving creator, who hates—yes, hates, and hates implacably—anything that spoils, defaces, distorts or damages his beautiful creation, and in particular anything that does that to his image-bearing creatures. If God does not hate racial prejudice, he is neither good nor loving. If God is not wrathful at child abuse, he is neither good nor loving. If God is not utterly determined to root out from his creation, in an act of proper wrath and judgement, the arrogance that allows people to exploit, bomb, bully and enslave one another, he is neither loving, nor good, nor wise.[46]

In Romans 1, Paul not only emphasises the reality of God's wrath but describes the primary method of its operation. The key word that appears three times in this passage is the verb *paradidonai*, which means 'to hand over.' Humanity is 'handed over' to sinful desires (v. 24), shameful lusts (v. 26) and to a depraved mind (v. 28). In this context, judgement is not primarily the retributive inflicting of punishment from outside, but is instead God allowing his people to experience the inbuilt consequences of their refusal to live in relationship with him. In other words, to rebel against God is to rebel against life.

Paul can therefore say that the 'wages of sin is death' (Rom. 6:23). Like Adam and Eve leaving the garden to embrace the lifelessness of the wilderness, our rejection of God always amounts to embracing death. But if, as argued, God's justice is primarily restorative rather than retributive, how does the cross enable restoration? Put simply, how does the cross bring life to those who have embraced death?

The Torah clearly stated that covenantal obedience would lead to blessing and covenantal disobedience would lead ultimately to the curse of exile and alienation from God. In the context of the first century, Israel were living under such a curse. They had rejected God, broken the covenant, and therefore God had 'handed them over' to live with the consequences of their decisions. Judgement wasn't simply some future event they were anticipating because of their unfaithfulness; it was present and active in the form of Roman oppression. Judgement was all around in the form of Roman taxes, the presence of Roman troops, images of Caesar and so on.

The doctrine of penal substitution states that Christ pays the penalty for sin in our place. This statement is more than just a theological statement; it's also a historical one. According to the narrative, Christ came to his own people in the place where they were already being justly punished (the curse of exile) and took upon himself the effects of their covenantal disobedience. As Paul states in Galatians, 'Christ redeemed us from the curse of the law by becoming a curse for us—for it is written, "Cursed is everyone who hangs on a tree"' (3:13 NRSV).

If God's wrath is experienced as alienation, then Christ entered that alienation to overcome the curse, bringing reconciliation and enabling blessings to flow through Israel to the Gentiles and to all of creation. The punishment here is not primarily retributive, but restorative. It's a punishment that does more than just pardon criminals by cancelling out their sin; it restores the covenant between God and his people through which he wants to restore all peoples in all places for all of time.

Substitutionary atonement is central to the gospel. When extracted from the story, however, this doctrine gets significantly distorted. Many people have rejected the doctrine because they have only heard the distorted version. It's clearly worth rejecting the caricature of an angry Father needing to find an innocent third party (his Son) to brutally die in my place because I had a lustful thought last night. But the caricature has hardly anything to do with the doctrine itself.

Firstly, Christ is one with God, so this is not just any substitute or third party who steps in to face God's wrath. As John Stott has stated, this is the 'self-substitution' of God.[47] Paul states in 2 Corinthians 5:19: 'God was reconciling the world to himself in Christ.' Secondly, the crime and the punishment aren't disconnected. In the caricature, the punishment (death) and the crime (a lustful thought) seem entirely disconnected. But if we define sin as ultimately rejecting God and his will for our lives, whilst acknowledging that walking away from the source of life must equate to death, then the punishment and the crime are very much related. Jesus embraces that death so that we can experience everlasting life.

It would be tempting to stop there. Jesus is our substitute. He died in our place. Job done. Move on.

But Jesus is more than just our substitute; he's also our representative. Christ is one with God, but he's also one with us, acting on our behalf in a way that involves us. Substitution therefore tells only half the story. We also need representation to explain how these events reverse the effects of the fall and restore God's order in the world. As Paul highlights in his letters, Christ didn't die so that we might escape death, but instead shared in our death that we might share in his. Through union with Christ, we don't stand back and spectate these events, but participate in them and therefore reap the rewards of them.

Only through Christ as our representative, and our subsequent participation in him, can Paul say that 'one died for all, and therefore all died' (2 Cor. 5:14), leading to his conclusion seven verses later that 'God made him who had no sin to be sin for us, so that in him we might become the righteousness of God' (v. 21). According to the narrative of the gospels, Christ participated in Israel's judgement, the curse of exile, that Israel might participate in his righteousness. This is the glorious exchange of the cross, and what is historically true is theologically true: Christ was clothed in our sin at the cross, dying our death, so that we might be clothed in his righteousness and share in his risen life. And that is unbelievably good news.

The Scene of Final Victory

But the good news gets better. If the doctrine of substitutionary atonement is one lens through which to view the events on Calvary, it certainly isn't the only lens. Perhaps the first lens we are introduced to in Scripture is the theory of the atonement often referred to as

'Christus Victor.' If substitutionary atonement emphasises how God deals with sin and guilt, the 'Christus Victor' theory emphasises how Christ conquers Satan, evil and death itself to liberate us for the fulness of life we were made for.

In Genesis 3, after Adam and Eve have eaten the forbidden fruit, God says to the serpent:

> Cursed are you above all livestock
> and all wild animals!
> You will crawl on your belly
> and you will eat dust
> all the days of your life.
> And I will put enmity
> between you and the woman,
> and between your offspring and hers;
> he will crush your head,
> and you will strike his heel. (vv. 14-15)

This reference to the offspring of Eve crushing the head of the serpent points forward to the conquest between Christ and the serpent, and ultimately to the victorious triumph of the cross. As 1 John 3:8 highlights: 'The reason the Son of God appeared was to destroy the devil's work.'

God's plan from the beginning was for Adam and Eve to multiply and bear fruit, expanding Eden until it filled the earth, and with it God's blessing and glory. This would involve pushing back the chaos of the wilderness by bringing the life of Eden to the inhospitable land that surrounds. This plan, however, is derailed as Adam and Eve submit to the serpent.

A reversal of the fall is therefore implied in the temptation narratives of Jesus in the wilderness. A conquest begins, and Jesus returns from the wilderness in the power of the Spirit and immediately begins to push back the darkness as he casts out demons and liberates the demonically oppressed. This is the beginning of Re-creation, and the conquest comes to its climax at the cross, the scene of ultimate victory.

This victory is experienced by God's people as freedom. As we've said before, the defining story for Israel was the Exodus narrative, whereby God overpowered the Egyptian army and Pharaoh himself through the plagues and the parting of the Red Sea.

A key part of this victory over Egypt was the story of the Passover Lamb. In the final plague, before the Egyptians were destroyed at the Red Sea, the firstborn son of every Egyptian was put to death. The firstborn sons of the Israelites were rescued by the blood of the lamb. This story becomes liturgy in the Passover festival, celebrated each year to remember the victory and freedom experienced by God's people. This liturgy builds expectation of another exodus, a second Moses, and another Passover lamb. It therefore seems fitting that Jesus' last meal with his disciples, the Passover meal, is celebrated in anticipation of the cross. When we read the accounts of the last supper, we read of the bread and wine associated with the Passover meal, but there is no mention of the Passover lamb. It would have been inconceivable to celebrate the Passover without the lamb, but Jesus does, and in doing so redefines the meal around himself. He is the lamb, offering his body and blood as the new pathway to freedom. This is what John the Baptist said when he first set eyes on Jesus: 'Look, the Lamb of God, who takes away the sin of the world!' (John 1.29). To describe Jesus as the true Passover lamb, as John and the other the New Testament writers do, underlines that the victory, freedom and redemption experienced at the Red Sea are now experienced in fulness through the events of Calvary.

At Calvary, Christ has overcome not just an earthly empire, but also all evil and all oppression. The serpent's head has been crushed. The prophecy of Genesis 3:15 has been fulfilled. The enemy has been defeated and the sons and daughters of God are finally free.

The cross is therefore the scene of ultimate triumph. Though this victory is gloriously confirmed at the resurrection, it is achieved through the events of Calvary. This is why Paul celebrates this victory in Colossians 2, stating that 'having disarmed the powers and authorities, he made a public spectacle of them, triumphing over them by the cross' (v. 15).

The cross has more than just dealt with our sin and guilt; it has equally overcome the powers of evil and oppression. The serpent of Genesis 3 has been defeated so that we can live the lives we were made for.

The Scene of Perfect Worship

A beautiful exchange takes place at Calvary. Christ takes what is rightfully ours (judgement and death) so that we might take what is rightfully his (righteousness and life). He reverses disorder in order to establish right order. In Jesus' life and death, he fulfils Israel's calling in perfect obedience to the Father, and by doing so reverses humanity's 'No' to God. Smail states:

> God in Christ becomes the one true representative of Israel who keeps the covenant when all others have broken it.[48]

The cross is therefore to be understood as perfect worship. Right order is restored at Calvary.

We see this demonstrated in the seven sayings of Jesus on the cross. Each of these sayings recorded in the gospels directly links to, or are quoted from, Psalm 22. This psalm, written five hundred years before crucifixion, which was a common form of torture, details the brutal physical experience of such a death. Jesus was perhaps reciting this worship song from the cross, triggering these seven sayings.[49]

In the first saying, 'My God, my God, why have you forsaken me,' Jesus quoted the first verse of the psalm. This was more than just a cry of desperation from the Son, who is experiencing separation from the Father as he is weighed down by the sin of the world; this was a cry of praise.

From the cry of verse 1, the psalm moves in verses 6-8 to the insults and mocking Jesus experienced at the cross. Jesus responded with 'Father, forgive them, for they do not know what they are doing' (Luke 23:34). The following verses of the psalm reference the psalmist's mother and of no one being present to help. This calls to mind memories of Jesus' own mother, and so he called out, 'Woman, here is your son,' and to the disciple, 'Here is your mother' (John 19:26-27). Even in his agony Jesus ensured that Mary has help in her time of trouble. Verses 14-18 of the psalm describe the agony of crucifixion, of bones being out of joint, the strain on his heart, his mouth drying up and his tongue sticking to the roof of his mouth. He therefore cried out, 'I am thirsty' (John 19:28). Verse 18 of the psalm even describes the mockers dividing his clothes and casting lots for his garments, which is precisely what happens in Matthew 27:35.

The psalm then moves on to verse 26, which says that the poor will eat and be satisfied as they seek the Lord and that their hearts will live forever. This is fulfilled as one of the criminals being crucified alongside Jesus asked, 'Remember me when you come into your kingdom.' Jesus responded to this poor man seeking God, 'Truly I tell you, today you will be with me in paradise' (Luke 23:43). The psalm then swiftly moves towards the theme of death. As Jesus recited the psalm, aware of his own approaching death, he cried out, 'Father, into your hands I commit my spirit' (Luke 23:46). And then it ends, as Jesus declares the final words of the psalm, 'It is finished' (John 19:30).

But what is finished? The answer is Jesus' mission has been accomplished. The law, perfectly lived out in Jesus' ministry, was fulfilled at Calvary. The idolatry that led to De-creation had been reversed in this perfect offering of worship at the cross. Re-creation is now both possible and inevitable.

The Scene of New Birth

So Calvary was the scene of ultimate judgement, final victory and perfect worship. The chaos and disorder of De-creation has been dealt with and reversed to enable right order to be restored. It is therefore important to recognise that the judgement that takes place at the cross was both an end and a beginning. Christ bore God's judgement, and in doing so the old humanity was put to death in order that a new humanity may be birthed. Often our views of the atonement tend to be retrospective, focussing on the past. A prospective view, however, emphasises what Paul emphasises in 2 Corinthians 5:17, that 'if anyone is in Christ, he is a new creation; the old has gone, the new is here!' This has to be the best news in the world.

In the death of Christ, sinful humanity is not simply covered, but is instead put to death in order that a new humanity might be born. At Calvary we see God in agony giving birth to a new creation. Julian of Norwich, a mystic from the Middle Ages, described the cross as the 'labour pains' of the new humanity. This explains the strange phenomena of Matthew 27. Verse 50 narrates the moment of Jesus' death, before adding:

> At that moment the curtain of the temple was torn in two from top to bottom. The earth shook, the rocks split and the tombs broke open. The bodies of many holy people who had died were raised to life. They came out of the tombs after Jesus' resurrection and went into the holy city and appeared to many people. (vv. 51-53)

At the very point of Jesus' death, new life was breaking out. Christ's death was the beginning of the end of the old creation and the inauguration of the new creation. The historian Josephus says that on the outer veil of the temple was needlework portraying the starry heavens.[50] The tearing of this veil therefore pointed to the beginning destruction of the old cosmos (the de-created order). The cross opened the door to a new order.

Humanity left Eden through the doorway of death, and every attempt to return had failed. The doorway had remained shut. The cross proclaims the glorious truth that the return to the life of Eden is also through the doorway of death, but this time it is through the death of the Messiah. Jesus is the way. He is the truth. He is the life. And no one gets to experience walking and talking with God except through him. This is the beautiful good news of the cross: the story of Re-creation.

Chapter 14

THE RESURRECTION AND THE BIRTH OF THE NEW HUMANITY

Vasco de Gama was a famous Portuguese sailor of the Middle Ages. At the time, people believed that it was impossible to sail around the southern tip of Africa. All attempts at rounding the Cape had failed, causing the headland to be named the 'Cape of Storms.' Wreck after wreck had dashed hopes. The inability to round the Cape meant that trade routes between Europe and India were blocked. However, in 1497, Vasco de Gama bravely decided to give it one more go.

Against all odds he successfully rounded the Cape. He returned to Lisbon victorious, and the treacherous headland, in light of his accomplishment, was renamed the 'Cape of Good Hope.' One man had been where no one had been before, and it brought hope to all. By opening the trade route between Europe and India, Vasco de Gama transformed the world by creating a new world of possibility.

This is the message of the resurrection: Jesus has rounded the Cape of Death, opening a route to the new creation, and bringing hope to all humankind. Re-creation and resurrection are therefore inseparable in the New Testament.[51]

Running from the Empty Tomb

In John 20 we read the moving story of Mary encountering the risen Jesus in the garden. The De-creation spiral began in a garden, before Adam and Eve were evicted from God's presence. But the story of Jesus is the story of the gardener taking on human flesh to come and seek and save that which was lost.

Genesis 3 states that after the Lord God had made garments of skin for Adam and Eve, he banished them from the Garden of Eden and 'placed on the east side of the Garden of Eden cherubim [angels] and a flaming sword flashing back and forth to guard the way to the tree of life' (v. 24). Interestingly, here in John's resurrection account, we have two angels welcoming Mary into a whole new world brought about through Christ's resurrection. The trauma of Genesis 3 is replaced with ecstatic celebration.

When Mary Magdalene and the other Mary realised that Jesus was alive, they 'hurried away from the tomb, afraid yet filled with joy, and ran to tell his disciples' (Matt. 28:8). These two women were the first witnesses of the resurrection, running with the message that would change the world. Their task is our task: to run as fast as we can to deliver the good news that Jesus is alive and a new age has dawned.

Two Meals: Genesis 3 and Luke 24

In Luke's account of the resurrection, we see two of the disciples discussing the events of the last few days as they journey on the road to Emmaus. The risen Lord Jesus joins the conversation without them realising his identity. He explains the events and reminds them of what the Prophets said would happen. They remained clueless. The breakthrough came at dinner:

> When he was at the table with them, he took bread,
> gave thanks, broke it and began to give it to them.
> Then their eyes were opened and they recognised
> him. (Luke 24:30-31)

What caused their eyes to open? Was it a sense of déjà vu, of being in the upper room with Jesus a few days before celebrating the Passover meal? At that meal Jesus also 'took bread, gave thanks, broke it and began to give it to them.' We can't know for sure, but over this post-resurrection meal, the lights turned on: the resurrected Jesus was at the table with them—the new creation had begun.

The meal in Luke 24 calls to mind another meal. If this is the first meal of the new creation, then it points back to that fateful meal that led to the unravelling of created order in Genesis 3:

> When the woman saw that the fruit of the tree
> was good for food and pleasing to the eye, and also
> desirable for gaining wisdom, she took some and

ate it. She also gave some to her husband, who was with her, and he ate it. Then the eyes of both of them were opened, and they realised that they were naked. (vv. 6-7)

In Genesis 3, the food is also taken, eaten and given before 'the eyes of both of them were opened.' Luke undoubtedly had this in mind. This post-resurrection meal replaced that meal in Eden, before Adam and Eve embraced the chaos of life beyond the garden. Jesus has done everything necessary to reverse the tragic effects of that meal in Genesis 3 that led to Adam and Eve departing Eden. The door to Eden was now open again.

A New Chapter in Cosmic History

The resurrection is therefore the hinge point in the whole story of God. This is why Paul states in 1 Corinthians 15:14 that 'if Christ has not been raised, our preaching is useless and so is your faith.' But Christ has been raised, and therefore everything has changed. In this new creation, resurrection life is the norm not the anomaly. In his brilliant book *Surprised by Hope*, Tom Wright states:

> The resurrection of Jesus offers itself not as a very odd event within the world as it is, but as the utterly characteristic, prototypical, and foundational event within the world as it has begun to be. It is not an absurd event within the old world, but the symbol and starting point of the new world.[52]

As this new creation dawns, the disciples understand what this all means. The implications of this change everything, not just for those first disciples, but for all those who down the ages have followed in their footsteps.

Firstly, Jesus is alive and can therefore be personally known. For the first disciples this meant that they didn't need to feed off past memories but could make new memories as they continued to walk and talk with their living Saviour. For us today, without the resurrection, we could know about the historical Jesus, but we couldn't know him personally. It's impossible to have a living relationship with someone dead. Our faith, however, isn't simply built around a historical figure. We worship a man who was dead and is alive again. We worship the risen Lord Jesus.

Secondly, the resurrection guarantees life after death:

> If only for this life we have hope in Christ, we are of all people most to be pitied. But Christ has indeed been raised from the dead, the firstfruits of those who have fallen asleep. For since death came through a man, the resurrection of the dead comes also through a man. For as in Adam all die, so in Christ all will be made alive. But each in turn: Christ, the firstfruits; then, when he comes, those who belong to him. (1 Cor. 15:19-23)

Christ goes before us, through death to new life, and then beckons us to follow. Now there can be assurance that a route has been opened to enable us to follow in his footsteps and enjoy the new world that has been created. Paul celebrates this in 1 Corinthians 15, declaring that 'death has been swallowed up in victory' (v. 54). Death itself has been defeated, leaving eternal life for those who follow the way of Jesus.

But life after death is one part of the promise. The promise of eternal life starts now, which means 'life before death' is also part of the package. The new creation has already dawned, and we can live in the light of the world to come now. As Paul constantly reminds us, it is through participation in these events that what has happened to Christ has also happened to us. He states in Romans 6:4 that we were 'buried with him through baptism into death in order that, just as Christ was raised from the dead through the glory of the Father, we too may live a new life.' This is more than just a future hope; it's a present invitation.

Jesus' resurrection more than just guarantees our own bodily resurrection when he returns; by being 'in Christ,' we can experience, at least in part, resurrection life now. Paul makes this clear in Romans 8:11: 'And if the Spirit of him who raised Jesus from the dead is living in you, he who raised Christ from the dead will also give life to your mortal bodies because of his Spirit who lives in you.'

Resurrection life is therefore coursing through our veins. God's Spirit, as Paul stresses on three separate occasions,[53] is the guarantee of our inheritance, the down payment that is both a foretaste of the future and a guarantee of that future. The fulness of life that Jesus promised is therefore more than just a promise of the quality of life available after death; it is a way of life before the grave for those who follow in the way of Jesus in the power of the Spirit.

Chapter 15

THE SPIRIT AND THE NEW CREATION

Robert Cornwall was the pastor of a small church in Salem, Oregon. He decided to volunteer some of his time to offer counselling at a nearby state mental institution. His first assignment was Building 37, a room that housed thirty-seven of the most severely mentally disturbed patients.

The guard escorted Robert to the building and unlocked the door to a padded cell containing half-clothed patients incapacitated by their drugs, with excrement all over the room. When he tried to talk with the patients, all he got was groans and grunts. The Holy Spirit prompted him to sing over the patients. So he found a space on the floor free from excrement and urine, and started singing, 'Yes, Jesus loves me, the Bible tells me so.' He sang that one refrain for a full hour, before the guard unlocked the door to collect him.

He returned the following week. And the week after. On the third week, whilst he sat on the floor singing the same refrain, a large lady approached him and began circling him, like a predator circling prey. Robert carried on singing, and the lady eventually sat down next to him and joined the chorus. Week by week the patients joined in with the singing. By the end of the month, thirty-six of the patients had been transferred from Building 37 to a self-help ward, and by the end of the year, all but two had been released from the mental institution. Many of them began worshipping at Robert's local church.[54]

There are definitely easier ways to grow your local church, but what blows me away about this story is the power of the Spirit to transform and bring life. The apostle Paul says that the Father pours his love into our hearts by the Spirit. As Robert Cornwall was singing, the Father was pouring out his love. The Spirit was roaming Building 37, bringing resurrection life. The miracle of Building 37 goes beyond medical explanation. It's a work of the Spirit, for where the Spirit of the Lord is, there is freedom. Where the Spirit of the Lord is, there is Re-creation.

Jesus and the Spirit

So far we have examined how the incarnation, cross and resurrection of Jesus reverse De-creation and the effects of the fall and enable Re-creation to take place. This all takes place by the Spirit, the agent of both creation and Re-creation. Of the incarnation, Luke recounts the story of Mary's encounter with the angel, who revealed God's plan for Mary to give birth to the Messiah: "'How will this be," Mary asked the angel, "since I am a virgin?" The angel answered, "The Holy Spirit will come on you, and the power of the Most High will overshadow you. So the holy one to be born will be called the Son of God'" (Luke 1:34-35).

A few chapters later Luke highlights that Jesus' ministry and mission, like the incarnation, was empowered by the Spirit. The Spirit comes to rest and remain on Jesus at his baptism, and then Jesus was immediately led by the Spirit into the wilderness, before later returning in 'the power of the Spirit.' It is at this point that Jesus famously declared, 'The Spirit of the Lord is on me' (Luke 4:18), empowering him to heal the sick, cast out demons and liberate the oppressed.

However, the same Spirit who empowered Jesus in his ministry also led Jesus to the cross. Hebrews 9:14 makes it clear that Christ offered himself unblemished to God through the eternal Spirit. So Jesus lived by the Spirit, but he also died 'by the Spirit.' In fact, more than that, he also rose by the Spirit. Paul highlights in Romans 8:11 that it is the Spirit who raised Christ Jesus from the dead. In summary, the mission of Jesus to fulfil Israel's (and thus humanity's) story through his life, death and resurrection all takes place by the Spirit.

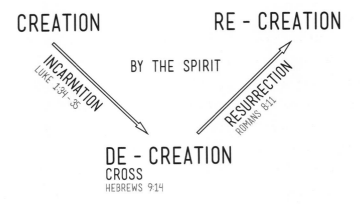

Every part of Jesus' mission is energised by the Spirit, and for his followers to share in his mission, they will need the same empowering presence to come and rest and remain. This is why the story of Pentecost is so central to the theme of Re-creation.

Pentecost, Re-creation and the Reversal of Babel

The reversal of De-creation was clearly taking place at Pentecost. It is hard to miss Luke's comparison of Pentecost and Babel in Acts 2. In the account of the Tower of Babel, recorded in Genesis 11, we see two key drivers: the pursuit of significance and the pursuit of a heavenly home and experience. In many ways, both pursuits reveal the longing to return to Eden, where a heavenly identity and a heavenly home were ours by nature of our relationship with God. Now, in isolation from God, humanity seeks to reclaim this lost identity and home by human endeavour. Such efforts, however, were thwarted by God who, in order to save humanity from itself, confused their languages and scattered the people.

This myth of human progress, of attempting to re-create Eden or establish our own utopia, now stands in direct contrast to the account of Pentecost in Acts 2. Instead of humanity working its way to the heavens, God by his Spirit brought heaven down. Instead of confusion regarding the languages, in Acts 2 there is suddenly understanding as each people-group heard the message in their own native language. Rather than the scattering in Genesis 11, we now have an ingathering in Acts 2.

Peter then proclaimed the gospel and three thousand responded, receiving the new life that Jesus by his Spirit brings. Now restored and rebirthed, Jesus' followers are sent out afresh, this time as God's servants rather than his rivals, with the great desire of making known the name of Jesus. These contrasts emphasise this moment of the outpouring of the Spirit as a critical ingredient in the movement from De-creation to Re-creation, as humanity is restored to its God-given identity as his image-bearers in the world.

Receiving Afresh the Breath of God

This theme of the Spirit as the agent of Re-creation is most powerfully evident in John's account of the giving of the Spirit. The language of Re-creation and new life are present in John's gospel from the very start, continuing right through his theological retelling of the story of Jesus. The theme of eternal life is in fact one of the distinguishing features of John's gospel, replacing the kingdom language that dominates the synoptic gospels (Matthew, Mark and Luke).[55] In John's account, Jesus is portrayed as the one who has the Spirit (who gives life) without measure (John 3:34), and therefore can't help but bring life wherever he goes.

This new life, Jesus declares to Nicodemus, is like being 'born again.' For any readers of this gospel, the language of rebirth in John 3 surely brings to mind the introduction to John's biography:

> Yet to all who did receive him, to those who believed
> in his name, he gave the right to become children
> of God—children born not of natural descent, nor
> of human decision or a husband's will, but born of
> God. (1:12-13)

To be born again must therefore mean the same thing as becoming 'children of God' (vv. 12-13). Jesus expands on his statement of being born again by saying that someone must be born of 'water and the Spirit' if they are to enter the kingdom of God (3:5). Several interpretations have been offered as to what this phrase actually means.[56] The most likely explanation is that Jesus was proclaiming the arrival of the end times when men and women would be cleansed of the idolatry that led to De-creation and restored to their original identity as God's children. Interestingly, when water is used figuratively in the Old Testament in conjunction with 'spirit,' it habitually refers to a renewal that cleanses God's covenant people from their idolatry and disobedience. Ezekiel 36 is perhaps the most vivid example. Here God states:

> For I will take you out of the nations; I will gather you from all the countries and bring you back into your own land. I will sprinkle clean water on you, and you will be clean; I will cleanse you from all your impurities and from all your idols. I will give you a new heart and put a new spirit in you; I will remove from you your heart of stone and give you a heart of flesh. And I will put my Spirit in you and move you to follow my decrees and be careful to keep my laws.... The desolate land will be cultivated instead of lying desolate in the sight of all who pass through it. They will say, 'This land that was laid waste has become like the garden of Eden.' (vv. 24-35)

Idolatry leads to death. Remember the warning of Psalm 135 that idols have 'ears, but cannot hear, nor is there breath in their mouths' (v. 17). These man-made idols are breathless, and because we become what we worship, idolatry will always lead to suffocation. But being 'born of water and the Spirit' results in renewal. The effects of idolatry are reversed and the land that was laid waste becomes like the Garden of Eden. Re-creation is essentially the issue at hand.

The theme of new life continues to dominate in John's gospel as people begin to experience the life of the age to come through healing, deliverance, forgiveness and the raising of Lazarus from death. However, as Jesus begins to involve his disciples in his ministry of extending his kingdom and bringing eternal life, a key question for the disciples emerges: how will they continue this ministry when Jesus has departed to be with the Father? This is perhaps the key concern of John 14-16. Jesus answers by promising that another 'Counsellor' will enable them to continue his ministry. The implication seems to be that the Spirit will take over from Jesus as the Counsellor.[57]

In the light of this, Jesus' promise not to leave the disciples as orphans and to come to them suggests that the fulfilment of this promise is to be found in the outpouring of the Spirit. The climactic moment is recorded in John 20:

> On the evening of that first day of the week, when
> the disciples were together, with the doors locked
> for fear of the Jewish leaders, Jesus came and stood
> among them and said, 'Peace be with you!' After

he said this, he showed them his hands and side. The disciples were overjoyed when they saw the Lord. Again Jesus said, 'Peace be with you! As the Father has sent me, I am sending you.' And with that he breathed on them and said, 'Receive the Holy Spirit.' (vv. 19-22)

This passage describes the moment Jesus breathed on (or perhaps better translated 'into') his disciples and said, 'Receive the Holy Spirit.' The use of the rare verb *emphusao* (to breathe on) would evoke two other memorable passages in which this verb is also used. The first is Genesis 2:7, which states that God breathed into Adam the breath of life. And the second is Ezekiel 37:9, which refers to God breathing into Israel's dry bones and bringing life again. These two passages are connected, particularly when one bears in mind the Eden reference we've just explored in Ezekiel 36. At the very beginning in Genesis 2, Adam and Eve came to life through the breath of God. The Hebrew word used here, *ruach*, can be translated as either 'breath' or 'spirit.' The promise of Ezekiel 37 is therefore that one day God will do again what he did in Eden and breathe his Spirit into dry bones to bring about new life.

Jesus breathing the Spirit into the disciples is therefore the fulfilment of the prophetic promise that had been given hundreds of years earlier through Ezekiel, as well as a reenactment of Genesis 2:7. The new age was dawning and the disciples were receiving the life of the age to come. Through the outpouring of the Spirit, the breath of God is given once again as God's redeemed humanity is restored to its original identity and mission.

The New Humanity as Agents of Re-creation

God's restored humanity, acting as agents of restoration, are both the means and the ends in God's purposes. Jesus tells Nicodemus that he needs to be born again, not simply for the sake of being born again, but in order to enter the kingdom of God. The implication seems to be that if the end goal is the regeneration and renewal of all things (Matt. 19:28), then this must be preceded by the regeneration and renewal of humanity.

This is evident in John 7:38, where Jesus states that streams of living water will flow from whoever believes in him. The context of this passage is Jesus interrupting the Feast of Tabernacles, which celebrated God's presence within the tabernacle as the people of Israel journeyed from Egypt to the Promised Land. On the final day of the feast, they would reenact the prophecy of Ezekiel 47 foreseeing a time when the Spirit of God would be poured out of the Temple as a river, bringing incredible life wherever it goes. To reenact the prophecy, the people would gather at the pool of Siloam and fill up water jars before processing up the mount to the Temple. They would then pour out the water over the altar, whilst reading out the prophecy from Ezekiel 47. This was a symbolic way of inviting God to fulfil his promise to pour out his Spirit in such a way that would turn their present wilderness experience into an Eden-type experience of the new creation.

Jesus interrupts the drama by saying, 'Let anyone who is thirsty come to me and drink. Whoever believes in me, as Scripture has said, rivers of living water will flow from within them' (John 7:37-38). In other words, stop reenacting the drama because it's all happening right now in your midst.

This one statement from Jesus contains two explosive truths. Firstly, he is claiming to be the source of this new life, the one who can satisfy their deepest longings for the age to come. He is the messiah, the one anointed by the Spirit to usher in a new world. But secondly, Jesus is stating that those who receive this new life will in turn become a Temple of the Holy Spirit.

To understand the weight of this idea, you need to know that according to the Jewish worldview, the Temple represented both the dwelling place of God as well as the meeting point of heaven and earth. This dwelling place and meeting point shifts in the biblical narrative from Eden to the Temple in Jerusalem, and eventually to Christ himself, who is described in the gospels as the new Temple. The kingdom of heaven breaking out around Jesus is to be expected if he is the place where heaven and earth now collide. However, to now describe the believer as the Temple of the Holy Spirit, as Paul does in his letter to the Corinthians, and as is implied here in John 7, is incredibly profound. The role of the Spirit to bring the life of the age to come is now at work in and through those who respond to Jesus' invitation. They are to become both recipients of the life of the age to come and agents of it. In other words, life flows to them as they breathe in and then through them as they breathe out to the rest of creation.

The giving of the Spirit answers the question of how the disciples are to continue Jesus' kingdom ministry of bringing life to creation. In fact, just before Jesus promises the 'Counsellor' in John 14, he famously says: 'Very truly I tell you, whoever believes in me will do the works I have been doing, and they will do even greater things than these, because I am going to the Father' (v. 12).

These 'works' are the proclamation of the kingdom's arrival, and the demonstration of its presence through acts of mercy and signs and wonders. The 'greater' therefore refers not to the quality of such works but to the quantity. Whereas Jesus operated in a fairly limited geographical area, and his primary mission was to seek and save the lost sheep of Israel, his disciples are now sent out to the ends of the earth and to all people groups. The ministry of Jesus is multiplied in and through his followers.

It is interesting that the narrative of John's gospel portrays Jesus, the one who has the Spirit without limit, as a healer,[58] a miracle-maker,[59] a prophet,[60] a teacher[61] and a man of wisdom. Paul, in his letter to the Corinthians, reminds the church of their role of continuing Jesus' ministry as the Spirit empowers them with gifts of healing, prophecies, words of wisdom, teaching and miraculous powers. Paul's clear implication is that the Spirit who empowers Jesus to do the works of his Father in the gospel narratives is the same Spirit who empowers the church in 1 Corinthians with gifts to continue such works.

In light of this, it should be expected that signs of Re-creation accompany the mission of the church today. In fact, to go one step further, ministering in the power of the Spirit is an absolute non-negotiable if we want to be both true to Scripture and effective in our mission today. The church cannot afford to reduce its mission to just the proclamation of a message. The message of the life available in Christ must equally be demonstrated in acts of compassion and through signs and wonders: for as recipients of life and Re-creation, we are now invited by Christ and through his Spirit to become agents.

Chapter 16

PERSONAL REFLECTIONS: FROM BROKENNESS TO BREAKTHROUGH

One of the worst days of my life occurred on 24th February 2018. We had taken the kids ice-skating with some close family friends when I received the phone call from our worship pastor, Tom Eccleshall. As a church we were getting ready to record our first-ever live worship album and had arranged to fly in two producers, Jeremy Edwardson and Andrew Jackson, from Redding, California. They were due to arrive that afternoon, and Tom and his wife, Sarah, were waiting at Heathrow to pick them up. But Jeremy and Andrew never made it that far.

The news eventually reached Tom, and that's when he phoned me. Andrew Jackson, 29, had started feeling unwell on the plane. Towards the end of the flight, things began to deteriorate. Andrew started to experience chest pains. The pilot was alerted that he should land the plane as soon as possible and to get an ambulance on standby at Heathrow. The pilot did so, and as Andrew was being wheeled off the plane, he went into cardiac arrest. The ambulance immediately rushed Andrew to Harefield Hospital.

Leaving Bee and the kids ice-skating, I began to navigate my way through London traffic to Harefield Hospital, praying my heart out and phoning friends and family to do likewise. I eventually arrived at the hospital and was greeted by Tom and Sarah. We made our way to the operating theatre, where medical specialists were working on Andrew. For the next hour, we prayed, waited, cried and prayed some more. The surgeons popped out from time to time to provide an update. The updates weren't great, but the surgeons were doing all they could.

I remember the moment of the final update. The surgeon came out and spoke to Jeremy. I gave Jeremy and the surgeon some space, but everything from the look on the surgeon's face to the body language of Jeremy's response made it clear what had happened. It's a horrific moment when everything you've feared and furiously prayed against becomes a reality. Time seems to stop. You feel sick. And then everything happens in slow motion. The surgeons invited us to say our final farewell to Andrew.

In a state of disbelief and shock, we walked into the operating theatre, caught somewhere between the most horrendous of nightmares and a heavenly moment where God's presence felt thick. We said to the doctors that we were Christians and, before we said goodbye, wanted to pray one last time for a miracle. We surrounded Andrew's bedside, laid on hands and began to intercede. Jeremy had managed to get through to Andrew's mum and dad in Redding. He held his phone to Andrew's ear so they could say their farewells as we continued to contend in prayer for a breakthrough.

It's hard to articulate what happened next. A deep peace was present in the room, and we knew it was time to transition from praying for healing to committing Andrew into the arms of his saviour. Our final goodbye was coinciding with heaven's welcome. And in the middle of the agony, trauma and shock, there was the peace that God's presence brings, and it really is a peace that passes understanding.

The next day we met up with Jeremy. A mixture of jetlag and trauma meant that he hadn't slept at all that night. We told him that he should go home and be with his family. The live recording he had come for was far less important than his emotional wellbeing and could easily wait for another time. But he was adamant that going ahead with the recording would be the best way to honour Andrew's life and legacy. Andrew was a passionate worshipper. He had spent the previous decade recording and producing much of the worship music that we sing in our churches and listen to at home. He believed in the power of worship to transform lives and communities. And having tasted the love of his Father in heaven, he wanted to create music that led people into that kind of encounter. Jeremy therefore wanted to finish what was to be Andrew's final project. Andrew had been excited about coming to London and had already spent hours in the studio refining and honing the songs for the recording. His fingerprints were all over each individual song. The live recording would provide a beautiful opportunity to capture Andrew's heart and his work, and to celebrate his life.

So less than a week after the trauma of Andrew's death, six hundred of us from KXC gathered in Scala, the iconic nightclub and gig venue of King's Cross. Andrew's parents had flown over from

Redding to join us in worship. We all knew this would be a powerful night as we came before God in total brokenness, bringing our tears as an offering of worship, whilst celebrating the story that defines us: a story of grace in which all brokenness will experience healing, all suffering will come to an end and death will be merely a gateway into everlasting life for those who respond to the love of Jesus. We had written eleven songs that would be our weapons for worship. Eleven unique songs with one unifying message, which has been the heart's cry of our church, that God is on a redemptive mission to make all things new. And if there was ever a time to declare the message, it was now.

As we gathered to worship, there was a deep sense that God had prepared us for this moment of worship and warfare. He had gone before us and left a trail to alert us that he wasn't absent from the pain and suffering, but present in it. One example of God's fingerprints reminding us of his presence came through the last song Andrew ever worked on as a producer. The song, 'With Me,' was written by two of our worship leaders, Rich and Lydia Di Castiglione, when Lydia's brother had tragically died in a car crash. The morning before Andrew boarded his flight to London, he had finished the demo for the song. He never knew it, but his last piece of work was to prepare a song that would help us in this moment of deep grief. The lyrics became our prayer that night:

> When I walk through the valley of the shadow of
> death
> And the grief that I carry is pounding on my chest
> I know, Jesus You are with me.

When sorrow has surrounded and I cannot
understand
I reach out in the doubting and hold onto your
hand
I know, Jesus You are with me

The songs then ends with a defiant declaration:

I will dance in the land of the living
I will shout and I'll never stop singing
You are good, and Your love endures forever.[62]

How can anyone dance in a moment like this? Why would people be singing in a time of such pain? The answer is that people can dance and sing when they know what God has prepared for those who love him. As we sang this song, I looked up to the balcony in Scala and saw Andrew's mum on her feet, hands in the air, worshipping and celebrating the God who makes all things new. I couldn't believe it. What an example of worship.

Another fingerprint pointing to God's presence with us in the pain came through a devotional reading that had been written two years previously. As a church we had created a devotional anthology called *Awaken*. It provided 365 daily readings, all written by people from within the KXC community, to help others journey through the year with Jesus. The Thursday morning of the recording, as I was preparing some thoughts to share that night to help guide our community through the tragedy of that week, I was interrupted by a phone call. It was a friend calling to ask if I had read the devotional entry for that day in *Awaken*. I hadn't but swiftly found my copy of the book and turned to the 1 March entry. The reflection was unpacking the story from Luke 7 of the sinful woman washing Jesus' feet with her tears. I read this:

> In the last few months I have cried more tears, sworn more profusely, felt more anger than I can remember. But the weirdest part is that in the middle of it all, I've also come to know more of God's immeasurable kindness....
>
> We worship a God who knows how to grieve. We worship a God who doesn't try and minimise the pain of loss. We worship a God who has mercy in our times of anger and frustration. We worship a God who knows when to speak and when just to hold us as we cry.
>
> Every human heart that has ever lived has experienced grief. Making the choice to worship in the middle of that pain has the power to transform it into something life-giving and beautiful. The tears will be cried either way—the choice we have is whether to pour them onto the feet of Jesus or not.

Out of 365 entries, God had chosen this one for 1 March. Perfect timing. The words were a gift, written two years before but ordained for such a day as this.

There's one particular moment from that night I'll never forget. In the months building up to the recording, I had a deep sense that it would be a significant moment of worship, intercession and break-through for us as a community. I had personally been studying the story of Joshua entering the Promised Land and sensed the Lord had taken us, like Joshua, on a journey of consecration in preparation for a new season and a new land. God had told Joshua, 'Consecrate yourselves, for tomorrow the LORD will do amazing things among you' (Josh. 3:5). We had been on such a journey and were praying for a corresponding move of God in King's Cross. I was planning on sharing this story at the live recording, before leading the church in a time of intercession.

Joshua and the people marched around Jericho seven times before raising a shout. The walls fell and the kingdom of God advanced. I thought it might be meaningful to do the same. Six hundred people walking around Scala seven times would look incredibly weird. So I decided we would instead just raise a shout of intercession, pray-ing for all the walls that stand in opposition to God's kingdom in King's Cross to come tumbling down: the walls of injustice, poverty, trafficking, greed, gang violence, the sex industry, the isolation of the elderly and the addictions that enslave people. So like Joshua in the face of the 'giants' of the land, we thought we'd raise a shout of intercession.

That was the plan in the months building up to Scala. But after Andrew's death and all that had happened in the week before the recording, raising a shout was the last thing on my mind. Humanly speaking, part of me just wanted to get through the evening. At best, I hoped the evening would provide a context for people to bring their own disappointments, pain and grief into a conversation with the God who heals and restores. I wasn't really expecting lament to turn to deep intercession. I didn't think people had the strength in them. But something happened in the worship.

As the Spirit began to move, intercession began to rise. It was like the sound of an army waking up ready to release a shout. Responding to what was stirring in the room, I shared the story of Joshua leading a tired, broken, yet consecrated, army into battle at Jericho. All God required of them was worship and prayer, and as they raised their voices, the walls that stood against God's kingdom came tumbling down. I suggested it was time to do the same. And we raised a shout. Six hundred of us. Six hundred hearts that had tasted grief and brokenness but had also tasted the love of the Father, the grace of the Son and the restorative power of the Spirit. And we roared, trusting that heaven could hear the sound of desperate hearts crying out for kingdom breakthrough. I've read enough Scripture to know that the roar of the broken releases the rule of heaven. And on 1 March 2018 in Scala, King's Cross, that was the sound I heard. I'll never forget it.

We follow Jesus in the midst of brokenness. Though we experience loss and taste grief, we don't lose hope because though Jesus died, he rose again, which means nothing is beyond his redemptive power. More than that, the power that raised Christ from the grave is coursing through the veins of his followers, empowering us to live in and live out this glorious story. It's time for the church to rediscover our confidence in the story, to shout it from the rooftops. For the life of the kingdom is available through the death and resurrection of the King.

PART V

THE CHURCH ON FIRE,
THE CITY ALIVE

Chapter 17

THE CHURCH AS THE KINGDOM ARMY

Towards the end of the Alpha Course my mum and dad had been leading, they did an exercise with their group to facilitate a discussion about where people were at on their journey of faith. They placed on the table a picture of a football stadium and asked people to place themselves somewhere on the picture: Were they in the stands, watching others play but still with big questions? Were they on the pitch, having made a commitment to follow Jesus, fully engaged in the game? Or were they on their way out of the stadium?

One by one the group named their place on the picture. The first guy in the group said that he was on the bench warming up. He hadn't grown up as a Christian but knew he wanted to be involved. He was metaphorically stretching, preparing to give his life to Jesus and get stuck in. Mum and Dad said, 'How exciting!'

The next to go was an engaged couple. The lady went first and began by asking, 'Is it okay if I'm really honest?' Mum and Dad said, 'Absolutely, this is a safe place.' She proceeded to share some of her past and present struggles, concluding with, 'I feel like I'm in the changing rooms having a shower. There is so much in my life I'm ashamed of, and I feel like God is washing me clean for a fresh start in life.' The group were visibly moved by her honesty, and Mum and Dad encouraged her vulnerability. 'How exciting!' they said once more. Her fiancé went next, and leaning towards Mum and Dad, asked, 'Is it okay if I'm really honest too?' Mum and Dad nodded emphatically. He then looked lovingly towards his fiancée, and cheekily said, 'If she's in the shower, then I'd quite like to be in the shower too.' The group nervously laughed, and Mum and Dad swiftly moved the conversation on.

I think that was the last time that my mum and dad did the exercise. But it's a great question: where are you in the stadium?

The story of Pentecost is the story of Jesus inviting his players on the pitch, empowering them with his Spirit to not just spectate but fully participate in his kingdom purposes.

Pentecost and the Birth of the Church

The church was birthed at Pentecost. The prophecy from Ezekiel 37 was more than just a promise of new life, it was equally a promise of a new community: a renewed Israel, redefined around Jesus, Israel's messiah. Ezekiel 37:9-10 states:

> Then he said to me, 'Prophesy to the breath; proph-
> esy, son of man, and say to it, "This is what the
> Sovereign LORD says: come, breath, from the four
> winds and breathe into these slain, that they may

live."' So I prophesied as he commanded me, and
breath entered them; they came to life and stood up
on their feet—a vast army.

The outpouring of the Spirit at Pentecost was the fulfilment of this prophecy. A vast army was formed, filled with the Spirit of God and a vision of serving God's purposes to make all things new.

The New Testament uses numerous images and metaphors to describe the beauty and power of the vast army. The church is a family, a household, the bride of Christ, a body with many parts and a Temple of God's Spirit. These metaphors are rich in meaning but don't provide a simple definition. Perhaps the closest we get to a definition comes from the Greek word used for church in the New Testament: *ekklesia*. This word is a compound word formed by fusing *ek* (meaning 'out of') and *klesia* (from the Greek verb *kaleo*, meaning 'to call'). Fused together, the word literally means 'called-out ones.'

In the world of ancient Greece, an *ekklesia* was an elected civil assembly that helped govern a city. Such a gathering had been called out to play a critical role in overseeing the affairs of the city to enable the people to flourish. For the New Testament writers to use the language of *ekklesia* to describe their gatherings is deeply subversive. They were claiming there was a new political assembly, called out by God himself, to govern over the affairs of the city. This new political assembly did not acknowledge the lordship of Caesar and instead proclaimed that Jesus was Lord. Equally, they weren't interested in the expansion of the Empire of Rome, instead awaiting the arrival of the kingdom of God throughout the earth. The Empire of Rome was busy creating colonies, where people worshipped the Roman pantheon of gods. But this true *ekklesia* gave itself to building colonies of heaven, where people worshipped the crucified and risen Christ.

The term *ekklesia*, whilst most commonly referring to a town council, was also used in different contexts. One such example was a gathering of Roman soldiers. If the emperor wanted to gather his army, or at least one section of the army, he would summon the troops. The summons was referred to as the *ekkaleo* (call out), and the summoned ones were the *ekklesia* (called-out ones).[63] In this context, the *ekklesia* was a group of Roman soldiers 'called out' by the emperor to extend the Empire of Rome. I like to imagine the early followers of Jesus intentionally using this loaded language to describe their identity and mission as God's 'called-out' civil assembly, sharing in his rule and reign, and his 'summoned' army, extending his kingdom in the world.

With this understanding of the term *ekklesia*, the church is to be seen as the worldwide community of Jesus followers, surrendered to his lordship and living to extend his kingdom and serve his purposes for the world.

A Worldwide Community of Jesus Followers

A few years ago I stumbled across an article about Delia Smith, the well-known British cook, and was surprised to read:

> Delia Smith never planned to become a cookery writer.... After leaving her secondary modern with no qualifications, she worked as a hairdresser and a shop assistant, and only learned to cook when a

boyfriend wouldn't stop talking about what a good cook his previous girlfriend had been…. Yet her greatest passion is no longer food, but football. Long-term Norwich City supporters, Smith and her husband joined the board of the team in 1996, and have since sunk £9m into the club. There's no chance of making any of it back, but as Smith, who has no children, explains: 'There's nothing else we would want to do with the money.' It's not just that she loves the game. She also believes that a well-run football club is one of the few places left where you'll find a community in its truest sense. 'When you see a community at a football match, that is how we're all supposed to be in the world,' she says. 'You're bonded with other people, sharing the same goal. You have joy and you have pain—not deep pain; perhaps for some people it might be. You understand what being human is, following a football team.'[64]

Delia illustrates a truth that the Judeo-Christian story emphasizes from beginning to end: human beings are made for community. Within the context of a football team, Delia suggests people share a sense of belonging ('bonded with other people') as well as a sense of purpose ('sharing the same goal'). As a big football fan myself, I understand what Delia is getting at, but I'm aware that however good the team you follow is, it will be unable to deliver the kind of community we crave. This God-given desire suggests that the fulfilment of the desire must be found in relationship with the giver. To be made in the image of a trinitarian God suggests that human flourishing must be dependent on communion with both God as well as his image-bearers.

Those who draw close to Jesus are always drawn close to his body, the church. The church is therefore the gathering together of those who follow Jesus from all across the globe: people from every tribe and tongue, from every sector of society, of every age, of every ethnic group and of every nationality. In Christ, and through the cross, the dividing walls are gone: 'There is neither Jew nor Gentile, neither slave nor free, nor is there male and female, for you are all one in Christ Jesus' (Gal. 3:28). A new family has been formed through those who have said yes to Jesus and chosen to follow in his way.

This drawing together of people from all walks of life and from all corners of the globe is central to our witness to the world. Jesus even said that the world would know that we belong to him through our unity and love for one another (John 13:35). It was also his prayer that still awaits complete answer, recorded in John 17, that the church might be brought to complete unity. It is this unity in diversity that communicates the power of the gospel to create a new family and therefore a new place of belonging in an age of isolation and loneliness. Lesslie Newbigin, in his book *The Gospel in a Pluralist Society*, underlines this point:

> I have come to feel that the primary reality of which we have to take account in seeking for a Christian impact on public life is the Christian congregation. How is it possible that the gospel should be

credible, that people should come to believe that the power which has the last word in human affairs is represented by a man hanging on a cross? I am suggesting that the only answer, the only hermeneutic of the gospel, is a congregation of men and women who believe it and live by it.[65]

Hermeneutics is the study of a text's meaning, so Newbigin is suggesting that people can only understand and make sense of the gospel when they see it lived out in community. Such Christian community, where the love and grace of Christ is present and practiced in the midst of all the brokenness and pain of life, not only illuminates the gospel, but also attracts peoples to it. It is not surprising to read in the book of Acts that 'the Lord added to their number daily those who were being saved' (2:47). The way the church looked after the poor and vulnerable, loved each other and lived with hope and purpose against a backdrop of Roman oppression created a gravitational pull.

Perhaps it's for this reason that the author of Hebrews stresses, 'Do not give up meeting together, as some are in the habit of doing' (Heb. 10:25). When we stop gathering, by very definition, we stop being the *ekklesia* (the assembly of called-out ones). When we stop gathering, we stop witnessing. To follow Jesus and give up on the church is ultimately to give up on Jesus, as Jesus has wedded himself to the wellbeing of his bride, the church. To follow Jesus is to love what he loves, and he loves the church, despite its hypocrisy, brokenness and dysfunction. St Augustine captured this sentiment well when he said, 'The church is a whore, but she's my mother.' Such language acknowledges the brokenness of the church and how it has failed to be faithful to the teaching of Jesus. And yet the church is where we find life, nurture and are named as the children of God.

Now is not the time to give up on church, but to re-envision a younger generation of the beauty and power, even in the chaos and complexity, of local church. For as George Eldon Ladd famously said, 'The church is the primary agency of the kingdom of God.' It's time to believe and put faith in what God believes and puts faith in, his community, body, bride, family, household, army, new Temple—his local church.

Surrendered to the Lordship of Christ

The church is a worldwide community, but as we stated earlier, it's more than that. This community has a centre around which everything revolves, and that centre is the crucified and risen Lord Jesus. We get a beautiful picture of this in John's sneak peak of the worship of heaven in Revelation 5:

> Then I saw a Lamb, looking as if it had been slain, standing at the centre of the throne, encircled by the four living creatures and the elders.... Then I looked and heard the voice of many angels, numbering thousands upon thousands, and ten thousand times ten thousand. They encircled the throne and the living creatures and the elders.... Then I heard every creature in heaven and on earth and under the earth and on the sea, and all that is

in them, saying: 'To him who sits on the throne and
to the Lamb be praise and honour and glory and
power, for ever and ever!' (vv. 6, 11, 13)

All of creation is gathered in the round, encircling the crucified and risen Jesus. This redeemed community exists because of his
sacrifice and lives to bring him praise. We centre our lives around
Jesus, both individually and corporately, as we bow down and proclaim that he is Lord. The very statement 'Jesus is Lord' is central to
dethroning other objects of worship. For the early Christians this
statement meant that Caesar wasn't Lord, and that kind of rebellion
could get you killed. Surrendering to the lordship of Jesus is always
costly business: it means placing his values and desires before your
own. And it affects everything: how we vote, where we spend our
money, how we treat our employer or employees, what kind of parent we become and how we treat our neighbours.

So how do we surrender to the lordship of Jesus? The answer is to
recognise, repent and replace the idols that have been enthroned in
God's place. Jesus begins his ministry with the declaration, 'Repent,
for the kingdom of heaven has come near' (Matt. 4:17). The word
'repentance,' from the Greek word *metanoia*, means 'to turn around.'
By inviting people to repent, Jesus is inviting them to shift their
thinking about how the kingdom would come and to turn around
and follow him.

Such a process begins by recognising we are heading in the
wrong direction—that we have fallen in love with the wrong things
and have been walking away from the source of all life. These 'wrong
things' may not even be bad things, but when good things become

ultimate things, they break the hearts of their worshippers. Once the idol has been named, it needs to be dethroned. This is the repentance part: turning away from the idol, severing the relationship, asking God to forgive and cleanse you. Then, having turned away from the idol, we turn towards Jesus and proclaim that he alone is Lord. In doing so we replace the objects of wrong worship with the object of right worship. The idols get dethroned as Jesus takes his rightful place on the throne, at the very centre of our lives.

This is the pathway to life and how the journey of faith begins. We respond to the invitation of Jesus, we turn towards him and then follow after him. The church is far more than an assembly of people who believe in Jesus: it is the army of those who follow him. Before the followers of Jesus were ever called 'the church,' they were referred to as 'People of The Way,' for they followed 'the way' of Jesus. This was manifest in the way they lived, the way they treated people and the way they conducted themselves. Everyone could identify a follower of Jesus because of the way they did life, and it was this lifestyle that enabled people to enjoy the life of the kingdom. As my good friend John Mark Comer says, 'If you want to experience the life of Jesus, you have to adopt the lifestyle of Jesus.' To surrender to the lordship of Jesus is more than giving mental assent to a set of beliefs and doctrine; it is to say yes with every part of who you are to Christ's plans and purpose. This is what it means to be church.

Living to Extend God's Kingdom

So how do we follow the way of Jesus and serve God's purposes in the world? The key to this lies in living in the full story of God.

Numerous writers have summarised the biblical plotline as a journey through Creation—Fall—Redemption—Renewal. One of the tragedies within church history has been the replacement of this full narrative with a truncated version. As a result, certain doctrines rose to prominence, and the journey of the individual from sin to salvation began to take centre stage.

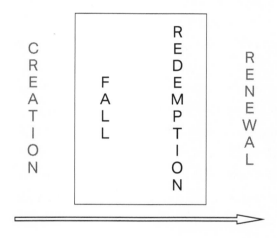

Evangelistic courses began (and often still begin) with the doctrine of original sin, and the rest of the story became about how the cross deals with the issue of sin in order to reconcile us to the Father. Genesis 1 and 2 are left behind, and we start the story in Genesis 3. The question of what it means to be human, being made in the image and likeness of God, is replaced with the question of what it means to be sinful and how one could be saved. The story then ends with the cross and resurrection, guaranteeing heaven when we die for those who believe in Jesus. The restoration and renewal of all things gets cut from the narrative. Heaven coming down, and God making his dwelling place with us on earth, gets replaced with us ascending to the heavenly realm to escape the sinful world around us. However, the mission of Jesus in the gospels and of the early church in Acts makes it clear that our story isn't one of simply being rescued from the world. We're rescued for the world to be agents of Re-creation within it.

The danger of a truncated story is that it leads to a truncated understanding of mission. A more holistic understanding of mission still emphasises the need to proclaim the message of the cross and call people to repentance, whilst equally emphasising the church's role to alleviate the poverty and suffering that rob people of life, to steward the creation we have been entrusted to look after and to work towards the renewal of the culture we are embedded within.

Within the full story, the job of a banker isn't simply to tell other bankers about Jesus and to be a good witness; it's equally to work towards the renewal of the banking industry and to infect this industry with the values of the kingdom of God. Those in the fashion world are called to reimagine an industry that glorifies God and leads to people flourishing. Teachers are invited to redeem the sphere of education with a kingdom vision, developing character and preparing students to live wisely and well. It's time to embrace the full story and therefore reclaim a fuller vision of what it means to be church, living in and living out the full story of God.

Part of living within this story means embracing the tension that exists between our future hopes and our present experience. Jesus declared that the kingdom of God was a present reality in his ministry and at the same time held that in tension with a future arrival of that kingdom. Jesus had inaugurated this kingdom, but its complete arrival awaited his second coming. The followers of Jesus also have to embrace this tension. One day there will be no death, grief, crying or pain, but in the meantime those hardships are constantly with us. We therefore live as people of hope, welcoming God's future into the present through prayer and acts of faith. At the same time, we mourn and suffer with those experiencing loss. We celebrate with people when the kingdom arrives and mourn with others when it doesn't.

Theologians often refer to this as the now and not-yet of the kingdom. The kingdom is both present and future. The new creation has been birthed, but we await its full arrival. Living in this tension is hard, and it's easy to see why some church traditions seek to break the tension either with an under-realised or an over-realised eschatology, or end-times theology. The former states that we shouldn't expect the signs and wonders of the kingdom anymore, and the purpose for the present is to cling on and remain faithful until Christ returns. The latter states that the entirety of the kingdom is accessible by faith, so if healing hasn't come and provision hasn't arrived, it must be because of some hidden sin or lack of faith. The pastoral damage from this approach is enormous.

Jesus made it clear in John 9:3 that sickness doesn't necessarily mean hidden sin. He also raised Lazarus from the dead, and dead men don't tend to have much faith. This doesn't mean holiness and faith aren't key ingredients in our partnership with Jesus in his mission—they very much are. But kingdom breakthroughs are a gift, not to be earned though moral endeavor, religious activity or spiritual intensity, but to be freely received. The right emphasis in kingdom activity is always on the grace and generosity of the king rather than the performance of the subjects.

So if the church is called to live in this tension, how do we do that well? The answer is that we start by acknowledging that the tension hurts. We shouldn't seek to eliminate the tension with bad theology, with an over-realised or under-realised eschatology, but instead embrace the fact that good theology sometimes hurts. In this case, inaugurated eschatology hurts.

Secondly, we remember the hope that has been set before us. We are shaped by the end we live for. We fix our eyes on Jesus, the author of the story and the one who will bring it to completion. This completion, of all things being made new, means that no situation now is beyond redemption or beyond Christ's reach. All will be healed, all will be put right, which creates incredible hope even in the midst of pain.

Finally, in this posture of pain and hope, we pray. And more specifically, we pray the kingdom prayer that Jesus taught us, that his 'kingdom would come on earth as it is in heaven.' The implication of the prayer is that God's will isn't always done. Most image-bearers, like Adam and Eve, like me and you, more often than not choose our own will rather than God's will, leading to the brokenness we see all around us. And so we take a stand against such a tide and pray for God's will to be done, and then align our lives with our prayers, seeking to be obedient to the way of Jesus.

Past, Present, Future

The church, as many writers have highlighted, has an upward dimension (worship), an inward dimension (community) and an outward dimension (mission). But these activities in the present, though rooted in time and space, also span time and space. We are a people shaped by the past and living for a defined future that affects all people and all places. Worship anchors us in our specific time and place so we can live out our story. This is why the Scriptures and sacraments are so central to church life. To anchor people in the Scriptures is to anchor them in the story of God.

The sacraments also draw us further and deeper into the story. Through baptism we enter both a family and a story. The story we enter is the story of Jesus, who in turn fulfils the wider story of God. The same is true of the Eucharist. This meal was first celebrated in anticipation of the cross, during the Passover festival. Jesus redefines an ancient meal that drew the Jewish people back to God's rescue at the Red Sea. This reminded them that they were called to be a kingdom of priests in the present whilst awaiting the fulfilment of promises given to their ancestors. The meal formed community, affirmed identity and stirred hope through a simple act of remembrance. Likewise, the Eucharist forms community and affirms identity as we give thanks for God's saving work at the cross. We are drawn into the story of Jesus, and therefore the story of Israel that he fulfils, reminded of our purpose to be partners in such a story. As such, we hope for the day when Christ will return and throw a party to end all parties. This idea of a future heavenly banquet was a loaded Jewish image that Jesus used on numerous occasions in his storytelling. The Jewish people believed that at the end of time, in the age to come, there would be a grand feast at the Temple. The Eucharist anticipates and is a foretaste of this banquet.

We are shaped by the past, but we live in the moment, fully present emotionally, spiritually and physically. This means embracing the hurt and disappointments of life, acknowledging that our faith does not provide immunity. It doesn't. It equally means embracing the joys, the highs and the ecstatic moments life offers. The central thesis of Peter Scazzero's book *Emotionally Healthy Spirituality* is that it's impossible to be spiritually mature whilst remaining emotionally immature. Our emotions are not a guide to follow but a voice to listen to, communicating the state of our inner being. A spirituality that encourages emotions to be suppressed in the context of worship is misguided. God intended the free expression of emotions as we worship him with hearts full of joy and sorrow, gratitude and grief.

The writer Richard Rohr says a significant part of spirituality centres on what we do with our pain. He states that there are essentially only two options: allow God to transform it or transmit it instead. When pain is not transformed, it bleeds out and the De-creation spiral continues. The church is intended to be a place, a community, where people are encouraged and empowered to let their pain be transformed by God. It is a shelter for the poor, the broken, the ashamed and the sick.

As we live in the present, allowing God to transform our pain, we are also mindful of the countless kingdom possibilities. We long for adventure as well as authenticity. We long for a home that is safe enough for us to heal, but we also need it to be adventurous and audacious enough to challenge ourselves to grow. Experiencing comfort is a key part of the healing journey, but comfort alone can stifle our growth. It is outside our comfort zones that faith grows fastest and deepest. It shouldn't surprise us that supernatural activity and miracles happen most often when God's people are away from the safety of home and demonstrating faith in the face of adversity.

Hebrews 11 catalogues many stories of the heroes of our faith, adventurers searching for home whilst bringing about God's purposes into the present. The stories inspire us to actively live out our faith in the world today, realising that our true home awaits us. We are, in the words of the apostle Peter, 'foreigners and exiles,' traveling through our earthly lives whilst dreaming of our eternal home.

But we are more than just dreamers, we are also builders of that future. We can live in the moment because we know what is to come. By living in the story, we live out the story, pushing forward God's purposes while waiting for his return. This dreaming and building requires a prophetic imagination. What would the arrival of the kingdom look like on your street? What would it look like in your workplace? How would it change your family dynamics? We imagine and then pray to one who can do far more than all we could ever ask for or imagine, according to his power at work within us.

As a church, we dream, we pray and we build. This is the task of the worldwide community of Jesus followers, living to extend God's kingdom and serve his purposes in the world. We are a people of worship, community and mission, shaped by the past, living in the moment and building towards the future. We are anchored in a story and live out that story in the world. It is messy and chaotic, but beautiful and glorious. It's the local church, Christ's bride and God's kingdom army.

Chapter 18

DISCIPLES SHAPED BY THE STORY OF GOD

Ernest Gordon was a British officer captured by the Japanese in World War 2. The Japanese treated their prisoners of war brutally, forcing them to work in horrific conditions to build the Burma-Siam railway through the thick jungle. More than eighty thousand men died as a result. The conditions in the prison camp were equally horrific, a dog-eat-dog existence as people fought for their own survival.

However, a breakthrough came one day. One of the returning groups was missing a shovel. The Japanese guard made it clear that if it wasn't returned immediately, he would kill the entire group. No one came forward, so the guard lifted his rifle to shoot. Immediately one man stepped up to take responsibility. The guard responded by beating him to death in front of the group. Traumatised by what they had seen, the group later found out that the guards had simply miscounted the shovels. This heroic act of courage and sacrifice transformed the camp. Gordon himself recalls:

Death was still with us, no doubt about that, but we were slowly being freed from its destructive grip. We were seeing for ourselves the sharp contrast between the forces that made for life and death. Selfishness, hatred, envy, jealousy, greed, self-indulgence and pride were anti-life. Love, heroism, self-sacrifice, sympathy, mercy, integrity and creative faith, on the other hand, were the essence of life, turning existence into living in its truest sense. These were the gifts of God to men.... True there was hatred, but there was also love, there was death but there was also life, God had not left us, He was with us, calling us to live the divine life of fellowship.[66]

In is his book *Rumours of Another World*, Philip Yancey explains how the rule of heaven pervaded the camp after this breakthrough moment. The prisoners began to choose love over hate, to serve rather than be served and to put others first. Ultimately, they chose life over death and started building a community in which everyone could flourish. As part of this, the prisoners pooled their gifts to form a jungle university. Gordon taught philosophy and ethics. Other prisoners taught history, economics, maths, natural sciences and at least nine languages. They created galleries exhibiting the work of artists in the community. They made instruments and performed their compositions to the camp. They even built a church as a place of worship.

Yancey describes their community as a picture of the kingdom and a foretaste of God's coming reign. It was a gathering of people living in and living out the story of God. The prisoners formed a community of compassion, courage and creativity. And their task is very much our task today: to plant 'settlements in advance of that coming reign.'

Changing the World by Becoming Like Jesus

If there is a strategy for cultural renewal, community transformation and kingdom ministry present in the gospels and book of Acts, it would have two solid foundations: become more like Jesus and follow the leading of the Spirit. Everything else is built on this.

Before Jesus ascended to be with the Father, he instructed his followers to wait in Jerusalem to be clothed with power from on high. Only then, empowered by the Spirit, would they be sent out as witnesses and disciples. The Great Commission of Matthew 28 makes this clear:

> Then Jesus came to them and said, 'All authority in heaven and on earth has been given to me. Therefore go and make disciples of all nations, baptising them in the name of the Father and of the Son and of the Holy Spirit, and teaching them to obey everything I have commanded you. And surely I am with you always, to the very end of the age.' (vv. 18-20)

To put it simply, we change the world by becoming like Jesus. This journey of discipleship is central to our mission, so let's explore Jesus' model for discipleship and how he multiplied his kingdom ministry through unschooled fishermen, despised tax collectors and ordinary people like you and me.

Discipleship in the First Century

At the very beginning of Jesus' ministry, after his baptism and anointing of the Spirit, he invited the disciples to 'Come, follow me.' These three words would have been totally life changing, and to understand why, we need to explore the educational system of first-century Judaism. The first stage of education, roughly equivalent to primary school in our context, was known as Bet Sefer (House of the Book). At Bet Sefer, the children would learn to read and write by immersing themselves in the Torah, the first five books of the Hebrew Scriptures. By the end of Bet Sefer, most children would have memorised the entire Torah.

The next step, for the boys with capacity for more learning, was Bet Talmud (House of Learning). At this stage of their education, alongside learning their family trade, the students would be immersed in the rest of the Hebrew Scriptures, memorising large portions, and becoming well versed in the Jewish tradition of 'question and answer,' learning to answer questions with further questions that lead to deeper revelation and understanding. At the end of Bet Talmud, the majority of students had hit their ceiling for learning and left school to work in the family business.

For those hungry for more, they could approach a rabbi and ask to become their disciple. This final school was known as Bet Midrash. The rabbi would subject the student to a gruelling interview to see if the student had what it took to begin the training to become a rabbi. For the unsuccessful student, the rabbi would encourage them to have children and pray that their children would one day become rabbis, and in the meantime to learn the family trade. For the successful student, the one who had shown he was the cream of the crop, the rabbi would say, 'Come, follow me.' These three words were the invitation to begin the journey of becoming a rabbi. This was the highest of callings, the greatest privilege, and what every parent wanted for their child.

In response to the call, the student would potentially leave the family home, leave their village and wider community, to follow their rabbi. The community would send them off saying, 'May you be covered in the dust of your rabbi.' In other words, may you follow the rabbi so closely that you not only get covered in his teachings, character and practices, but also the dust from his sandals on the journey. This discipleship journey was marked out by three ingredients: being with the rabbi, becoming like the rabbi, and doing what the rabbi did. As rabbis raised up disciples, they would then begin to multiply their influence across a region.

Being with Jesus, Becoming Like Jesus

Matthew 4 tells the story of Jesus first calling out the disciples:

> As Jesus was walking beside the Sea of Galilee, he saw two brothers, Simon called Peter and his brother Andrew. They were casting a net into the lake, for they were fishermen. 'Come, follow me,' Jesus said, 'and I will send you out to fish for people.' At once

> they left their nets and followed him. Going on from there, he saw two other brothers, James son of Zebedee and his brother John. They were in a boat with their father Zebedee, preparing their nets. Jesus called them, and immediately they left the boat and their father and followed him. (vv. 18-22)

This story tells us that Peter, Andrew, James and John had dropped out of school so were at home working in the family business. For these unschooled fishermen to hear the three words 'Come, follow me' would have been remarkable. Normally the student approached the rabbi, but here the rabbi approached them and invited them into the greatest adventure on offer. No wonder they immediately left their boats, nets and even their father to follow Jesus.

In Mark's account, he highlights the first step of the discipleship journey:

> Jesus went up on a mountainside and called to him those he wanted, and they came to him. He appointed twelve that they might *be with him* and that he might send them out to preach and to have authority to drive out demons. (3:13-15)

The top priority of following Jesus is being with him. In the hyperactive world we live in—where we are always connected, accessible and hyper-alert—many of us find it difficult just to be still and enjoy spending time with Jesus. Like the story of Mary and Martha, most of us choose the path of Martha as we rush around flustered and 'upset about many things.' Mary, however, understood 'what was better' and chose to sit at Jesus' feet, enjoying his presence (Luke 10:41-42). Sitting at the feet of a rabbi was the identifiable posture of a disciple, indicating here Jesus' radical inclusion of women in the discipleship journey, breaking the socials norms of the day. This posture also indicates the priority of abiding before trying to be fruitful, of resting before working and of presence before productivity. Discipleship begins with friendship.

In *The Message* translation of Matthew 11, Jesus says to his disciples:

> Are you tired? Worn out? Burned out on religion? Come to me. Get away with me and you'll recover your life. I'll show you how to take a real rest. Walk with me and work with me—watch how I do it. Learn the unforced rhythms of grace. I won't lay anything heavy or ill-fitting on you. Keep company with me and you'll learn to live freely and lightly. (vv. 28-30)

The language of 'unforced rhythms of grace' beautifully paraphrases Jesus' teaching in Matthew 11 in which he offered an easy and light 'yoke,' a first-century reference to one's interpretation of the Torah and the way of living it out. Unlike other rabbis who would lay heavy burdens on their disciples, offering teachings that were impossible to live up to, Jesus offers a different path. He offers a gentle and humble path, centred on imitating these rhythms of grace.

These words contain Jesus' wisdom on the art of becoming, much of which has been neglected over the last two thousand years. Since the Enlightenment, we have embraced the view that behavioural change is initiated by new patterns of thinking. To act differently, we need to think differently. Behind this is a distorted understanding of what it means to be human, and as this Enlightenment thinking invaded the church, our discipleship programmes and courses became almost entirely focussed on the mind. Good doctrine must result in Christ-shaped living. My life, and I'm guessing yours, provides ample evidence for the insufficiency of this view.

Jesus, however, had a far more holistic understanding of our human identity. Of course we are rational beings, which is why he calls people to repentance. He invited his followers into a new worldview, a new way of understanding the Scriptures and the kingdom he was inaugurating. But more than just shifting worldviews, he wanted to redirect their desires to his vision of the kingdom rather than a nationalistic alternative. And when it comes to redirecting desires, offering more information and new worldviews won't cut it. What we need are rhythms of grace.

In his book *Desiring the Kingdom*, James KA Smith builds on the work of Augustine, writing centuries before the Enlightenment began, by acknowledging that though we are thinking and believing beings, we are fundamentally desiring beings. We are driven more by our appetites than by our reasoning. And therefore to embrace change, we need more than just renewed minds, we need redirected desires.

Ancient wisdom from philosophers and theologians such as Aristotle, Augustine and Aquinas emphasises two central aspects of this process of redirecting our desires and becoming more virtuous. Firstly, we need to imitate, and secondly, we need to practice. This process of imitation and practice is how we learnt to walk, talk and ride a bike. What once felt unnatural soon becomes second nature. If our current nature represents the things we do without even thinking, then the discipleship journey is about imitating Jesus and practising his rhythms of grace until his nature becomes our second nature. This is obviously a work of the Spirit, who is active in the process, transforming us into the image of Jesus (2 Cor. 3:18). This is more than just human effort; it is the willing cooperation with the Spirit's work in our lives.

FIRST NATURE UNFORCED RHYTHMS **SECOND NATURE**
CURRENT NATURE ——————▶ NATURE OF CHRIST
          OF GRACE

These practices begin to reorient our hearts and point our desires in the direction of God's kingdom. In turn, these redirected desires begin to move us towards the kingdom as we begin to do the things that Jesus did. A great example of this appears in Matthew 14:

> Shortly before dawn Jesus went out to them, walking on the lake. When the disciples saw him walking on the lake, they were terrified. 'It's a ghost,' they said, and cried out in fear. But Jesus immediately said to them: 'Take courage! It is I. Don't be afraid.' 'Lord, if it's you,' Peter replied, 'tell me to come to you on the water.' 'Come,' he said. Then Peter got down out of the boat, walked on the water and came towards Jesus. But when he saw the wind, he was afraid and, beginning to sink, cried out, 'Lord, save me!' Immediately Jesus reached out his hand

and caught him. 'You of little faith,' he said, 'why
did you doubt?' (vv. 25-31).

Peter knew the discipleship journey: be with Jesus, become like
Jesus, do the stuff. By this point in the gospel narrative, Jesus had
sent out the twelve to minister. They had been healing the sick, casting out demons and proclaiming the gospel. They were becoming,
slowly and incrementally, like Jesus. So when Peter wants to test out
whether this ghostly figure is in fact Jesus, he suggests a challenge:
'Jesus, if it is you, and if you are the rabbi training us up to do the
things you do, then surely you should be training me to walk on
water like you do. Therefore invite me onto the water.' The logic is
strong, and Jesus seems impressed. Finally the disciples understand
discipleship. Jesus says, 'Come.'

Sadly, much preaching on this text emphasises Peter sinking as
he takes his eyes off Jesus. That's obviously part of the story, but
those who emphasise this aspect miss the wood from the trees. The
incredible, paradigm-shifting event is that Peter walked on water. He
was becoming like Jesus. This is what is on offer when Jesus invites us
to come and follow him. It's more than just an invitation to friendship and more than just an invitation into character formation; it's
a journey of becoming intimately involved in Jesus' kingdom work.

Recapturing a Jesus-centred Approach to Discipleship

When comparing the Jesus model for apprenticeship to the dominant model of discipleship in the church, it is clear there is a

significant chasm. Predominantly within the evangelical tradition of the western church, I have encountered four main distortions of discipleship. Firstly, discipleship gets reduced to theological education, and therefore being with Jesus and becoming like Jesus gets replaced with knowing stuff about Jesus.

BEING WITH JESUS, BECOMING LIKE JESUS
AND DOING THE STUFF JESUS DID

KNOWING STUFF ABOUT JESUS

I'm a huge fan of theological formation, but it is mindboggling how many churches approach discipleship with an Enlightenment worldview and therefore try to find a course with the right content to help people become like Jesus. Forget spiritual practices and rhythms of grace and ancient wisdom. Let's immerse people in the biblical worldview and watch the change unfold. The problem is that whilst their minds might be marinating in a biblical worldview, their hearts are marinating in consumerism and the practices of the culture. Most pastors I meet are disillusioned and discouraged by the discipleship culture within their church. People keep looking for courses in the hope of finding a silver bullet, but the solution is far more costly than a course. Theology and doctrine are essential, but not enough. The most essential aspect of discipleship is proclaiming Jesus as Lord and learning to follow his teaching and his way.

The second distortion is reducing discipleship to character formation. In this distortion, being with Jesus and becoming like Jesus gets replaced with being good or becoming a better person.

BEING WITH JESUS, BECOMING LIKE JESUS
AND DOING THE STUFF JESUS DID

BEING GOOD

Discipleship becomes about moral improvement: swearing less, watching less porn, being kinder to work colleagues and more patient with our kids. Clearly, following the way of Jesus involves our character being formed into the character of Christ, but when this gets separated from evangelism and mission, it disempowers the church from effective engagement in the world. Jesus forms the disciples' character as they engage in his kingdom mission and proclaim his gospel. It's this gospel that saves and transforms, not the disciples' goodness or righteousness. Character formation is essential, but alone still falls short of Jesus' model for apprenticeship.

The third distortion is reducing discipleship to working towards the common good. Being with Jesus, becoming like Jesus and doing the stuff he did gets replaced with doing good in the world. When people talk about the kingdom these days, they often refer to serving the vulnerable, making poverty history, reducing our carbon footprint and caring for creation. All of that is fantastic, but did Jesus mean more than that when he referred to the kingdom of God? The answer is a resounding yes.

BEING WITH JESUS, BECOMING LIKE JESUS AND DOING THE STUFF JESUS DID

DOING GOOD

Don't get me wrong. I'm a huge advocate of the church intentionally and intelligently engaging with culture. I love the language of 'cultural renewal,' 'human flourishing' and 'the common good.' But at the same time the popularity of these terms within the wider church also concerns me. Everyone has a vision of human flourishing, so when using such a term we need to define it biblically. That's because Jesus' vision of human flourishing will not match the political, cultural and national visions that surround us and subtly shape us.

Jesus' priority wasn't the common good as the culture of his day defined it, but the will of his father, and it is the will of the father that defines what is good throughout the Scriptures. Today's culture may define 'good' one way, but the followers of Jesus have always been submitting to his definition of what is good and pleasing. Underneath this distortion often lies the heresy that our good works can save the world. The gospel alone is what saves, renews and transforms. And whilst the good deeds and moral character of Christians throughout the ages have pulled people towards the church, it's always been the message of Jesus' life, death and resurrection that has transformed lives.

The apostle Peter encouraged the church to 'live such good lives among the pagans that … they may see your good deeds and glorify God on the day he visits us' (1 Pet. 2:12). But he also encouraged the same people to 'always be prepared to give an answer to everyone who asks you to give the reason for the hope that you have' (1 Pet. 3:15). Followers of Jesus should be salt and light in the world, demonstrating God's love in acts of mercy, kindness and compassion. But our vision for discipleship has to go beyond simply working for the common good.

The final distortion is replacing discipleship with a church-growth agenda. As a church leader, I find the constant temptation is to emphasise programmes for church growth rather than emphasise becoming like Jesus. The temptation is to focus our energy on what is more measurable rather than embracing the costly work of loving people through ups and downs, mentoring people in the spiritual disciplines and training people to live out their faith.

This doesn't mean I'm against church growth. I love it, pray for it and desperately want it. Healthy organisations grow, and though that growth may be multifaceted, numerical growth must surely be an aspect of it. Nor does this mean that I think smaller churches are better or more effective at discipleship. I don't believe that either. It simply means that all churches must more intentionally pursue discipleship and evangelism. The end goal is never a larger church but redeemed lives, renewed cities and a restored creation.

If this is our end goal, we should with humility acknowledge the distortions that have crept into our ministries and churches. Where we have prioritised knowing stuff about Jesus, being good and doing good, perhaps it's time to follow again the way of Jesus, to imitate his example and practice his rhythms of grace.

Any reading of the gospel accounts will soon remove any gloss from what this actually looks like. Amongst the disciples are those with anger problems (the sons of thunder), those wrestling with doubt (Thomas) and those struggling with greed (Judas the betrayer); there are zealots who saw violence as the obvious path to peace (Simon) as well as tax collectors who saw compromise with Rome as the key path (Matthew). Imagine the arguments. Perhaps we get the clearest picture of the discipleship journey from Peter. He's the one who walks on water, first confesses Jesus' identity as the Christ and the one who is named as the 'rock' on which the church will be built. But he's also the one to whom Jesus says, 'Get behind me Satan!' He's the one who falls asleep in Jesus' hour of need and disowns him on the journey to the cross. Peter, who many scholars argue is the source of Mark's gospel (Mark being Peter's interpreter and scribe), allows these stories to be told to demonstrate what this discipleship journey is like. It is messy. There are high and lows, breakthroughs and breakdowns. The change is incremental, but as we daily deny self and follow the way of Jesus, our personal change impacts the world around us.

Becoming Like Jesus for the Sake of the World

What are the unforced rhythms of grace? In his book *The Spirit of the Disciplines*, Dallas Willard talks of the disciplines as being focussed on abstinence and engagement. The disciplines of abstinence are the ones that enable us to deny ourselves of something good for something greater. Willard suggests that these disciplines help us to counteract the 'sins of commission,' which are the sins we often gravitate towards, such as gossip, pride, greed, lust, gluttony and laziness. The disciplines of abstinence therefore include solitude, silence, fasting, simplicity, chastity, secrecy and sacrifice. We say no to food, noise, company or shopping so we can say yes to Jesus. In these practices we are using our bodies to lead our hearts, minds and spirits towards Jesus. We are redirecting our desires towards the kingdom. These disciplines often focus on emptying, but it is critical to understand that emptiness is not the end goal. The end goal is to be filled with the presence of Jesus. We let go in order to grab hold of what he has for us. We deny ourselves so that we can give ourselves wholly and completely to him and his purposes.

This emptying leads us to filling, focussing on the disciplines of engagement. These disciplines help us overcome the 'sins of omission,' the good works and activities we are called to but often ignore as our lives become busy and overcrowded. Such disciplines include study, worship, celebration, service, acts of compassion, prayer, Scripture reading, evangelism, fellowship, confession and submission. As we say no to some of the dominant practices of the surrounding culture—such as busyness, over-consumption and constantly checking our status on social media—we replace them with practices modelled in Jesus throughout the gospel accounts.

Willard describes this rhythm of abstinence and engagement as the out-breathing and in-breathing of our spiritual lives. They are disciplines of emptying and filling, of dying to self and rising with Christ, of descending and ascending. This shouldn't surprise us when we consider the journey of Jesus. If we are to follow the way of Jesus, who fulfils the whole narrative of Scripture through his life, death and resurrection, then the shape of his life must inevitably become the shape of our lives.

A Narrative Approach to Discipleship: Becoming Compassionate Followers

Let's explore the downward journey of the incarnation, which illuminates the compassion of God. One of the key texts of the Old Testament describes God's character with the following words:

> The LORD, the LORD, the compassionate and gracious God, slow to anger, abounding in love and faithfulness, maintaining love to thousands, and forgiving wickedness, rebellion and sin. (Ex. 34:6-7)

This passage comes in the context of God having recently revealed his name (Yahweh, meaning 'I AM'), and therefore his identity, to Moses. These words begin to fill in the blank of Yahweh's name: I AM _____. Interesting that the first word used is compassionate. This is a compound word, formed by bring together *com* meaning 'with' and the verb *passio* meaning 'to suffer.' To have compassion is simply to 'suffer with,' and the Exodus story makes it abundantly clear that when we suffer, God suffers too. He hears the cries of his people and is moved to action. As with all mission, it starts in the heart of God and overflows eventually into our actions through the following process:

GOD'S BEING $\Longrightarrow$ GOD'S DOING $\Longrightarrow$ OUR BEING $\Longrightarrow$ OUR DOING

God's *being* becomes visible in God's *doing* at the incarnation. In the person of Jesus, God suffers with us as he 'makes himself nothing' by taking 'the very nature of a servant.' The Creator steps into the De-creation. Why? The answer is in order to heal and re-create us. To borrow the language of Psalm 40, he 'lifts us out slimy pit' and 'out of the mud and the mire' by first jumping into the pit with us.

A friend told me the story of when she was taking her two children for a walk. Whilst getting the kids ready, she managed to get the buggy with her youngest out of the front door. A gust of wind then slammed the door shut behind her, trapping her other child inside the house. She reached for her keys to open the front door but couldn't find them. By this point, the toddler locked inside started screaming for help, wanting to go on the walk with mummy. The mum began to panic, frantically searching her pockets and bag for the keys, before realising she had left her keys on the kitchen table. She started giving instructions to her child, but the kid couldn't hear the mother through her own crying. The mum started shouting instructions over the screams of the toddler but still couldn't be heard. At this point my friend prayed and felt God clearly say, 'Stop giving instructions and comfort your child instead.' So the mother got to her knees, opened the letterbox on the front door and reached in towards her child, saying, 'Mummy's here. It's all going to be okay. Mummy's not going to leave you. Everything is okay.' The screams gradually became a whimper before the child was comforted as she held her mother's hand. The mum then explained that her keys were on the kitchen table. The child ran off to get them, placed them through the letterbox before the door was opened and a reassuring embrace began.

This is a beautiful picture of the incarnation. God doesn't yell instructions behind a locked door. He came to 'suffer with,' to enter our condition, and comfort us in our pain in order to open the door to freedom. The incarnation reminds us that the first move God makes in mission is towards the pain, the hurting, the lost and the lonely. Some people have a picture of a distant, angry deity yelling instructions through a locked door. That isn't the God of the Scriptures. Quite the opposite. When he first unpacked his name and nature, he describes himself as compassionate. He wants to hold our hand in the pain and gives us a reassuring embrace. And if this is the God we worship, the God we image to the world, then it should be one of the defining characteristics of God's people.

God's compassion is ultimately demonstrated at the incarnation, but is then constantly demonstrated through Jesus' ministry and teaching. Matthew 9 tells that 'when he saw the crowds, he had compassion on them, because they were harassed and helpless, like sheep without a shepherd' (v. 36). This compassion results in Jesus sending out the twelve to heal the sick, cast out demons and preach the kingdom. Matthew 14 states that 'when Jesus landed and saw a large crowd, he had compassion on them and healed those who were ill' (v. 14). Again and again in the gospel accounts when you read that Jesus had compassion, you can guarantee a tidal wave of kingdom activity is about to be released.

God's doing then shapes our being. We have been forever changed by the compassion God has shown towards us. In Christ we are new creations, with a new wardrobe to wear as we clothe ourselves with the character of Christ. And as Paul makes clear in Colossians 3:12, as God's chosen people, holy and dearly loved, we must clothe ourselves 'with compassion, kindness, humility, gentleness and patience.' Compassion was the first characteristic named in Exodus 34:6, and here it is the first item of the new wardrobe. If God's first move in mission is towards the pain, then the first move of his followers must also be towards the pain. We have freely received, and now we must freely give. In doing so, our being begins to shape our doing.

Incarnational mission means 'suffering with.' By definition it has to hurt. It's not clicking a button to like a cause on social media, and it's not charitable giving from the safe distance. It's wedding yourself to the wellbeing of your neighbours, your community and your city. When they hurt, we hurt. When they suffer, we suffer. It is this connection that brings comfort and motivates us to partner with God in bringing freedom to his people.

A Narrative Approach to Discipleship: Courageous Followers

The incarnation leads us to the cross. Jesus becomes obedient to death, even death on a cross. To be shaped by the story therefore means living a cross-shaped life. In response to the mercy of the cross, we have a message to proclaim and an example to follow, both of which require courage.

The word *courage* finds it root in the Latin word *cor*, meaning 'heart.' To be courageous is to live from your heart and to speak from your heart. The cross is at the very heart of the gospel message and the biblical story. It is the place from which God communicates the depths of his heart to us. To communicate the gospel to a surrounding culture resistant to the Christian faith requires a whole-hearted approach. To become like Jesus, to be shaped by the narrative, means embracing the path to courageous living.

The apostle Paul declared, 'I am not ashamed of the gospel, because it is the power of God that brings salvation to everyone who believes' (Rom. 1:16). Shame is what causes us to hide and shrink back. It is what Adam and Eve experienced when they hid from God in the garden and became aware of their nakedness. The temptation for any church seeking to relevantly engage in culture is to cover up the parts of our message and story that cause offence. Driven by the desire to protect our own reputation and to proclaim a message that people want to hear, we hide the cross. The problem is, when we extract the cross from the story, we are left with a sanctified form of humanism, and sanctified humanism doesn't have the power to save. Paul was fully aware of this. Whilst his battle wasn't against secularism, he was very much battling against strong worldviews, ideologies and philosophies that resisted and laughed at the message of a crucified messiah ruling the world. In 1 Corinthians 1:18 he therefore exclaims that 'the message of the cross is foolishness to those who are perishing, but to us who are being saved it is the power of God.' The power for salvation, transformation, restoration and renewal flows from the cross. For the sake of the world, we can't afford to hide the message of the cross. Instead we need to find spiritual practices that form us into courageous followers running with the good news of the cross.

The cross is a message to proclaim, but it is also an example to follow. Jesus said to his disciples, 'Whoever wants to be my disciple must deny themselves and take up their cross and follow me' (Matt. 16:24). This means dying to self and living for Christ and the cause of his kingdom. Church history is littered with the stories of people living this cross-shaped life and ushering in the work of the kingdom as they do so. The Moravians are a great example.[67] In 1731, Count Zinzendorf met an African slave from the Danish West Indies who described the horrific conditions of the plantation workers there. Zinzendorf began to highlight the wellbeing of these African slaves to his community in Herrnhut. In response, two of the Moravians volunteered to go to the West Indies, ready to sell themselves into slavery in order to reach the slaves. That's what you call 'suffering with'!

For the next eighteen months they gave themselves fully to the mission. But despite the sacrifice and hard work, they managed to gain only one convert in that time. Seventeen more Moravians joined them in June 1734, eight of whom died of yellow fever. Eleven more missionaries arrived the following February, four of them dying within two months. In 1735, most of the missionaries were forced to return to Herrnhut, three of whom drowned in a shipwreck on the journey back. The early church theologian Tertullian famously said that the blood of the martyrs is the seed of the church. These missionaries emptied themselves for the sake of the gospel and planted the seeds for a revival. In 1736, Zinzendorf himself went to visit the colony. Not expecting to see much fruit after all the discouragements his fellow Moravians had experienced, Zinzendorf discovered a church of eight hundred people that had heard the good news from the Moravian missionaries. This is the power of the cross and the cross-shaped life.

The phenomenal growth of the church in the first few centuries can also be explained through the compassion and courage of Jesus' followers. In his book *The Rise of Christianity*, Rodney Stark outlines that one of the contributing factors to the church's growth was the epidemics and plagues sweeping through the urban centres of the Roman Empire. The elites would flee the cities, leaving behind the poor, the sick and the vulnerable. The followers of Jesus remained present to care for the them: to feed the hungry, to nurse the sick and proclaim the gospel. This created fertile soil for the rapid growth of the church. Not only did the pagan religions and surrounding philosophies have nothing to offer in terms of an explanation or hope in such a crisis, neither did they have a practice of 'suffering with.' A God who both suffers *with* and suffers *for* his people and then takes them by the hand to lead them out of suffering and into the life of his kingdom will always be attractive to a people in pain. Large numbers became open to the person of Jesus as they saw his message of hope lived out in his followers.

Christianity spread like wildfire in the cities, and when the wealthy elite returned to the cities once the epidemics had passed, the poor were once again displaced but carrying with them the message of salvation. The wildfire of the gospel spread from the cities across the empire. This is what happens when people courageously proclaim and follow the way of the cross.

A Narrative Approach to Discipleship: Creative Followers

The final movement—an upward movement—focusses on the ascension and resurrection. Jesus is exalted to the highest place as the new world order breaks in upon us. As we follow the way of Jesus we become ministers of his new creation, living as people of the future in the midst of the present. We are citizens of God's future reality in heaven, but we are also residents on earth. Filled with resurrection hope and the Spirit of God's new creation, we begin to creatively engage with the surrounding culture and partner in God's mission to make all things new.

It is time we recapture the centrality of creativity in our mission and ministry. We are made in the image of an artist, so creativity is part of our DNA. Picasso once famously said, 'We are all born as artists. The challenge is to remain an artist.' Ken Robinson, whose TED talk has been viewed by over 50 million people and is the most watched TED talk of all time, similarly challenges our current systems of education by suggesting that we are 'educating people out of creativity.' The question for the church is whether we are discipling people out of creativity. I think we potentially are.

What would it look like to develop spiritual practices that help the followers of Jesus think more creatively and entrepreneurially? How can we equip God's people to more effectively engage in their spheres of industry? How can we prepare them to reimagine what politics, business, education and media might look like if they were pervaded by the kingdom of God? How do we encourage people to use the God-given gift of their imagination? If a large part of the creative process is ordering chaos, then perhaps we need to get better in the church at acknowledging chaos. In the story of God, the pain and brokenness all around us become raw materials in the hands of our saviour as he restores and renews. For us to become more like him, perhaps we need to become less afraid of these raw materials and more honest about the chaos that needs ordering within.

As we freely receive his restoration, we might more freely give, and therefore journey towards the kind of creativity that renews culture.

This calling is both our history and our destiny. It was the creation mandate given to Adam and Eve to establish culture and extend it throughout the earth. It is also our Re-creation mandate, to redeem culture and extend God's redemption throughout the earth. Creativity is a non-negotiable for such a task.

Discipleship and Cultural Engagement

A narrative approach to discipleship means immersing ourselves in the story to such an extent that our lives mirror both the shape of the narrative and the shape of Jesus' fulfilment of the narrative. As we follow the way of Jesus, we become compassionate, courageous and creative.

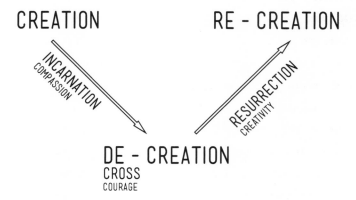

This shape is beautifully articulated in the words that Paul uses to describe the model of Jesus. He says in 2 Corinthians 8:9 'that though he was rich, yet for your sake he became poor, so that you through his poverty might become rich.' In other words, though Jesus was rich in terms of life, fully alive by the Spirit, he became poor by embracing the cross. However, this poverty led to us experiencing the richness of Christ's risen life. This is the model of Jesus. And as we embrace his example, emptying ourselves for the sake of others, our poverty brings life to all around.

This narrative shape also gives us a model for cultural engagement. The message of the incarnation is that our first move must be to 'stand in' culture. Before we are ever countercultural, we first acknowledge that we are part of the culture. In fact, we have to humbly admit that we have contributed to the culture in all sorts of ways, and are therefore part of the problem even if our deep desire is to be part of the solution. The incarnation is an affirmation of creation and our humanity, and likewise our cultural engagement is at its best when we can affirm the good that surrounds us, and that which already finds its home in God's kingdom.

The cross reminds us that having stood within the culture, we must then stand against culture, and the evil and injustice that we encounter there. Having made such a stand, we finally offer the world a new culture, the culture of heaven.

So we affirm the good, we oppose the evil, and we usher in God's kingdom. We 'stand in,' we 'stand against' and we 'offer a new' culture. This is the shape of Jesus' fulfilment of the story. This is our shape as we follow his example. And this is the shape of our cultural engagement. It starts in the heart of God and bleeds out to redeem and restore the culture around us.

Chapter 19

PERSONAL REFLECTIONS: FROM REVIVAL TO AWAKENING

The more you intentionally indwell the narrative of Scripture, the more you will care passionately about the renewal of culture. Let me now add another conviction: the more you care passionately about the renewal of culture, the more you will long for revival.

The church needs to be revived if the city is to be awakened. The people of God need to be on fire if the city is to come alive. In King's Cross, the scale of the task and the tepid state of our own spirituality have combined to ignite this longing. We have therefore started praying and fasting for such a move of God, whilst simultaneously feasting on stories of previous awakenings and revivals. What's incredibly encouraging is that as we look around, both locally, nationally and beyond, people are sensing the same stirring. Prophetic voices around the world seem to be singing from the same hymn sheet, that we are beginning to hear the rumblings of a fresh move of God. It might not yet be a heavy rain, but a cloud as small as a man's fist is perhaps present on the horizon.

This longing for revival, at least personally, has emerged from what feels like a desert experience in my life. We have been through a number of significant challenges and transitions as a church in the last few years. These have left me emotionally and spiritually drained. In this last year particularly, there have been moments when I've doubted my own leadership and questioned my own suitability to lead such a young church in the heart of such a demanding city. Thankfully, in these moments of vulnerability and insecurity, I have met God and heard his still, small voice, affirming both identity and calling. Such encounters have birthed fresh faith, not in my own leadership or gifting, but in what God could do through a broken, exhausted and surrendered life.

I began reading through some of the stories of significant moves of God over the ages. I was surprised to observe a common thread: such outpourings not only took place when both the culture and the church were in crisis, but also when the key leaders associated with such movements were experiencing their own spiritual wilderness. In fact, it was often whilst they were in the wilderness that the rains began to fall.

Martin Luther, for example, the great thinker and theologian of the Reformation era, was led to such a place of dryness where his heart and soul began to yearn for heavy rain. He referred to these spiritual crises as his 'Anfechtungen'—a German word meaning trial or tribulation—which included cold sweats, nausea, constipation, crushing headaches, ringing in his ears, together with depression and anxiety. These physical manifestations were brought on by spiritual wilderness experiences where Luther felt a deep sense of being abandoned by God's grace.

The struggles, however, drove Luther to the Scriptures, and in the Scriptures Luther found Paul's teaching on justification by faith. The crisis created longing and the longing led to an outpouring of grace. Luther was changed, and as a result a reformation swept through the church, transforming the spiritual, political, social and economic landscape of an entire continent. Reflecting on his journey, Luther wrote, 'Until a man is nothing, God can make nothing out of him.' For Luther, the wilderness was the place of preparation for the outpouring.

John Wesley had a similar experience. Before his breakthrough moment at a Moravian prayer meeting in Aldersgate, where his heart was strangely warmed, he faced his own desert experience. He had gone to be a missionary in Georgia. In fact, it was on his journey there where he first encountered the Moravians. His ship was caught in a storm and people began shrieking, thinking they were about to die. The Moravians on the ship, however, were unfazed, unafraid of death because of their deep faith in Christ. Their example caused Wesley to question his own salvation, and this led to a period of soul searching.

The two years that followed in Georgia were hard years, marked out by disputes and controversies. Wesley was forced to return to England in December 1837. Discouraged and dejected, he was encouraged by a friend to go to a prayer meeting of the Moravians. He went along, and upon hearing someone read from Luther's *Preface to the Epistle to the Romans,* he encountered the Spirit. This was the moment of his 'conversion' and, according to some, the beginning of the Evangelical Awakening in the British Isles.

God led Wesley into the wilderness, which created a deep thirst, and it was this deep thirst that led Wesley in search of water. The revival that followed transformed the culture. The church was set on fire, and it brought the city to life. Wesley and his contemporaries gave their lives to the proclamation of the gospel and the renewal of culture. Wesley rode up and down the country on horseback preaching the gospel. Thousands upon thousands came to faith. At the same time, however, he dedicated himself tirelessly to social change. He was one of the pioneers of ending slavery, writing *Thoughts Upon Slavery* thirteen years before the abolition of slavery. In fact his last letter, written from his deathbed, was to encourage a young William Wilberforce in such a pursuit.

Wesley also championed the living wage and prison reform, handing on the baton to John Howard and Elizabeth Fry. He took on the legal system, highlighting inconsistencies in the penal system that disadvantaged the poor. He took on the political system, trying to stamp out bribery and corruption in politics. He campaigned against medieval practices in medicine. He championed funeral reform. He and his brother Charles got the nation singing, writing nine thousand songs. Such was his passion for justice and social change that he asked for there to be no coach or hearse at his funeral, instead leaving instructions that six poor men, in need of employment, be given a pound each to carry his body to the grave.

The revival of the church led to an awakening in the culture. Even secular historians name the evangelical awakening as one of the key reasons why the revolutions and civil wars on the continent didn't make it to the British Isles. The culture was in crisis and the people were drowning their sorrows in gin. But a different type of revolution hit the Isles, a movement of the Spirit that began in the thirsty hearts of followers of Jesus in crisis. A revival began in the heart of Wesley. The fire spread, and led to the Great Awakening.

The charismatic renewal movement of the 1980s has a similar story. John Wimber had been through a desert experience of his own. He described a night in his Detroit hotel room when he was exhausted and depressed from continual travel. He heard God tell him, 'John, I've seen your ministry, and frankly I'm not that impressed. But now I would like to show you mine!' This encounter was the breakthrough moment that led to the founding of the Vineyard movement and the charismatic renewal movement that swept through the church in this country. For Luther, Wesley and Wimber, the streams began to flow in the desert.

Is something similar stirring at this time? There is a desperation that is birthing fresh faith. There is a hunger and thirst that is drawing people to their knees, and historically these outpourings are always preceded by fresh movements of prayer, as people gather together to pull God's promises into the present. The relatively recent revival in the Outer Hebrides in the 1950s is a great example of this. The revival began with two ladies, Peggy and Christine Smith, both in their eighties, grabbing hold of the promise from Isaiah 44:3, for God to 'pour water on the thirsty land, and streams on the dry ground.' Others began to join them in prayer for such an outpouring. I love the following account of one of their prayer meetings, highlighting this deep thirst present for God to move:

> So we're praying and the going was hard. We prayed
> till twelve or one o'clock in the morning, when I
> turned to the blacksmith.... Half an hour he prayed,
> then he paused for a second or so, and looking up

to the heavens he cried, 'God, did you know that your honor is at stake? Your honor is at stake! You promised to pour floods upon dry ground and, God, you're not doing it!' ... Then he went on to say this: 'There are five ministers in this meeting and I don't know where any one of them stands in your presence, not even Mr. Campbell. But if I know my own poor heart, I think that I can say, and I think that you know, that I'm thirsty! I'm thirsty to see the devil defeated in this parish! I'm thirsty to see the community gripped ... I'm longing for revival and, God, you're not doing it! And I'm thirsty and you've promised to pour water on me.' Then a pause, and then he cried, 'God, I now take upon myself to challenge you to fulfil your covenant engagement!'

Now it was nearing two o'clock in the morning. And what happened? The house shook. A jug on a sideboard fell onto the floor and broke.... My mind went back to the Acts, chapter four, when they prayed and the place was shaken. When John Smith finished praying at twenty minutes past two, I pronounced the benediction and left the house. What did I see? The whole community alive! Men carrying chairs, women carrying stools and asking, 'Is there room for us in the churches?' And the Arnol Revival broke out. And oh, what a sweeping revival! I believe there wasn't a single house in the village that wasn't shaken by God.[68]

When you read into revival history, you will always find thirsty hearts that have gone in desperate search for water. People start praying with a greater sense of urgency. People start longing for a deeper sense of holiness, of being right with God. They begin to yearn for a move of the Spirit to bring about a tidal wave of salvation, just like the first Pentecost, and just like previous revivals.

At a time of cultural crisis, God says to Habakkuk, 'Look at the nations and watch—and be utterly amazed. For I am going to do something in your days that you would not believe, even if you were told' (Hab. 1:5). Habakkuk knew that the Babylonian armies were advancing with a mission to overcome and destroy Jerusalem. He was therefore already looking at the nations and watching nervously, but God invites Habakkuk to look through a different lens to see things from God's perspective. Judgement may be approaching, but beyond there is restoration. Habakkuk responds by declaring: 'LORD, I have heard of your fame; I stand in awe of your deeds, LORD. Repeat them in our day, in our time make them known; in wrath remember mercy' (Hab. 3:2).

This prayer of Habakkuk in a time of cultural crisis has become the cry of my heart: 'Lord, do it again. What happened in the Acts of the Apostles, do it again. What happened through the last Great Awakening, do it again. What happened in the Outer Hebrides, do it again.'

This has been the journey: a passion for Scripture has fuelled in us as a church a passion for cultural renewal, and this longing for renewal has birthed a deep desire for a fresh move of God. This is what we are praying for. Mark Batterson says that our prayers are essentially prophecies: 'They are the best predictors of your spiritual future. Who you become is determined by how you pray. Ultimately, the transcript of your prayers becomes the script of your life.'[69]

The culture is in crisis and the church is on its knees. This is a threshold moment, and it is time for the church to press in and press on. It's time to tune in to the prophetic voices inviting us to ready ourselves for a fresh move of God. Emma Heddle, who works closely with Bee and I at KXC, is one such prophetic voice and wrote the following in April 2018:

> Threshold moments are equally beautiful and ter-
> rifying. They have the capacity to make or break
> the vision. As you stand on the cusp of everything
> you've ever dared hope for, you survey the land that
> now lies before you, your eyes tracing the intricate
> shapes that settle on the horizon, too good to imag-
> ine. This is what has been stirring for so long. This
> has been the cry of your heart for years, hidden,
> deep down, but now here it is, that first glimpse
> of dream turned reality, within reach, right before
> your very eyes. So nearly there. And as you stand
> there, at the threshold of everything you've ever
> dared dream about, with that cocktail of excite-
> ment and fear rising in equal measure, that other
> voice kicks in. The one that gently tells you to take
> a step back from the threshold. It whispers to you
> that passing through that door will have its costs.
> It's too good to be true. Or even worse, what lies in
> front of you is all a mirage and you'd be foolish to

walk through. It will disappear as soon as you enter. It's better to survey the land from the doorway, to distance yourself from it, just in case. To stand at the threshold just watching. It's better to quietly let the dream die now, before sacrifices are made, bridges are burned, and there's no safe way back.

Threshold moments have power. Many see them as the end of a long journey, they've finally glimpsed what their hearts have longed for, but they stop, exhausted and find themselves settling in the doorway to all they've hoped for, never actually crossing through and taking hold of it. Tired and exhausted they find contentment in the reasoning that they've made it this far, that they can see it from a distance. But the truth is that these threshold moments are just the start of the adventure, they're only just the beginning.

Step in. Take courage. And move forward. You have been called. For such a time as this.[70]

The Lord has done it before, and he can do it again. Perhaps he might be saying to us what he said hundreds of years ago to Habakkuk: 'Look at the nations and watch—and be utterly amazed. For I am going to do something in your days that you would not believe, even if you were told.'

PART VI

AN END TO LIVE FOR

Chapter 20

RETHINKING HELL: THROWING THE SERPENT OUT OF THE GARDEN CITY

Not many people know this, but I have an extremely sensitive gag reflex. I discovered this during a week of mission on a local estate near King's Cross. We were working with local churches and some local organisations to proclaim and demonstrate God's love through social action projects, evangelistic events and community fun days. One of the organisations we partnered with were doing the most phenomenal work amongst young people in some of the most deprived parts of London. Their vision was to take the love of Jesus into every school, onto every estate and into every neighbourhood, and as they did this, to 'love the hell out of the community,' they found themselves in.

What does this practically look like? Well, the first job each morning of the mission was to clear the park area in the middle of the estate so we could host a barbecue and some five-a-side football games. And by clear, I mean put on rubber gloves and pick up every bit of dog poo on the park. So I put on my gloves, hoping people would see this public demonstration of servant leadership, and bent down to pick up the first poo. I immediately wretched. I'm not sure whether it was the smell or the texture, but the combination of the two was overwhelming. I put the poo in a bag and moved on.

The next poo had the same effect. I wretched again. This time I needed a few moments to recover, to practice some mindfulness and prepare myself for poo number three. Multiple questions were raging within: 'What do they feed the dogs around here? Did that last dog survive, for surely that was the poo of a dying dog? How many dogs live on this estate, because this park has quite literally become a dumping ground?'

I took a deep breath and bent down once more, desperately trying not to wretch. I failed miserably. The cumulative effect of the three wretches was taking its toll. I was right on the edge of vomiting. I was doing the best I could to demonstrate servant leadership and trying to love the hell out of this park. Each poo provided a very real manifestation of hell. But it all became too much. A lovely lady in our community approached me, and looked at me with compassion, before asking me to find a different job as I was distracting everyone with my wretching. I took off the gloves and watched the army of volunteers press on by getting their hands dirty and transforming the park into a garden of delight. Within hours there was a party atmosphere with barbecues, bouncy castles and football, all accompanied with the sound of laughter and delight as the community came together. It felt like a tiny foretaste of heaven.

Jesus said that he would build his church and that the gates of hell would not prevail against it. The implication is that hell is more than just a future reality; it's also a present one. Jesus' vision was and is to use his church, his hands and feet, to push back the darkness and flush from his creation all forces that would oppose his kingdom purposes. What we were doing for the park in the middle of the estate, God wants to do for the world he so loves. Why? Because he loves the hell out of his creation.

Heaven and Hell

The Bible ends with the vision of God returning to make his dwelling place with humanity on earth again. All things are reconciled to God, all things restored to how they were meant to be. No death, no grief, no crying and no pain. We've already stated that this ending is different from the teaching many of us grew up with, where upon death our souls ascend to a disembodied bliss to spend eternity with God in the clouds. Within that framework, those who choose life without God spend eternity separated from him in hell. Most evangelism therefore frames this as a choice we make now about a future and eternal destination.

The problem with that framework is that it doesn't do justice to the biblical narrative. It's not that there are no truths contained within this framework; there are, and we will explore them within this chapter. It's that this framework is heavily dualistic, separating the material and immaterial, the physical and the metaphysical, and the present and the future. Throughout the gospels, heaven is more than just a future reality. It's the sphere and realm in which God's will is done, and whilst there absolutely is a future dimension to it, there is also a present one.

In his book *The Skeletons in God's Closet*, Joshua Ryan Butler highlights that if you were to do a biblical word search for 'heaven hell' to find the number of verses and passages where these two 'future destinations' appear side by side, you may be shocked to find the answer is zero. Heaven and hell never appear together as counterparts in the same verse. More than that, in the seven gospel sermons in the book of Acts, hell is never mentioned.

Any retelling of the gospel that reduces Jesus' message to a choice between a ticket to heaven or a ticket to hell is at best simplistic and at worst totally unbiblical. It may be a well-known strategy for 'winning souls' and getting people to make 'decisions for Christ,' but there is a big difference between what Scot McKnight calls the 'decided' and the 'discipled.' If you want people to make decisions, then it seems sensible to raise the stakes by talking about heaven and hell, using fear to motivate people to make a decision against 'eternal torment.' If, however, you want to invite people into relationship with Jesus, to follow his way, to become his disciple, for now and all eternity, then the simplistic 'heaven or hell' strategy must be replaced by the full gospel message and the full narrative of Scripture.

I'm guessing at this point, some are either nervously clenching their buttocks or alternatively getting very excited, thinking that I'm about to come out as a universalist. For the excited, prepare yourself for significant disappointment. For the nervous, just because I am deconstructing the distorted and simplistic understanding of hell and judgement doesn't mean I'm about to throw out the baby with the bathwater.

So back to the biblical word search: 'heaven hell' yielded zero results. But 'heaven earth' comes up with almost two hundred results. The primary counterpart for heaven is not hell but earth. In the story of creation, God created 'the heavens and the earth.' In the story of Re-creation, God reconciles 'the heavens and the earth.' The story of De-creation is the story of sin separating earth and heaven, but the ministry of Jesus centres on reuniting that which has been divided. In Colossians 1:19-20, Paul says of Jesus that 'God was pleased to have all his fulness dwell in him, and through him to reconcile to himself all things, whether things on earth or things in heaven, by making peace through his blood, shed on the cross.' Similarly, in Ephesians 1:7-10 Paul says,

> In him we have redemption through his blood, the
> forgiveness of sins, in accordance with the riches of
> God's grace that he lavished on us. With all wisdom
> and understanding, he made known to us the mys-
> tery of his will according to his good pleasure, which
> he purposed in Christ, to be put into effect when

the times reach their fulfilment—to bring unity to
all things in heaven and on earth under Christ.

The biblical story is about heaven and earth. The ministry of
Jesus is about heaven and earth. So how does hell fit in?

De-creation, Hell and the Destructive Power of Sin

De-creation is the result of sin tearing apart God's created order.
Violence enters the story, suffering enters the story and death enters
the story, creating hell on earth. These evil powers stand in opposition to God's kingdom and God's created order. The hope for the
arrival of the kingdom therefore must involve the casting out of hell,
and with it an end to the violence, suffering and death all around us.

Joshua Ryan Butler offers the following diagram to summarise
this:

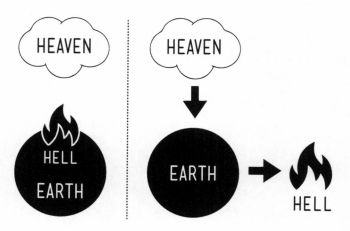

He explains:

> In the gospel story, heaven and earth are currently torn
> by sin. Our world is being ravaged by the destructive
> power of hell. Sin has unleashed it into God's good
> world, and God is on a mission to get it out, to rec-
> oncile heaven and earth from hell's evil influence to
> himself through the reconciling life of Christ. The
> time is coming when God's heavenly kingdom will
> come down to reign on earth forever, when Jesus will
> cast out the corrosive powers of sin, death, and hell
> that have tormented his world for so long.[71]

Hell exists where the will of the evil one is done. Back in Eden,
listening to the serpent and surrendering to its will was the deadly decision that unleashed the forces of hell into the world. Jesus, however,
began his ministry by announcing the arrival of his kingdom and then
enacted it by casting out demons and pushing back the darkness of
demonic oppression. He then called his disciples, giving them authority to do the same. Jesus and his followers began to drive back the
forces of hell, in anticipation of the day when heaven and earth fully
become one and hell itself will be flushed from God's new creation.

Jesus' Teaching on Hell

Jesus' clearest teaching on hell appears in the Sermon on the Mount
as he provides his ethical framework for life in the kingdom of God.
He says:

> You have heard that it was said to the people long ago, 'You shall not murder, and anyone who murders will be subject to judgement.' But I tell you that anyone who is angry with a brother or sister will be subject to judgement. Again, anyone who says to a brother or sister, 'Raca,' is answerable to the court. And anyone who says, 'You fool!' will be in danger of the fire of hell. (Matt. 5:21-22)

Prior to these statements, Jesus declares that he has come to fulfil the law, not to abolish it. And then throughout the sermon, he uses the formula, 'You have heard that it was said … But I tell you …' Jesus therefore points back to the law given from God himself as well as pointing forward to the ethics of the new creation. In his commentary on the Sermon of the Mount, Scot McKnight refers to this as the 'ethics from above' and the 'ethics from beyond.' The Torah (ethics from above) was given as a signpost to life in God's kingdom (ethics from beyond).

The law could therefore set parameters around the external behaviour of God's people, but it was powerless to transform hearts and minds. What people needed was the law to be 'written on their hearts.' This inward change would inevitably lead to outward obedience to the law. Jeremiah 31:33 prophesied such a time, and Jesus' teaching suggests that this time had arrived.

Jesus then provides some specifics. The Torah made it clear that murder would lead to judgement and that judgement would result in death. This deals with the external behaviour. Jesus then intensifies things to go after the internal transformation of the heart. Murder is the external action, but it is motivated by anger. To be specific here, the Greek word *orgizomenos* is used, which is a particular type of anger, referring not to the type of anger that flares up quickly and dies down quickly; this kind of anger brews over time. It's also a present participle and is therefore best translated 'whoever is choosing to remain angry' or 'whoever is nursing a grudge.' This type of anger, if unprocessed, can eventually lead to murder. Murder in turn leads to judgement. And judgement leads to hell.

ANGER ⟶ MURDER ⟶ JUDGEMENT ⟶ HELL

anyone who is angry with a brother or sister... will be in danger of the fire of hell.

This is cause and effect. What starts with the choice to remain angry ends in hell. Notice, the 'fire of hell' in the context of Matthew 5 is primarily a present rather than future danger. Jesus is warning of something totally destructive that can be unleashed in the present if not immediately dealt with.

Jesus then turns his attention to lust. He says:

> You have heard that it was said, 'You shall not commit adultery.' But I tell you that anyone who looks at a woman lustfully has already committed adultery with her in his heart. If your right eye causes you to stumble, gouge it out and throw it away. It is better for you to lose one part of your body than for your whole body to be thrown into hell. And if your right hand causes you to stumble, cut it off

and throw it away. It is better for you to lose one part of your body than for your whole body to go into hell. (Matt. 5:27-30)

The Torah stated that adultery would lead to judgement and that judgement would result in death. But like before, Jesus raised the stakes by highlighting the outward action of adultery begins with lust hidden in the human heart. That lust sets in motion a set of dominoes that can ultimately lead to hell.

LUST ⟶ ADULTERY ⟶ JUDGEMENT ⟶ HELL

Remember, the primary focus isn't hell as a future reality, but a present one of pain and destruction. Anyone who has experienced the betrayal of adultery knows firsthand the hell that Jesus is referring to. All of this has future ramifications, which we will get to in due course, but the focus here is a destructive force opposing God's kingdom and undoing God's created order in the present.

Hell: The Destructive Fire

A world without death, grief, crying and pain is a world without murder and adultery. The Ten Commandments, God's guidelines for human flourishing, make this abundantly clear. But Jesus outlines the pathway towards this future reality: it's not just about banishing murder and adultery; it's about driving out anger and lust. They create a fire that destroys God's good creation, and try as we may to put some boundaries around these fires to limit their destruction, the fire rages on.

Fire is one of the defining metaphors used in the biblical narrative to address the devastating effects of idolatry and sin. Proverbs 16:27 states that 'a scoundrel plots evil, and on their lips it is like a scorching fire.' James 3:5-6 similarly highlights the destructive power of our sinful words: 'The tongue is a small part of the body, but it makes great boasts. Consider what a great forest is set on fire by a small spark. The tongue also is a fire, a world of evil among the parts of the body. It corrupts the whole body, sets the whole course of one's life on fire, and is itself set on fire by hell.'

What starts as a spark of anger or lust can eventually, when left unchecked, destroy the entire forest. As Joshua Ryan Butler states:

> Hell gains entrance into God's good world through us. We are the agents of destruction, the architects of demolition. God is not the architect of hell, the creator of its soul-destroying power; we are. We unleash its wildfire flame into God's good world.[72]

We, as followers of Jesus, have a social responsibility to deal with the wildfires of injustice we see all around us, but we first have to recognise our personal responsibility to deal with the sparks within. When our focus predominantly remains on the problem 'out there,' we fail to recognise that the source of the fire is the sparks of our own hatred, lust and idolatry.

This is why the central message of Jesus was repent and believe, for the kingdom of God is at hand. The Sermon on the Mount was Jesus' way of declaring that God's future order was breaking in. And in this future order, not only do adultery and murder have no place, neither do lust or anger. The spark needs to be snuffed out. This is also why the cross is the climactic moment in the story of Jesus. For the wildfire to be overcome, the sin that leads to the wildfire needs to be addressed and banished: separated from us as far as the east is from the west.

At the cross we encounter grace and freedom, and this grace leads us on a journey to becoming more like Jesus and following after his way. The pursuit of holiness (dealing with the internal sparks) and justice (dealing with the external wildfires) is our response to his grace. Grace is the only fuel that can sustain these pursuits.

Hell: The Place Where We Cheat on God

The word for hell used by Jesus in the Sermon on the Mount, and the word most used throughout the New Testament, is *gehenna*. This word referred to a place as well as an idea. To this day, you can visit the valley that bears the name Ge Hinnom.

This valley had a dark history that Jesus was bringing to mind in his teaching. The valley was associated with idolatry, evil and injustice. In the book of 2 Chronicles, we find this description of the hellish reign of King Ahaz:

> He burned sacrifices in the Valley of Ben Hinnom
> and sacrificed his children in the fire, engaging
> in the detestable practices of the nations that the
> LORD had driven out before the Israelites. (28:3)

We've already highlighted that one aspect of the creation, De-creation, Re-creation journey is the story of God and Israel's covenant relationship (wedding, divorce, wedding). God and Israel were wed at the covenant of Mt Sinai, but sin led to separation. God eventually spoke through the Prophets of a time when he would return as a husband to take back his bride. But prior to that hell, the Valley of Ben Hinnom was the place where Israel went to cheat on God with other lovers. The place of idolatry then becomes the place of injustice, as the people offer up their children as a human sacrifice to these bloodthirsty gods. In such a context, idols more than just break the hearts of their worshippers; they also devour their children. Idolatry always leads to death. It always leads to hell.

When Jesus talks about *gehenna* with imagery of fire and the language of 'your whole body going to hell,' the mental pictures of human sacrifice in the Valley of Ben Hinnom would have flooded the mind, serving as a warning. We are all free to worship whatever we want, but when we worship the wrong things, we start fires that begin to destroy us. Jesus says repent. Turn around. Run from the fire.

Hell: The Garbage Dump Outside the City

In Jesus' day, this well-known valley with a dark history had become the garbage dump on the southwest corner of the city of Jerusalem, just outside the city walls. Without the sophisticated systems of waste disposal that we know today, people would take their garbage to *gehenna*, where it would be consumed in a fire that never stopped. All of the rubbish that didn't belong in the city burned outside of the city.

Jesus' teaching was therefore loaded with meaning. Murder, adultery, anger and lust don't belong in God's city. Jerusalem was created to be a place of *shalom* (the name literally means 'city of shalom'), and Jesus was on a mission to overcome all the forces that violated that shalom. Jesus overcame such forces at the cross, making a public spectacle of them. He then rose as the firstborn of the new creation, ascending to the Father whilst promising to return to finish what he started. In other words, there would be a day when all such forces would be driven out of the New Jerusalem to be consumed in *gehenna*.

These forces that violate shalom desperately want to be inside the city. Like those who visited the Valley of Ben Hinnom to cheat on God and worship the idols, they still wanted to come back to their husband's home at night. Those who visited the valley to sacrifice their children in the fire still wanted to live in and enjoy the city of shalom. The problem is that the worshippers in the valley smuggled the idols back into the city, and before long the city of shalom had become a city of idolatry and injustice like the valley itself. This is why Jesus wept over Jerusalem.

The future promise is therefore of a day when the flames of desire of the valley are not allowed in the city. The city will be a place of shalom, and anything that violates this shalom will have no access. It will be left on the garbage dump of *gehenna*, burning outside of the city.

Future Judgement and the Wrath of God

From the very beginning of this book, I have argued that for De-creation to be reversed there needs to be both judgement and restoration. The forces that violate shalom need to be destroyed, and right order needs to be established. Some people seem to want the latter without the former, nervous of a God that gets angry and brings judgement. Tom Wright highlights that just as some people rejected the childish images of God as a bearded old gentleman sitting on a cloud, presuming they must now be an atheist, others rejected the image of hell as an underground torture chamber with fire and worms, presuming they must now be a universalist. But just as it is both possible and desirable to reject the caricature of a passive bearded deity in the sky for the image of God revealed in the person of Jesus, so too is it both possible and desirable to reject the caricature of hell in order to embrace God's vision for flushing out evil so that shalom can be established.

The imagery of fire and worms points to a deeper reality. To focus on the imagery and ignore the reality is a huge mistake. The fire and the worm suggest something being consumed in an act of judgement. But this judgement flows from God's heart of love. Judgement is good news if you care about justice. It's good news for those who want an end to poverty, genocide and human trafficking. Those who want God's shalom, but don't want judgement, fail to realise that God's judgement is the only path to his shalom. Evil must be dealt with before there can be reconciliation.

Hell is therefore primarily about protecting shalom. A distorted vision of hell emphasises torment and torture, but not only does this misunderstand the character and nature of God, it also misunderstands the teaching of the Scripture. Hell is not primarily a place of torture, but a place outside of God's city containing evil so that it can no longer violate God's created order.

Zechariah 2:4-5 states: "'Jerusalem will be a city without walls because of the great number of people and animals in it. And I myself will be a wall of fire around it," declares the LORD, "and I will be its glory within."' This echoes the words of Revelation 21 that 'on no day will its gates ever be shut, for there will be no night there,' and 'nothing impure will ever enter it, nor will anyone who does what is shameful or deceitful' (vv. 25, 27). In other words, the invitation is to all. God has torn down the walls to let the people in. But at the same time, the fire of his presence protects the city from the evil outside. The abusers and bullies, those who exploit and enslave, are left outside. This is more about protecting shalom than it is about torturing sinners. Joshua Ryan Taylor concludes:

> God's glorious presence is a boundary that safe-guards the city, preventing the destructive power of sin from invading his kingdom. Inside are the fields, mountains, and rivers of the new world; outside is the wildfire that tore apart the old. Inside is intimacy with God given graciously; outside is the self-inflicted darkness of his absence.[73]

Hell reminds us that a day is coming when the perfect love of God will cast out all fear and all the forces that lead to fear. Evil will be judged and cast out of the city. What will be left is love and shalom, where humanity can flourish and live the lives they were made for. This is incredibly good news. Hell is incredibly good news.

Rejecting Eternity with God

So the invite goes out to all. The gates are open and the city has no walls. But any force that stands in opposition to God's created order cannot pass through the fire of his presence. Those who want to respond to the invite and access the city have to turn from worshipping the idols that belong in the valley. Jesus' death has done all that is necessary for our sins and idolatry to be forgiven and separated from us as far as the east is from the west. But to receive that grace, to RSVP to the invite, there has to be a turning towards Jesus in faith. This is why Jesus' primary message was, 'Repent, for the kingdom is at hand.'

God doesn't impose his grace upon his children. God always invites. He initiates, and then waits, allowing us with the free will he gave us, to respond or reject the invite. This is why universalism doesn't work. For hell to be eventually unpopulated, free will must be taken away, and God must impose his reign upon his creatures. Neither of these happen throughout the narrative of Scripture.

So all are invited, but not all respond. For those who don't want to turn from living life centred around themselves, they miss out on the embrace of the Father, and face exclusion from the city. Note here, however, God is the rejected one. He is the one inviting, with arms wide open. He's the wounded lover. All of this is seen at the cross. The rejected and wounded Saviour with arms outstretched inviting sinners into paradise communicates something of the very heart of God and the very essence of the biblical narrative. The point is, hell is primarily the choice of the individual rather than the choice of God.

In his book *The Great Divorce*, CS Lewis states that there are two kinds of people in the end: those who say to God, 'Thy will be done,' and those to whom God says in the end, 'Thy will be done.' In other words, God honours the free will he gifted his children in Eden. With that free will comes the capacity to reciprocate God's love and enjoy relationship with him. But it also comes with the capacity to turn inwards. Like Adam and Eve in the garden, who chose the pursuit of being king and queen in their own kingdom above being servants in God's abundant kingdom, so too some people would rather reign in hell than serve in heaven.

Rejecting eternity with God and saying yes to our sinful desires eventually means being devoured by those desires. Sin wants to feed on God's good creation, but like a parasite feeding on a host organism, once the host organism ceases to exist, it represents the end for the parasite. This is why sin must be separated from God's good creation. Without an ability to feed off the shalom of God's new creation, separation represents death. To rebel against the life found in God must inevitably lead to death.

The Second Death: Annihilationism and the End of Evil

In his book *The Problem of Pain*, CS Lewis writes, 'Hell was not made for men. It is in no sense parallel to heaven; it is "the darkness outside," the outer rim where being fades away into nonentity.'[74]

Though the historic and traditional reading views hell as a place of eternal conscious torment for those that reject God, there are strong biblical grounds for what CS Lewis is describing and what is commonly called the 'annihilationist' position, namely that those who reject God's gift of eternal life eventually cease to exist. Before we examine some tricky passages with some pretty intense language, let's remember that hell is primarily the choice of the individual who rejects the grace of God. Within this annihilationist framework, God is not the distant angry deity wanting to torture his children but the gracious Father and the wounded Saviour inviting his children home. As such, he risks the pain of rejection.

What is clear from Scripture is that on the day Christ returns, all will be raised to life. In Acts 24, Paul says, 'There shall certainly be a resurrection of both the righteous and the wicked' (v. 15 NASB). Jesus warns in John 5, 'For an hour is coming, in which all who are in the tombs shall hear His voice, and shall come forth; those who did the good deeds to a resurrection of life, those who committed the evil deeds to a resurrection of judgement' (vv. 28-29 NASB). So all will be raised. All will stand before Jesus, the risen King. Those who respond to his invitation receive the promise of eternal life, but what happens to those who reject it? Does the rejection of eternal life mean eternal conscious torment or simply a second death?

Firstly, Paul highlights that immortality is not an innate human characteristic, but something only God possesses as of right and gives as a gift to those who are 'in Christ.'[75] Eternal conscious torment therefore only makes sense if you ignore such passages and assume the soul is immortal, which is what Augustine did in carrying on some of the ideas of his Platonic past.[76] Alternatively, you have to believe that God gifts immortality to the wicked. This, however, is never clearly stated in Scripture. In fact, in Genesis 2, living forever was conditioned upon eating from the tree of life. This tree appears again in Revelation 22 in the New Jerusalem, but those outside the city would not be able to access this tree. This seems to imply extinction rather than everlasting torment.

Secondly, the Old Testament points towards an ultimate judgement that involves death, not torment. The Old Testament says nothing about hell (the word is never used).[77] It does, however, say a lot about the fate of those who set themselves against God. Edward William Fudge, in his brilliant book *Hell: A Final Word*, highlights principles from the Psalms, prototypes from the Law (Torah) and prophecies from the prophetic writings to illustrate this.

Let's start with the psalms that use more than fifty verbs to assure us of the certainty of God's justice. For example, the wicked will 'wither,' 'perish,' 'vanish,' 'be destroyed,' and 'be no more.' The implication is death, not torment. Over seventy similes are used to describe the fate of the wicked: they will be 'chaff blown away,' 'grass cut down,' 'wax that melts,' 'a clay pot broken' and 'smoke that vanishes.' These descriptions point not to torment but extinction.

The prototypes for judgement from the Old Testament also imply destruction, not everlasting torment. The first prototype is the flood, in which Noah and his offspring, and all the animals in the ark, are rescued for the sake of Re-creation. But those outside of the ark are destroyed. As 2 Peter 3:5-7 states:

> But they deliberately forget that long ago by God's word the heavens came into being and the earth was formed out of water and by water. By these waters also the world of that time was deluged and destroyed. By the same word the present heavens and earth are reserved for fire, being kept for the day of judgement and destruction of the ungodly.

The logic seems to be that God previously judged evil by water, flushing it from the earth for the sake of new creation. In the future, evil will be consumed by fire for the same purpose. In both cases, destruction, not eternal torment, is the focus. The second prototype is the destruction of Sodom and Gomorrah. As 2 Peter 2:6 highlights: 'He condemned the cities of Sodom and Gomorrah by burning them to ashes, and made them an example of what is going to happen to the ungodly.' Jude 7 also highlights the fate of Sodom and Gomorrah by stating that 'they serve as an example of those who suffer the punishment of eternal fire.' It would be easy to assume the 'eternal fire' here is a fire that burns forever and ever, tormenting the wicked. But Sodom's fire is not still burning. The fire went out. It is therefore an 'eternal fire' not because it *burns* forever but because it *destroys* forever. Eternal conscious torment doesn't seem to fit the Old Testament prototypes used by Peter and Jude.

The prophetic literature of the Old Testament affirms the principles and the prototypes. Malachi 4:1-3 states:

> 'Surely the day is coming; it will burn like a furnace. All the arrogant and every evildoer will be stubble, and that day that is coming will set them on fire,' says the LORD Almighty. 'Not a root or a branch will be left to them.... They will be ashes under the soles of your feet on the day when I act,' says the LORD Almighty.

The prophecy is of destruction, not torment. Isaiah 66, prophetically pointing towards the new creation and the accompanying judgement of the wicked, echoes this:

> 'As the new heavens and the new earth that I make will endure before me,' declares the LORD, 'so will

> your name and descendants endure. From one
> New Moon to another and from one Sabbath to
> another, all mankind will come and bow down
> before me,' says the LORD. 'And they will go out
> and look on the dead bodies of those who rebelled
> against me; the worms that eat them will not die,
> the fire that burns them will not be quenched, and
> they will be loathsome to all mankind.' (vv. 22-24)

Again, it would be easy to focus on the worm that will not die and the fire that will not be quenched, but the fate of the wicked is very clearly death. The worm and the fire are images of destruction, not to be taken literally. Though these images are used by Jesus, it is important to highlight that they are used to make the same point Isaiah was making: evil will be destroyed.

In fact, Jesus makes it incredibly clear in Matthew 10:28: 'Do not be afraid of those who kill the body but cannot kill the soul. Rather, be afraid of the One who can destroy both soul and body in hell.' It's hard to interpret any other meaning than destruction from these verses. John 3:16 uses similar language to make the same point. Jesus says that those who believe in him will not perish but have eternal life. Note, he doesn't say that those who believe in him will not suffer eternal conscious torment, but have eternal life. To read the latter into John 3:16 requires some serious hermeneutical gymnastics.

But how do we deal with Matthew 25:46, which states that some 'will go away to eternal punishment, but the righteous to eternal life'? It seems to clearly point to eternal conscious torment. But does it? As we've noted, Jude 7 talks about the 'eternal fire' that destroyed Sodom and Gomorrah. The fire itself had an end, but its effects were irreversible. In other words, it's an eternal fire not because it burns forever, but because it destroys forever. Could that not be the same here? The eternal punishment is therefore permanent rather than unending.

Edward William Fudge convincingly argues that the adjective *eternal* is used here in Matthew 25:46 to emphasise that this specific life and punishment belong to the age to come and not to the present age. The New Testament speaks of eternal salvation (Heb. 5:9), eternal redemption (Heb. 9:12), eternal judgement (Heb. 6:2), eternal punishment (Matt. 25:46) and eternal destruction (2 Thess. 1:9). In each case the 'eternal' points not to an unending process, but to a process with an end result in the age to come. Eternal punishment and eternal destruction are therefore a process with an end result that lasts forever. They do not describe an unending torment.

This is supported by how the New Testament constantly describes the fate of the wicked, which aligns with the fate of the wicked throughout the Old Testament. Though the word for hell, *gehenna*, appears only twelve times in the New Testament, numerous references to judgement are present. The vast majority of the texts highlighting the fate of the wicked suggest finality.[78]

The overwhelming evidence points to death being the end of the story for those who reject God. This is spelt out in Revelation 20, the final scene before the marriage of heaven and earth.

The Death of Death and the Lake of Fire

It is not a coincidence that in the chapter before Revelation 21 and
John's vision of the new heavens and earth, we have the vision of 'the
death of death.' In Revelation 20 we have the famous imagery of the
lake of fire. Those thrown into the fire to be tormented day and night
forever include: Satan; his chief officer 'the beast' (a symbol of the
oppressive human empires that have claimed authority higher than
God's); and the 'false prophet.' As Fudge explains:

> This is the only text in the whole Bible that speaks
> of anything being tormented forever. The statement
> applies to the devil, Beast, and False Prophet, nei-
> ther of which is a human being. Scripture nowhere
> says that any human being will be tormented for-
> ever. Jesus does say the wicked will suffer "eternal
> punishment" (Matt. 25:46), which Paul explains to
> be 'eternal destruction.' (2 Thess. 1:9)[79]

Following the scene of Satan being thrown into the fire comes
the destruction of both death and hades. Note here that 'hades,' the
place called 'sheol' in the Old Testament, is simply the unseen realm
of the dead, often translated 'the grave.' Jesus spoke of this place on
numerous occasions, and a major mistake has been to equate hades
(or sheol) with hell. For example, in Jesus' parable of Lazarus and
the Rich Man, the rich man died and went to hades, where he was
tormented by fire. You might notice that Jesus never mentions hell in
the story. Moreover, given that this parable uses imagery not meant

to be taken literally, and given the immediate narrative context, this parable is far more about stewardship and obedience to God's commands than it is about final punishment. The story takes place in the here and now, before the resurrection of Jesus, not in some future setting of judgement. The King James Version gets it wrong in stating:

> And *in hell (hades)* he lift up his eyes, being in torments, and seeth Abraham afar off, and Lazarus in his bosom. And he cried and said, Father Abraham, have mercy on me, and send Lazarus, that he may dip the tip of his finger in water, and cool my tongue; for I am tormented in this flame. (Luke 16:23-24)

It's not hard to see how this mistranslation poured fuel on the fire (pun intended) for those holding the position of eternal conscious torment. But it is nothing short of a complete misunderstanding of what Jesus was saying, and thankfully the New King James Version rectified the error. Hades is not hell; it is an intermediate state for both the wicked and the righteous between death and resurrection.

So back to Revelation 20. Before death and hades are destroyed, the Book of Life is opened up. Hades gives up its dead, then verse 15 states that 'anyone whose name was not found written in the book of life was thrown into the lake of fire,' which is described as the 'second death.' Note here that the fire does not point to eternal conscious torment but to extinction. This has been the choice all along. The choice was present in the Torah when God said, 'See I have set before you life and death.' He did not say, 'life and eternal conscious torment.'

The choice is present in Jesus, who states that those who believe in him shall not perish but have eternal life. This is the choice offered in the preaching of Paul, who states that 'the wages of sin is death, but the gift of God is eternal life in Christ Jesus our Lord' (Rom. 6:23). The choice has always been a matter of life and death. People will be raised to eternal life or raised for a second death. After this there will be no more death, grief, crying or pain. No more gnashing of teeth. No more injustice. No more darkness. Evil will have been flushed outside of the city and consumed in the flames of the Valley of Gehenna. Life's ultimate obstacle, death, will have been thrown into the fire (Rev. 20:14). All that will be left is God's new creation, which sets the scene for Revelation 21, and the marriage between heaven and earth.

Chapter 21

HOME SWEET HOME: THE MARRIAGE OF HEAVEN AND EARTH

As I write this, I am currently planning my three-month sabbatical after a decade of ministry at KXC. To say I'm excited is an understatement. As part of the sabbatical, we as a family are planning a few different trips, adventures and holidays. The time and energy I have devoted to research is potentially concerning, revealing perhaps both my need of a sabbatical as well as my raw excitement about three months of rest and replenishment. We've booked the flights and I know what restaurants I want to eat at, what beaches to visit, what the temperature is likely to be (30°C, if you're asking!) and what I want to read by the pool. I can close my eyes and almost taste the food and feel the sea breeze on my face. In fact, knowing what's to come has provided the energy to finish this decade of ministry well rather than just hobble towards the finish line before collapsing.

It's perhaps disconcerting that I've spent more time in my life contemplating and researching holidays than I have researching heaven. I've spent hours and hours preparing for a three-month rest, fuelling the imagination with Google images of restaurants and beaches. But when it comes to my eternal rest, I have a starved imagination.

For many of us, our picture of heaven has tragically become one of disembodied souls floating in the clouds caught up in an eternal church service, singing my brother's song 'Here I Am to Worship' on endless repeat. That was my upbringing, and I'm really hoping for something more in heaven. Even in the best of Sunday services, I'm normally struggling after ninety minutes. All of eternity would be a stretch. Let's face it: this is a vision that most people don't really want to acquaint themselves with. But it is a result of settling for a less-than-biblical imagination regarding the future.

JC Ryle captures all of this well:

> The man who is about to sail for Australia or New Zealand as a settler is naturally anxious to know something about his future home, its climate, its employments, its inhabitants, its ways, and its customs. All these are subjects of deep interest to him. In the same way, you are leaving the land of your nativity—and you are going to spend the rest of your life in a new world. It would be strange indeed if you did not desire information about your new abode. Now surely, if we hope to dwell forever in that 'better country, even a heavenly one'—then we

ought to seek all the knowledge we can get about it. Before we go to our eternal home—we should try to become acquainted with it.[80]

So let's acquaint ourselves with our future home.

Setting Our Hearts on Things Above

In his book *Heaven*, Randy Alcorn tells the story of a pastor questioning him on whether it was possible to write a book on heaven, quoting 1 Corinthians 2:9 that 'no eye has seen, no ear has heard, no mind has conceived what God has prepared for those who love him.' Surely we can't know what God has prepared for us in heaven. But Alcorn reminds us of the words that immediately follow: 'But God has revealed it to us by his Spirit.' In other words, feeding on God's revelation in Scripture fuels the imagination regarding what Christ has prepared for us. This is why Paul declares in Colossians 3:1-2, 'Set your hearts on things above, where Christ is, seated at the right hand of God. Set your minds on things above, not on earthly things.'

This may sound like escapism, but it is in fact quite the opposite. It is in the process of setting our hearts and minds on heaven that we prayerfully begin to pull God's future into the present. As CS Lewis suggests:

> If you read history you will find that the Christians who did most for the present world are just the ones that thought the most of the next. The Apostles themselves, who set on foot the conversion of the

Roman Empire, the great men who built up the
Middle Ages, the English Evangelicals who abol-
ished the Slave Trade, all left their mark on Earth,
precisely because their minds were occupied with
Heaven. It is since Christians have largely ceased
to think of the other world that they have become
so ineffective in this. Aim at Heaven and you'll get
the earth 'thrown in': aim at earth and you'll get
neither.[81]

Life after Death

Throughout this book we have highlighted that the end of the
Christian story is a renewed heaven and earth. Heaven (God's home)
and earth (our home) will become one, and we will enjoy God's new
creation in our resurrected bodies. This is what will happen when
Christ returns. But what happens to those who die before Christ
returns? The traditional answer is that those who die 'in Christ' go to
be with him in paradise. But is paradise the same as heaven?

Tom Wright makes the helpful distinction between what he calls
'life after death' (paradise) and 'life after life after death' (heaven).
The latter refers to our resurrection state in the new creation, the
former to an intermediate state in the presence of Jesus whilst awaiting his return. Randy Alcorn, like Wright, also wants to differentiate
between the two, referring to the former as the 'intermediate heaven'
and the latter as the 'eternal heaven.' Whilst this book has focussed
on the eternal heaven, let's briefly explore the idea of paradise or the
'intermediate heaven.'

Jesus said to the thief on the cross, 'Today you will be with me in paradise' (Luke 23:43). This was clearly not a reference to the 'eternal heaven,' enjoying a resurrected body in God's fully redeemed creation. It does, however, indicate a 'life after death' in the presence of Jesus. In his letter to the Philippians, Paul begins to contemplate his own death. He says, 'For to me, to live is Christ and to die is gain ... I desire to depart and be with Christ, which is better by far; but it is more necessary for you that I remain in the body' (1:21, 23-24). Again, this departing is not a reference to the final resurrection, but instead points to being present with Jesus in a deeper way than is available on earth right now.

Elsewhere, Paul talks about being 'asleep in Christ,' a euphemism for death, used to describe the outward appearance of those who have died. Some have interpreted this phrase as a period of unconsciousness between death and resurrection. This, however, is not what Paul had in mind. When we die, our outward being (what Paul refers to as our 'earthly tent') may 'sleep' awaiting resurrection, but our inward being is present with Jesus, experiencing his perfect peace, limitless love and immeasurable joy. This is why Paul describes it as 'better by far.'

So before Christ returns and we experience the fulness of his new creation in our resurrected bodies (what Paul refers to as our 'heavenly dwelling'), we will enjoy paradise. The word *paradise* comes from the Persian word *pairidaeza* meaning 'an enclosed garden.' In the Greek translation of the Old Testament, the word for paradise is used to describe the Garden of Eden, referring not simply to wild nature, but also to nature under humanity's dominion. The theologian Alistair McGrath writes:

> The idea of a walled garden enclosing a carefully cultivated area of exquisite plants and animals was the most powerful symbol of paradise available to the human imagination, mingling the images of the beauty of nature with the orderliness of human construction ... The whole of human history is thus enfolded in the subtle interplay of sorrow over a lost paradise, and the hope of its final restoration.[82]

Paradise became the place in the Jewish imagination where humanity and divinity met. It was not understood as mere allegory, but as an actual physical place where God and humanity dwelt together. Just as Adam and Eve walked and talked with God in Eden (a physical place), and just as we will dwell with God in our resurrected bodies in the new creation (a physical place), we need to recapture the idea of paradise (or the intermediate heaven) as a physical place. In fact, if we believe that the resurrected Lord Jesus resides there now with a physical body, paradise having physical properties is a non-negotiable. This might be hard for us to get our heads around, but makes sense within the overarching narrative of Scripture and emphasises continuity in the story of Eden.

Super String Theory and the Unseen Realm That Surrounds

Let's consider for a moment paradise as an unseen (yet physical) realm that interacts and overlaps with reality as we know it. This shouldn't be beyond our imaginations. Scientists today suggest there are multiple unobservable dimensions and potentially an infinite number of unobservable universes. For example, in string theory, space-time is ten-dimensional (nine spatial dimensions and one time dimension), while in M-theory it is eleven-dimensional (ten spatial dimensions and one time dimension). We're obviously only aware of three of these spatial dimensions. So if the leading scientists of the day believe in multiple unobservable dimensions, then it shouldn't be beyond our reach to consider one such dimension, the spiritual realm including paradise.

The Bible is full of stories of people momentarily glimpsing the reality of this unseen realm. For example, in Acts 7, Stephen, full of the Holy Spirit, saw an open heaven and the Son of Man standing at the right hand of God. The text suggests that this was something Stephen actually saw rather than just imagined. Similarly, Elisha in 2 Kings 6 asked God to give his servant a glimpse of the invisible realm. The Lord responded by opening the servant's eyes, enabling him to see the hills full of horses and chariots of fire all around Elisha. These texts are historical accounts, not apocalyptic or parabolic literature. The implication is that the servant actually saw something of the spiritual realm present in his physical surroundings. The physical and the spiritual are not opposites or contradictory. The physical realm has a spiritual dimension to it and the spiritual realm has a physical dimension to it. Angels can take on physical form (Heb. 13:2), and a human being with a physical body (Jesus) currently resides in paradise. The two realms coexist and interact.

This is actually critical for our understanding of paradise. The story of creation, De-creation, Re-creation is the story of heaven and earth. Heaven and earth were united in Eden, separated at the fall, and will be perfectly reunited when Christ returns to complete what he began through his death and resurrection. Eden will be restored.

One of the defining features of Eden is the tree of life (Gen. 2:9). This same tree is present at the end of the story in Revelation 22: 'Then the angel showed me the river of the water of life, as clear as crystal, flowing from the throne of God and of the Lamb down the middle of the great street of the city. On each side of the river stood the tree of life, bearing twelve crops of fruit, yielding its fruit every month' (vv. 1-2).

The implication is that the original Eden has become the garden at the centre of the New Jerusalem. Eden has expanded, as was always the plan in the beginning. Perhaps what we've described as paradise (the intermediate heaven) links Eden and the New Jerusalem.

Revelation 2:7 seems to support this. It states that 'whoever has ears, let them hear what the Spirit says to the churches. To the one who is victorious, I will give the right to eat from the tree of life, which is in the paradise of God.' The same tree that was physically present in Eden, and will be physically present in the New Jerusalem, is present here, prior to Christ's return, in paradise. The temptation here is to surrender again to the dualism that separates the material and the immaterial, the spiritual and the physical. In this case, the tree of life must become non-physical in paradise, a symbol pointing to what was in Eden and what will be again. However, it is this dualism that has robbed us of fully understanding the story that we belong to.

So if paradise, or the intermediate heaven, has physical properties and isn't simply a disembodied bliss waiting for a physical expression, how does it relate to the present earth that God will make new?

The answer is that these two realms, though separated by sin, interact and overlap. We experience the pain of separation as well as the joy and comfort of momentary interaction. Both create a yearning for future reconciliation. Eden is therefore more than a distant memory; it is equally a future hope of which we experience foretastes. Alcorn states:

> We are told that after the Fall, God 'drove the man out; and at the east of the garden of Eden He stationed the cherubim and the flaming sword which turned every direction to guard the way to the tree of life' (Genesis 3:24, NASB). It appears that Eden's Paradise, with the tree of life, retained its identity as a physical place but was no longer accessible to mankind.... Eden was not destroyed. What was destroyed was mankind's ability to live in Eden. There's no indication that Eden was stripped of its physicality and transformed into a 'spiritual' entity ... God is not done with Eden. He preserved it not as a museum piece but as a place that mankind will one day occupy again.[83]

This future home therefore both awaits us and in some sense surrounds us. This idea is captured in the beautiful vision in Hebrews 12 of the great cloud of witnesses cheering us on as we run the race marked out for us. Notice that these witnesses, the departed saints who have gone before us, now surround us. They cheer us on in the present. This is what the church means by the 'communion of saints.' Both departed saints and we ourselves are 'in Christ,' and when we celebrate the Eucharist, for example, we join together with the angels and archangels and remember what has been and what is to come. Heaven is closer than we think, and we yearn for it to be reunited with earth as it was in the beginning.

Creation Reborn

The realm of heaven (in its intermediate form) surrounds us and is beyond us. There is both 'nearness' and 'distance,' and with this comes the comfort of nearness and the pain of distance. Paul reminds us in Romans 8 that the whole of creation has been groaning as in the pains of childbirth. In childbirth there is the joy and excitement of the imminent arrival of the baby, but this runs alongside the agony of labour. Paul adds that we ourselves, who have the firstfruits of the Spirit, also groan inwardly as we wait eagerly for the redemption of our bodies. Like creation itself, we too feel the pain of the disconnection. Notice here the link between humanity and creation. It was the fall of Adam and Eve that led to created order unravelling. But a fallen creation now groans for the redemption of humanity, because therein lies the hope for redemption of all created order. As humanity goes, so goes all of creation.

Childbirth is the perfect analogy to describe all of this. Something old gives birth to something new. The fallen but redeemed humanity will be transformed into the sinless image-bearers that we were originally created to be. The fallen creation will give birth to a new creation in which there is no death, grief, crying or pain. Alcorn beautifully captures this theology of suffering in Romans 8 by stating:

There's the groaning of those dying without hope, and in contrast, the groaning of those in childbirth. Both processes are painful, yet they are very different. The one is the pain of hopeless dread, the other the pain of hopeful anticipation. The Christian's pain is very real, but it's the pain of a mother anticipating the joy of holding her child.[84]

The birth of God's new creation is front and centre in the New Testament from beginning to end. The gospel accounts introduce Jesus with language and imagery borrowed from Genesis in order to highlight that the events to follow will usher in a new creation. In Matthew 19:28, Jesus himself talks about this 'renewal' of all creation. He says to his disciples, 'Truly I tell you, at the renewal of all things, when the Son of Man sits on his glorious throne, you who have followed me will also sit on twelve thrones, judging the twelve tribes of Israel.' The Greek word used here for 'renewal' is *paligenesia*. This is a compound word formed by fusing *palin*, meaning 'again,' and *genesia,* which means 'birth' or 'beginning.' Jesus is pointing towards a future moment when he will sit down on his throne, and all things will be 'reborn.' Christians often speak of being 'born again,' using the language of John 3 to highlight the importance of the spiritual rebirth that takes place when we give our lives to Jesus. Our gospel proclamation is therefore that through Jesus we can be 'born again' and become a 'new creation.' That's unbelievably good news, but the point of Matthew 19:28, and the gospels at large, is that it's even better than that. All of created order will be 'born again.'

This is what Revelation 21-22 is about. God returns to dwell with humanity, and 'He who was seated on the throne said, "I am making everything new!"' Notice the connection with Matthew 19. God sits down, a sign of his work being complete, and all things are 'born again' or 'made new.' The New Jerusalem descends from the heavens, and all things are restored to how they were in the beginning. The life, death and resurrection of Jesus secured in the middle of the story lead to the glorious end of the story, which is described in Revelation 21-22.

The Marriage Ceremony of Heaven and Earth

The current heaven (paradise) and earth will be reborn, and in this renewal there will be the full reconciliation of these realms. This was Paul's message in Ephesians: through the cross, Christ has revealed the mystery of his will 'to be put into effect when the times reach their fulfilment—to bring unity to all things in heaven and on earth under Christ' (Eph. 1:10). This is echoed again in Paul's letter to the church in Colossae, where he explains that God in Christ has reconciled to himself 'all things, whether things on earth or things in heaven, by making peace through his blood, shed on the cross' (Col. 1:20). Rebirth and renewal bring reconciliation. Heaven and earth are reunited. The imagery therefore moves from childbirth to marriage, and this is how the Scriptures conclude. The marriage of heaven and earth ... the marriage of God and humanity ... and marriage of Christ and the church.

The Bible opens and closes with marriage: with two becoming one. In Eden, heaven and earth, God and humanity and Adam and

Eve become one. But sin leads to separation. Heaven and earth separate and God and humanity become estranged. The narrative from Genesis 3 onwards is a story of redemption that finds its climactic moment in the life, death and resurrection of Jesus. Sin, which led to disconnection from God, is dealt with at the cross. Death, which entered the story in Genesis 3, is overcome through Jesus' resurrection.

Right in the middle of the story we find these defining events that guarantee the end of the story. Heaven and earth and God and humanity embrace at the cross, but full reconciliation awaits Christ's return and the bodily resurrection of his followers. This resurrection will result in the resurrection of creation itself. As Romans 8 highlights, 'creation itself will be liberated from its bondage to decay and brought into the freedom and glory of the children of God' (v. 21). Then, and only then, will all things be new. The wedding bells will ring. The celebrations will begin. Pain and disappointments will be a distant memory. No sin. No sickness. No suffering. We will be fully alive, enjoying the new heavens and the new earth, walking and talking with God. We will party like there's no tomorrow, for the simple reason that the 'tomorrow' we have been living for and waiting for will have become our today.

Living with the End in Sight

This is the end we live for, and the end fuels hope. It was this joy set before Jesus that enabled him to endure the cross, and it is this joy set before us that enables us to endure the challenges that life throws our way. We need to recover the practice of meditating on and anticipating heaven. Such a practice relieves pain and despair, reminding us that suffering and death are temporary. They are not the end, but simply a gateway into the wide-open space. Such meditation isn't escapism but preparation, and this preparation for what's to come brings perspective and meaning to the present. The best parts of life become tiny foretastes of what we will feast on eternally. The worst parts, the wounds and regrets, create longing for wholeness. This longing becomes a signpost for such healing, pointing us towards what is set before us.

Similarly, we gravitate towards our inward longing. The greater the longing, the greater the forward movement. We therefore need to feed our longing for heaven. I love these words of Alcorn:

> I've never been to Heaven, yet I miss it. Eden's in my blood. The best things of life are souvenirs from Eden, appetizers of the New Earth. There's just enough of them to keep us going, but never enough to make us satisfied with the world as it is, or ourselves as we are. We live between Eden and the New Earth, pulled towards what we once were and what we yet will be ... Desire is a signpost pointing to heaven. Every longing for better health is a longing for the New Earth. Every longing from romance is a longing for the ultimate romance with Christ. Every desire for intimacy is a desire for Christ. Every thirst for beauty is a thirst for Christ. Every taste of joy is but a foretaste of a greater more vibrant joy than can be found on Earth as it is now.[85]

We spend so little time meditating on what's to come and so much time worrying about how to satisfy the present internal longings of our hearts. We've got the order wrong. It's time to set our hearts on what's to come and allow this deep desire to redefine every aspect of our current existence and redirect every longing. We've been blessed with God-given imaginations, so let's use them. Imagine this: being in a resurrected body on a resurrected earth, enjoying resurrected friendships in a resurrected culture, whilst walking and talking with the resurrected Jesus. Imagine the food, joy, laughter, intimacy and depth of friendships. Imagine the beauty of the landscape, the sights and the smells.

Now let's recognize the limitations of our fallen imaginations. However good it was in your imagination, know this: it will be infinitely and incomparably better. Join in with the apostle Paul's enthusiastic proclamation:

> Now to him who is able to do immeasurably more than all we ask or imagine, according to his power that is at work within us, to him be glory in the church and in Christ Jesus throughout all generations, for ever and ever! Amen. (Eph. 3:20-21)

Amen indeed!

Chapter 22

PERSONAL REFLECTIONS: GRIEVING WITH HOPE

Over the years I have conducted quite a few funerals. It's a huge privilege to support families in such moments of grief and vulnerability, pointing them to the person of Jesus and the hope of the gospel. The funeral of someone who has followed Jesus always has a dimension of celebration and joy amidst the grieving and the tears. The awareness that our mourning coincides with heaven's welcome transforms the atmosphere of a Christian funeral.

Despite this, funerals always throw up lots of questions. They are moments when the rubber hits the road regarding our beliefs. Do we really believe this stuff? Are our loved ones safe? Where are they? Will I see them again? Is there really life after death? The role of the priest in these moments is to comfort, speak hope and allow people to bring these big questions to Jesus. The temptation to provide simple answers deprives the questioners an opportunity of encountering Jesus in the place of their pain and doubt. The challenge for a priest is when you are not the one offering hope but the one needing it. This happened to me on 7th June 2018.

A few weeks before, I had been at a leaders' gathering at KXC. I'd turned my phone off to be entirely present to the gathering. When it was over, I turned it on to see multiple missed calls from my wife. Expecting to be in trouble for not unloading the dishwasher or tidying up the breakfast (again!), I called back. She answered and I immediately knew something horrific had happened. She was sobbing uncontrollably, trying to speak through her sobs. I couldn't make out what she was saying. I thought something awful had happened to one of the kids. Feeling panicked myself, I said that I couldn't understand and asked her to slow down and explain what had happened. The next four words I could hear clearly: 'My dad is dead.'

The shock hit like a tonne of bricks. There must be a mistake. He can't have died. Trying to comfort my wife whilst struggling to absorb what she had just said was a challenge.

Bee's mum and dad had been on holiday in Pembrokeshire, Wales. Nick, aged sixty-five, had woken up that morning and decided to go for a walk to have his quiet time. He found a spot on top of the hill overlooking Dale, opened his Bible to Psalm 63 and began reading. It was then and there that Nick experienced heart failure. We don't know much of what happened, but a dog-walker later found him dead with the open Bible by his side.

The dog-walker found Bee's mum, Rachel, walking up the hill to find Nick. She knew something was up because Nick had been gone for too long. The walker broke the horrific news and asked Rachel if anyone else was with her in the cottage, and if so to go back and get them. Bee's sister Alice and her family were thankfully down in Dale with Nick and Rachel, staying in the same cottage. Rachel grabbed Alice, and together they rushed to the top of the hill to where Nick's body lay. An ambulance soon arrived, but it was too late. Alice called Bee from the top of the hill. It's the kind of phone call we all dread.

Bee was away with a close friend at the time, so we decided that I'd pick up the kids from school, meet Bee back at home and then together drive down to Dale. Telling the kids that Papa Nick had died was even worse than receiving the call from Bee. They utterly adored Papa Nick, and this was their first experience of death. They were heartbroken, struggling to understand how the world would continue without Papa Nick in it.

I think the way kids respond to death is perhaps the most natural response. Death shouldn't exist. It's as if kids are more aware of the story of Eden and the New Jerusalem than adults are, that we were made for a world without death, grief, crying and pain.

So we made the long drive down to Dale and spent the next few days weeping, laughing, sharing memories and coming to terms with what felt like a new world, a lesser world, without Nick in it.

Those who have experienced this kind of loss know that funeral admin kicks in fairly quickly. So much to organise in a short space of time. So many small decisions. It becomes overwhelming. Inconsequential decisions (such as what font to use on the service sheet) feel crucially important, particularly if it provides another distraction from the deep grief that lies waiting. How do you make any decisions when your heart is in agony?

Then comes the funeral. As the service begins, and there is no admin to hide behind, emotions begin to stir. I would be giving the address at Nick's funeral. It was my opportunity to honour his life ... and to thank him for raising the most amazing daughter, my wife, and for being an incredible friend to me. Additionally, it was an opportunity to explain his remarkable life to those gathered who didn't understand Nick's faith. Nick was utterly adored. Over seven hundred people gathered at St John the Baptist Church in Burford. They not only needed an overflow room, there was also an overflow to the overflow room. People had arrived to celebrate Nick, to mourn with others because grieving alone is too much for the soul to bear, and pay tribute to a man whose life radiated the glory of God.

Writing the address was hard but therapeutic. I still had questions for God and disappointment to process. There was a lot I didn't know, but the address provided clarity as to what I did know. I knew that Nick walked and talked with God, and enjoyed a closeness with Jesus that should cause us to be jealous. After significant knockbacks and tough seasons in his early life, Nick found Jesus in his twenties, becoming more fully alive in his faith in his forties as he encountered the person and work of the Spirit. An amazing healing work began. Nick began immersing himself in the story of God, both living in and living out that story. Time in the presence of Jesus resulted in the fruit of the Spirit being more and more evident in his life: love, joy, peace, patience, kindness, goodness, faithfulness, gentleness and self-control. Nick became a magnet. People wanted to be with him because, even though many didn't realise it, being with Nick felt like being with Jesus, and this is what we were made for.

Hundreds at the funeral shared Nick's faith and through the tears were celebrating his arrival in glory. Hundreds there, however, didn't know Jesus but knew there was something compelling about Nick's life. The apostle Peter encouraged us to 'always be prepared to give an answer to everyone who asks you to give the reason for the hope that you have' (1 Pet. 3:15). Nick had lived in such a way that people at the funeral were leaning in, curious about the hope that he had. My job was to give the answer Nick had been giving all his life, but now to give it at his death. So as we near the end of this book, I want to share the words I offered at my father-in-law's funeral:

… Finally, I want to talk about his faith. If there was one friendship that formed and shaped Nick beyond any other, it was his friendship with Jesus. Nick immersed himself in the Scriptures, and knew that in the story of Eden, humanity walked and talked with God in the cool of the day. That's what human flourishing looks like, that's what we were made for, that's what Nick spent his life doing—walking and talking and enjoying friendship with his Creator.

Nick died in 'God's own country,' which is how he always referred to his Welsh homeland, and he died whilst reading Psalm 63, in other words, walking and talking with God. The psalm is such a fitting text for Nick, partly because it talks about the richest of foods, and I can imagine that Nick's mind would have drifted off at that point to a glass of claret and a succulent piece of steak. But the verse that jumps out is the psalmist declaring that God's love is better than life itself. In fact God's love is what leads to life itself. Perhaps the most famous verse in Scripture highlights this: 'For God so loved the world, that he gave his only begotten Son that whoever believed in him shall not perish but have eternal life.' This eternal life isn't just a reference to life beyond the grave but to a quality of life present this side of the grave, even in the midst of challenge, adversity and disappointment.

Nick stood out in this life because he knew that at the core of his being he was loved, and that knowledge is the pathway to peace, the key to contentment and the way to fulness of life. Martin Luther, the

Reformation theologian, put it like this: 'Christians aren't loved because they are attractive. They are attractive because they are loved.' Now, I'm not saying Nick wasn't physically attractive. Rachel definitely found him very attractive and we have photographic evidence in our booklets. What I am saying is that Nick was most attractive because he was loved.

There was a gravitational pull towards Nick because here was a man at peace. A man who had found the key to contentment. A man who had tasted the life of Eden, and we all wanted to be around Nick because we wanted what he had.

Thomas Merton, the Catholic writer, famously said, 'A man's life is shaped by the end he lives for.' So I want to tell you about the end Nick was living for. Nick never rammed his faith down anyone's throat, but neither did he ever hide it. And I would love to strike that balance with these closing remarks. Nick's approach was deeply invitational, mirroring the approach of the Apostles when they constantly said, 'Come and see.' I'm sure there are numerous people in the room who have received multiple invitations from Nick to evangelistic events, and of all the things you will deeply miss about Nick, those invitations probably won't be one of them. Therefore on Nick's behalf, can I offer one final invite into the greatest story ever told, for the simple reason that the story you live in is the story you live out, and this was the story that Nick lived in, and we all tasted the fruit of it in his life. This was the end he was living for.

It's a story of God on a mission to redeem and restore all the brokenness and pain we see all round us. He does this by taking on human flesh in the person of Jesus, who lived a perfect life, showing us what it means to be human, and then dies a brutal death in which all the sin, selfishness and narcissism that leads to disconnection from God, and therefore disconnection from life, was loaded upon him so that he could die the death we were facing, and gives us the life for which we were longing.

You see, the reason Jesus cries out on the cross 'My God my God why have you forsaken me' is that he experiences the disconnection from God that is the result of human sin. He experiences it so that we don't have to. Three days later Jesus rose from the dead and then invites people to follow him along the path of resurrection life.

This is the Christian hope that meant Nick never feared death and embraced every second that life had to offer. Nick believed that God would one day return and finish what he started. Upon his return, heaven and earth would become one, and suddenly there would be no more death, or grief or crying or pain. Tears, like the ones present today, would be wiped away, and then God would sit down on his throne and say, 'Behold I am making all things new.' Now in the Greek of the New Testament, there are two words for 'new.' There is *neos* which means brand new, and *kainos* which means something old made new, or restored to its former glory. When God sits down on his throne he says, 'Behold I am making all things "kainos."' In other words, 'I am restoring all things to how they were in the beginning, in Eden, where there was no sin, no sickness and no suffering, where humanity was fully alive in relationship with me and in relationship with one another.'

That was the story Nick was living in and that was the end he was living for. It was the story that told him he was loved perfectly and eternally, that his life had purpose and meaning, and that his role as an actor within this story was to join in God's mission of restoration and redemption by loving people as Jesus loved them, sharing his offer of salvation, to care for the poor and the broken, to give dignity to those from whom it had been stolen, to encourage the fainthearted and to bring hope to the hopeless. This was Nick's reason for living, and we want to join the chorus of heaven and say to you, Nick, 'Well done, good and faithful servant.' Yours was a life well lived, a life to emulate and a life to be grateful for.

So count this as Nick's final invitation to taste and see that the Lord is good, to explore this story of God restoring and redeeming all things, to explore this love that is better than life itself in the hope that God alone can satisfy the deepest longings of your heart.

So, Nick, we love you. We will never ever forget you. We will always be grateful for what you deposited in our lives. And we are grateful to God for blessing us with the most amazing husband, dad, Papa Nick, brother and friend we could have ever wished for.

I sat down, holding back the tears, and felt relieved. The weight of emotion on the day meant I stumbled my way through parts of the address. But in that moment I genuinely could sense the pride and affection of both my Father in heaven and my father-in-law now in paradise. I had done my one job, which happened to be the same call that inspired this book, to preach the gospel 'afresh to every generation.'

Every life has a message. Every life points in a direction. So what's the message of your life? Not the message you want it to be, but the actual message your actions communicate? In what direction is your life currently pointing? For those like me wanting to live a life that communicates the gospel and points people towards Jesus, here's the task: immerse yourself in the story of God. Live in it. Live it out. And as you do, you will join God's story of Re-creation, his mission to make all things new.

THE STORY WE LIVE OUT

So back to the beginning. The genesis of this book and the genesis of KXC were rooted in the same call of God to 'preach the gospel afresh to every generation.' At a time when millennials were being described as the 'lost generation' in the church, with the ones remaining increasingly biblically illiterate, Bee and I felt called to plant a church in the heart of London, helping people indwell the full narrative of Scripture and follow the way of Jesus.

The last ten years have been the most incredible journey. There have been huge highs and huge lows. We began with very little experience but high levels of faith as to what might be possible if we took the Scriptures seriously, opened ourselves to the power of the Spirit and pursued Jesus wholeheartedly. We were naïve and therefore made lots of mistakes. We were light on strategy, partly because we had no idea what we were doing, but also for theological reasons. I've lost count of how many times I've told people at KXC that 'we don't have a map because we have a guide.'

God didn't give Moses or the Israelites a map on the journey from Egypt to the Promised Land, instead providing a cloud by day and a fire by night as manifestations of his presence. Why? Because relationship matters. Faith matters. The spirituality that emerges with a map is to keep your head down and execute the plan. The spirituality that emerges in the wilderness wanderings, and throughout Scripture, is to keep your head up and follow the guide, God himself. Jesus said he only did what he saw his Father doing. That is a 'heads-up' spirituality. Paul spoke about keeping in step with the Spirit. That is too. So without experience, light on wisdom and without a map in our hands, we began the journey trying to keep our heads up and follow the promptings of the Spirit.

The first prompting was to prioritise the Scriptures: not simply to teach the Scriptures, but to teach people how to personally feed on the Scriptures and live in them. If people were immersed in the story of God, perhaps they would be rescued from drowning in the surrounding stories of secularism, relativism and consumerism. So we began teaching our way through the story.

Here's what we learnt. Firstly, the more you indwell this story, the closer you get to Jesus. This was Martin Luther's discovery. He described the Bible as the 'cradle wherein Christ is laid.' If you want people to meet Jesus, get them reading Scripture. Jesus is described in Hebrews 12 as the 'author and perfecter of the faith.' In reading the Scriptures you draw close to the author.

Secondly, the more you indwell the narrative, the more you long for the completion of the story. For Jesus is the author, but he's also the perfecter, the completer and finisher of the story. He's the alpha (beginning), but he's also the omega (the end). Having experienced numerous church cultures in which one would suspect that church growth was the end goal of the story, reading the Scriptures provided a far more glorious and exciting vision than church growth: the renewal of all things.

As we embarked on this journey as a church, people became more excited about their careers and workplaces. In the church-growth story, the workplace is relatively unimportant. What matters is leading a small group, serving at Alpha courses, inviting friends from work to church. The career may pay the bills, but the important work is the 'work of the kingdom,' by which we mean the work of the church. Millennials are increasingly dissatisfied, though, with a spirituality that doesn't really work from Monday to Friday. But if the end goal is the renewal of all things, then our careers are incredibly important. As followers of Jesus we are tasked to be agents of renewal to every sector of society. We partner with Christ in the renewal of politics, education, business, entertainment and the arts. The full glory of that renewal awaits Jesus' return, but every endeavour in line with this vision now will last for eternity.

Scripture led us to Jesus, and Jesus drew us into his vision for the redemption of all things. This shouldn't surprise us, for the story we live in is the story we live out.

Tom Wright brilliantly captures this theme of living within and being shaped by the narrative of Scripture, providing the following illustration. He suggests that we imagine a new Shakespearian play being discovered for the first time, but with most of the fifth act missing. In order to stage the play, the first four acts and what remains of Act V are given to well-trained and experienced Shakespearian actors, who immerse themselves both in the first part of the play and in the culture and time of Shakespeare. They are told to work out the concluding fifth act for themselves.

The final act requires the actors to speak and perform with both consistency and innovation. The first four acts would contain its own cumulative forward momentum that would demand that the play be concluded in a way that authentically fits with that energy. The actors would therefore have the responsibility of carrying forward the logic of the play and pushing the story towards completion, concluding things in a way that is coherent with the earlier parts of the play.

Wright goes on to describe the biblical narrative as a five act play. Act I is the story of creation, Act II covers the fall, Act III tells the story of Israel, and Act IV covers the ministry of Jesus. The church has been given the responsibility of immersing themselves within the first four acts of the narrative to such an extent that they can push the story (Act V) towards its natural conclusion.

This has become our passion as a church. It starts by knowing the story intimately. The dominoes then begin to fall. As my friend Pete James says, 'Story knowers become story tellers become story writers.' If we want to rewrite the stories of our cities and communities, it starts when we begin living in the story of God. We then begin to find our voice, communicating the good news of the story wherever there is opportunity, and the opportunities are endless for we live at a time of such spiritual hunger.

In 2008, around the same time I began writing this book, Julian Barnes wrote a memoir on mortality entitled *Nothing to Be Frightened Of*. He opens the book with the punchy line: 'I don't believe in God, but I miss him.' In that one statement Barnes captured the mind-set of this secular age, as well as the generational yearning for something transcendent. He summarised the dominant script of our time whilst simultaneously highlighting the cracks in that same narrative.

A recent poll, published by ComRes in January 2018, highlights that 51 percent of the British population pray. Compare that with the 4.7 percent who currently attend church, and it suggests that more and more people 'don't believe in God' but more and more people 'miss him.' The spiritual longing of the British public is truly alive and well.

The *Talking Jesus* publication (2015) on perceptions of Jesus, Christians and Evangelism in England suggests a similar trend. The research highlights that one in five non-Christians, having heard a Christian talk about their faith, want to experience the love of God for themselves. We need to jettison the old thinking that no one is interested in Christianity, Jesus or prayer. The facts show it to be a lie. People are hungry. The cultural moment we find ourselves in is creating a deep spiritual longing. People feel lost and are looking for a better story. The Austrian philosopher Ivan Illich put it like this:

> Neither revolution nor reformation can ultimately change a society, rather you must tell a new powerful tale, one so persuasive that it sweeps away the old myths and becomes the preferred story, one so inclusive that it gathers all the bits of our past and our present into a coherent whole, one that even shines some light into the future so that we can take the next step ... if you want to change a society then you have to tell an alternative story.[86]

People are desperately looking for an alternative story. Despair is all around us. Hope deferred makes the heart sick, and people are craving a story that will birth fresh hope and overcome the (home) sickness and despair of our times. The story the world craves is the story we have been entrusted with: the story of God, the story of Jesus and the story of humanity.

Throughout this book we have shared this story in three layers. The first layer emphasizes the wider narrative from creation to De-creation to Re-creation. The second layer emphasizes how Jesus fulfils this narrative through the incarnation, the cross and the resurrection. That is the gospel message. The third layer emphasizes our discipleship as Jesus invites us to follow in his footsteps by becoming a people of compassion, courage and creativity, living gospel-shaped lives and pushing this story of Re-creation towards its completion.

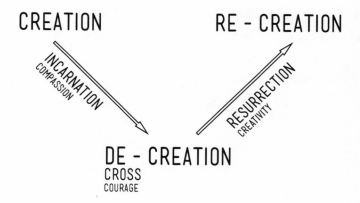

Now is the time for the church to rediscover its public voice and share the story it has been entrusted with. We owe it to the world to courageously tell it: the story that starts in Eden and ends with a renewed heaven and earth; the story of God becoming human to find us; the story of God embracing death so that we could taste everlasting life; the story of God rising again in order to bring resurrection life to his redeemed humanity and the world he so loves.

The need is great. The hunger is deep. So for the sake of the world, let's feed on this daily bread, and teach others to do the same. Let's immerse ourselves in the greatest story ever told. There we will find Jesus, the one who offers life in all its fulness and satisfies the longing of every human heart. He is the author. There we will also find purpose, to join Jesus in his mission to restore and redeem all things. For he is also the perfecter and completer of the story. He was there at the beginning, for through him all things came to be, and he will be there at the end, the redeemer sat on his throne, enjoying his finished work.

Our job is therefore simple:

To live in the story.

To live out the story.

To enjoy relationship with the author.

And to partner with his purpose to make all things new.

ACKNOWLEDGEMENTS

This book is the result of many people, over many years, investing in my life. A huge thanks to:

My incredible wife, Bee, whose patience, love and constant encouragement has fueled this project from beginning to end.

My mum and dad for modelling a life shaped by Scripture. The way you both live so wholeheartedly for Jesus constantly inspires me. Thanks to Tim and Rach and Steve and Becky for not just being great brothers and sisters-in-law, but for being the greatest of friends and for sharing in this adventure. Thanks also to my Jones family. Nick never got to read the final manuscript, but his fingerprints and yours are all over this book.

The many mentors and leaders that have encouraged my faith. In particular, Mike Pilavachi. So much of what I do now is the fruit of your investment in my life, and I'll be forever grateful.

The many theologians whose work has caused me to fall more in love with Jesus and the story he fulfils. Two theologians in particular have shaped this book. The first, Tom Wright, through his writing, and the second, Crispin Fletcher-Louis, through his friendship. The best insights contained in this book are most likely stolen from them. The heresies will almost certainly be mine.

My church family, KXC. Your spiritual hunger has forced me to dig deep week by week for fresh revelation from Scripture. The theological journey highlighted in this book has been your journey as much as it has been my journey. Thanks for never settling for less than full immersion in the story, and for always seeking to live the story out in the context of London and King's Cross. Particular thanks to the amazing KXC staff team for helping Bee and I carry the weight of leadership of the church, and to Emma Heddle for being a phenomenal EA and reading and commenting on so many drafts.

Finally, thanks to the David C Cook family, particularly Ian Matthews for believing in this project and persevering with me through the ups and downs, and for Keith Wall, my editor, for bringing fresh energy and grace to help us cross the finish line. We made it!

NOTES

1. Paris, M., 'As an Atheist, I truly believe Africa needs God,' *London Times,* 27 Dec. 2008.

2. Dr. Tim Fox, 'Global Food Waste Not, Want Not,' *Institution of Mechanical Engineers,* Jan. 2013, p.2.

3. Gaarder, J., *Sophie's World: A Novel About the History of Philosophy* (London: Phoenix House, 1995), p.12.

4. I've borrowed these worldview questions from Middleton and Walsh's book *Truth Is Stranger Than It Used to Be: Biblical Faith in a Postmodern Age.* J. Richard Middleton & Brian J. Walsh, *Truth Is Stranger Than It Used to Be: Faith in a Postmodern Age* (Carol Stream, Illinois: InterVarsity Press, 1995).

5. Witherington, B., *The Indelible Image: The Theological and Ethical Thought World of the New Testament* (Carol Stream: Illinois: InterVarsity Press, 2009), p.41.

6. Fretheim, T., *The Pentateuch* (Nashville: Abingdon Press, 1996), pp.22-35.

7. Dawkins, R., *The God Delusions* (London: Transworld Publishers, 2006), p.269.

8. Becker, C. L., *The Heavenly City of the Eighteenth-Century Philosophers* (New Haven, Connecticut: Yale University Press, 1932), p.15.

9. After all, as the theologian Gerhard von Rad states, 'The central point in Old Testament anthropology is that man is dust and ashes before God and that he cannot stand before his holiness.' Gerhard von Rad, 'Divine Likeness in the OT,' in Gerhard Kittel (ed.), *Theological Dictionary of the New Testament (TDNT),* trans. G. W. Bromiley, 10 vols (Grand Rapids: Eerdmans, 1964-76), vol. 2, 390.

10. *Elohim* is normally translated as 'God' in the Old Testament, but some translations insert 'angels' or 'heavenly beings' here in Psalm 8 instead.

11. Fretheim, T. E., *God and World in the Old Testament: A Relational Theology of Creation* (Nashville: Abingdon Press, 2005), p.49.

12. In his brilliant book *The Liberating Image*, Middleton writes that 'the paucity of biblical references to the *imago Dei* contributes to the diversity of opinion over what it means to be made in God's image. The problem is exacerbated by interpreters treating the immediate context of Genesis 1:26-27 as unimportant for determining the meaning of these verses.' The result of this inattention to context caused many interpreters to turn to extrabiblical, usually philosophical, sources to interpret its meaning. Middleton adds that 'most patristic, medieval, and modern interpreters typically asked not an exegetical, but a speculative question: In what ways are humans like God and unlike animals?' The result is that throughout the history of interpretation, this open-ended term 'the image of God' has been pressed into the service of contemporary philosophical and religious thought. Middleton, J. R., *The Liberating Image: The Imago Dei in Genesis 1* (Grand Rapids: Brazos Press, 2005), p.17.

13. The theologian Greg Beale states: 'They were to reflect God's kingship by being his vice-regents on earth ... they were to extend the boundaries of the garden until Eden covered the whole earth. They were on the primeval hillock of hospitable Eden, outside of which lay the inhospitable land. They were to extend the smaller liveable area of the garden by transforming the outer chaotic region into a habitable territory.' Beale, G.K., *The Temple and the Church's Mission: A Biblical Theology of the Dwelling Place of God* (Downers Grove, Illinois: IVP, 2004), pp.81-82.

14. See Numbers 3:7-8; 8:25-26; 18:5-6; 1 Chronicles 23:32; Ezekiel 44:14.

15. The Hebrew word often used to describe the wilderness or desert (*tohu wa-bohu*) is the same term used in Genesis 1:2 to describe the primordial chaos out of which God created the world. This is where Adam and Eve now find themselves.

16. Lewis, CS, *The Weight of Glory* (New York: HarperOne, 2000), p.31.

17. See Isaiah 6; Jeremiah 5; Ezekiel 12; Matthew 13:15.

18. Giglio, L., *The Air I Breathe: Worship as a Way of Life* (Oregon: Multnomah, 2003), p.13.

19. Interestingly, the flood story is used in the New Testament to describe this journey from judgement to the renewal of creation. See 2 Peter 3:6-7; Matthew 24:37. In theological language, eschatology (the study of the end times) recapitulates protology (the study of the beginning times). Watts. R., "The New Exodus/New Creational Restoration of the Image of God," in John G. Stackhouse Jr. (ed.), *What Does It Mean to Be Saved?* (Grand Rapids: Baker, 2002), p.16.

20. Jeremiah 34:18-19 also speaks about this type of oath-making.

21. Watts. R., "The New Exodus/New Creational Restoration of the Image of God," pp.15-41.

22. The Scriptures often refer to creation with architectural and, specifically, temple language. C.f. Job 38:4-22.

23. See Fretheim, T., *The Pentateuch* (Nashville: Abingdon Press, 1996), p.120.

24. See Birch, B.C., Brueggemann, W., Fretheim, T.E., Petersen, D.L., *A Theological Introduction to the Old Testament* (Nashville: Abingdon Press, 1999), p.168. Accordingly, the prohibition given humankind in Gen. 2:16-17, the response to which means life or death, parallels Moses' words to Israel about the commandments also leading to life or death (Deut. 30:11-20).

25. Winnett, R., 'Britain named the European capital of drug addiction,' *The Telegraph*, 1 Sept. 2013, www.telegraph.co.uk/news/uknews/10279600/Britain-named-the-European-capital-of-drug-addiction.html.

26. See 1 Kings 15:25-26, 33-34; 1 Kings 16:19, 25, 30.

27. Hunter, I., *Malcolm Muggeridge: A Life* (Vancouver: Regent College Publishing, 2003), pp.40-41.

28. Hunter, I., *Malcolm Muggeridge*, p.41.

29. Hunter, I., *Malcolm Muggeridge*, p.41.

30. In fact, in the Jewish tradition, the marriage ceremony between a man and a woman provides a reenactment of what took place at Sinai.

31. Isaiah 54; Hosea 2.

32. McKnight, S., *Kingdom Conspiracy: Returning to the Radical Mission of the Local Church* (Grand Rapids: Brazos Press, 2014).

33. In fact, he says to David himself in 2 Samuel 7:16: 'Your house and your kingdom will endure forever before me; your throne will be established forever.'

34. 1 Kings 22:17; 2 Chron. 18:16; Jer. 23:1-4; Ezek. 34:1-8.

35. Luke 4:3, 9.

36. The themes of creation, the Exodus and the kingdom also come together in Psalm 74 and Isaiah 51. The Exodus is thus seen as an act to restore creation and bring salvation upon the earth, and all of this is the work of Yahweh the King.

37. See Psalm 135:15-18 and Psalm 115.

38. As Tom Wright has convincingly argued, this is a story of both Israel's past (the Exodus) and Israel's present (the exile). For Wright, Israel awaiting rescue from exile is a key theme for understanding the ministry of Jesus.

39. See Kenneth Bailey's work on this parable: Bailey, K., *The Cross and the Prodigal: Luke 15 Through the Eyes of Middle Eastern Peasants* (Carol Stream, Illinois: InterVarsity Press, 2005).

40. 2 Samuel 7:16.

41. As quoted by Tim Keller in 'Gospel-Centered Ministry 1 Peter 1:1-12 and 1:22-2:12,' 11 Sept. 2010, https://issuu.com/gospeldelta/docs/tim-keller -gospel-centered-ministry.

42. John 19:30.

43. For example, the story of the prodigal son (previously explained) and Matthew 21:33-46 in which Israel is the vineyard and Jesus is the son who is killed before the vineyard is given to new farmers who receive an incredible harvest.

44. Smail, T., *Once and For All: A Confession of the Cross* (London: Darton Longman and Todd, 1998), p.77.

45. Wright, N.T., 'The Cross and the Caricatures,' *Fulcrum,* Eastertide 2007, https://fulcrum-anglican.org.uk/articles/the-cross-and-the-caricatures.

46. Wright, N.T., 'The Cross and the Caricatures.'

47. Stott, J., *The Cross of Christ* (Carol Stream, Illinois: InterVarsity Press, 2006), pp.133-164.

48. Smail, T., *Once and For All: A Confession of the Cross*, p.101.

49. This is proposed by Marcus Green in his book *Salvation's Song* (Kingsway Publications: 2004).

50. Josephus, *Wars* 5.5.4; Josephus, *Ant* 3.6.4; 3.7.7.

51. As Greg K. Beale notes, 'The equivalence of resurrection with new creation is apparent also from noticing that three of the four most explicit new creation texts in the New Testament refer to Christ's resurrection (2 Cor. 5:14-17; Col. 1:15-18; Rev 1:5 and 3:14).' Beale, G.K., 'The Eschatological Conception of New Testament Theology', in Brower, K.E., and Elliott, M.W., *The Reader Must Understand: Eschatology in Bible and Theology* (Carol Stream, Illinois: InterVarsity Press, 1997), p.19.

52. Wright, N.T., *Surprised by Hope: Rethinking Heaven, the Resurrection, and the Mission of the Church* (New York: Harper Collins, 2008), pp.67-68.

53. 2 Corinthians 1:22, 2 Corinthians 5:5 and Ephesians 1:14.

54. This story is told by Judson Cornwall and Michael Reid in *Whose Love Is It Anyway?* (New Jersey: Sharon Publications, 1991), pp.58-59.

55. Kingdom language is almost entirely absent in John's gospel, used on just two occasions.

56. Though many suggest that water refers here to baptism, this seems unlikely as it fails to make sense of Nicodemus' inability to understand what Jesus is saying.

57. The Greek word 'Paraclete' is perhaps best translated 'Advocate,' though some translations use the word 'Counsellor.' Brown argues that the 'one whom John calls "another Paraclete" is another Jesus. Since the Paraclete can come only when Jesus departs, the Paraclete is the presence of Jesus when Jesus is absent.' Brown, R., *The Gospel According to John, Vol 29* (Cambridge: Cambridge University Press, 1970), p.114.

58. John 4:43-54 (heals the official's son); 5:1-15 (healing at the pool); 9:1-12 (heals the blind man).

59. John 2:1-11 (water into wine); 6:1-15 (feeds 5,000); 6:12-24 (walks on water); 11:38-44 (raises Lazarus from the dead); 21:1-14 (miraculous catch of fish).

60. John 4:19; 6:14; 7:40; 9:17.

61. John 1:38; 3:2,10; 8:4; 11:28; 13:13-13; 20:16.

62. WITH ME (DAVID'S SONG) Words and Music by Rich & Lydia di Castiglione. © 2017 KXC Publishing (BMI)/Capitol CMG Paragon (BMI) (adm. at CapitolCMGPublishing.com). All Rights Reserved. Used by Permission. CCLI #7098626.

63. Brown, C., *The New International Dictionary Of New Testament Theology*: Vol. 1 (Grand Rapids: Zondervan Publishing House, 1986), p.291.

64. *The Week*, 23 February 2008.

65. Newbigin, L., *The Gospel in a Pluralist Society* (Grand Rapids: Eerdmans, 1989), p.227.

66. As quoted by Yancey, P., *Rumors of Another World* (Grand Rapids: Zondervan, 2003), p.175.

67. This story of the Moravians is told by Pete Greig in his book *The Vision and the Vow* (Eastbourne: Relevant Books, 2004).

68. Campbell, D., *Revival in the Hebrides* (Kraus House Publishing, 2016), pp.47-48.

69. Batterson, M., *The Circle Maker* (Grand Rapids: Zondervan, 2011), p.16.

70. This was written to articulate what she sensed the Lord was stirring at KXC and beyond.

71. Butler, JR, *The Skeletons in God's Closet* (Nashville: W Publishing Group, 2014), p.16.

72. Butler, JR, *The Skeletons in God's Closet*, p.24.

73. Butler, JR, *The Skeletons in God's Closet*, p.47.

74. Lewis, CS, *The Problem of Pain* (New York: Macmillan, 1962), p.127.

75. See 2 Timothy 1:10 and 1 Corinthians 15:50-54.

76. Augustine, because of his firm belief in the immortality of the soul, could not contemplate the annihilationist position. Eternal conscious torment was therefore his only option.

77. Unless it is used to mistranslate the word *sheol*, for example.

78. See Sprinkle, P., 'Biblical Support for Annihilation,' *Patheos*, 3 February 2015, http://www.patheos.com/blogs/theologyintheraw/2015/02/biblical-support -for-annihilation/#disqus_thread.

79. Fudge, EW, *Hell: A Final Word* (Texas: Leafwood Publishers, 2012), p.140.

80. Ryle, JC, *Heaven* (CreateSpace, 2015), p.7.

81. Lewis, CS, *Mere Christianity* (London: HarperCollins Publishers, 2009), p.134.

82. McGrath, A.E., *A Brief History of Heaven* (Oxford: Blackwell Publishing, 2003), p.40.

83. Alcorn, R., *Heaven* (Carol Stream, Illinois: Tyndale House Publishers, 2007), p.56.

84. Alcorn, R., *Heaven*, p.126.

85. Alcorn, R., *Heaven*, p.442.

86. Illich I., 'Storytelling or Myth-Making? Frank Viola and Ivan Illich,' *Proclamation, Invitation & Warning*, July 2007.

Made in the USA
Columbia, SC
10 May 2024

35527204R00202